PRAISE FOR *TE*

MW01492544

Dr. Rueter has combined his experience as an educator in the congregation and university with thorough research and insight to produce a text that explains catechetical instruction and equips the reader to realize its benefits. The history, doctrine, wisdom, and practical means of providing catechetical instruction contained in *Teaching the Faith at Home* make it a greatly needed resource for Christianity.

—Michael Eschelbach
Professor of Theology
Concordia University Irvine

The partnership of parents and church leaders is a powerful combination for both the instruction of children in the Christian faith and encouraging their vital and growing expression of that faith. *Teaching the Faith at Home* will both challenge and encourage you to make teaching the faith a priority at home and church, and give you workable ideas for how to do so in ways that honor your children's questions and foster a reasoned and owned faith. This is a wonderful resource for church leaders and parents to draw from in their work together for the sake of their children.

—Dr. Kevin E. Lawson
Editor of the *Christian Education Journal*
Director, PhD and EdD programs in Educational Studies
Talbot School of Theology, Biola University

Teaching the Christian faith and forming disciples of Christ is an ongoing challenge for congregations in this postmodern, fast-paced, distraction-filled world. To this context, Dr. Rueter applies both simple encouragement and practical ideas to teaching the Christian faith at home and within the "family of faith." This book helps parents, church leaders, and members assess their confirmation process and practice as well as give hope for the future. Many of the ideas are time tested and ensconced in congregations and families and Dr. Rueter provides a grace-filled nudge to put our faith in Christ into action. At the heart of it, Dr. Reuter reflects the body of Christ's shared care and responsibility for young people.

—Rev. Mark Kiessling
Interim Director, LCMS Youth Ministry

This is an excellent, reader friendly book, championing the cause of lifelong learning and lifespan catechesis. Rueter recognizes the responsibility of the whole church for raising disciples. He makes the case that catechesis is something church and family do together. Anyone concerned about teaching the faith to children, youth, and adults through the entire span of life will find plenty to chew on.

Chapter 3, "What Went Wrong?," provides an outstanding analysis of the challenge of teaching God's universal truth in a postmodern world. This chapter alone is worth the price of the book. Rueter provides generous insights from other sources (e.g., Christian Smith in the National Study of Youth and Religion, Eugene Roehlkepartain at Search Institute, David Kinnaman, Gabe Lyons, and many more) to reinforce his points.

The second half of the book targets parents with ideas for teaching the catechism to their children. Again, great for parents but also very helpful for any instructor. Rueter's reflections on the Six Chief Parts of the Small Catechism could easily be read devotionally by parents, pastors, DCEs, deaconesses, or small group leaders preparing to teach a confirmation class.

This book should find a place on the bookshelf of any person teaching the faith.

—Rev. Dr. Terry Dittmer
Senior Director, Youth Ministry Specialist
LCMS Office of National Mission

Teaching the Faith at Home will effectively equip and encourage church workers and parents alike as they work hand-in-hand to "train up a child" (Proverbs 22:6). In this excellent resource, which is both engaging and practical, author David L. Rueter provides an eye-opening approach to confirmation instruction—a philosophy of ministry that may be fundamental to building and maintaining a viable "catechesis culture" in the church and its families today!

—Deb Burma
Author of *Raising Godly Girls* (CPH, 2015)
and *Stepping Out: To a Life on the Edge* (CPH, 2013)
Youth Ministry Leader

TEACHING THE FAITH AT HOME

WHAT DOES THIS MEAN?
HOW IS THIS DONE?

Peer Reviewed

DAVID L. RUETER

CONCORDIA PUBLISHING HOUSE • SAINT LOUIS

Published by Concordia Publishing House
3558 S. Jefferson Ave., St. Louis, MO 63118–3968
1-800-325-3040 • www.cph.org

2 3 4 5 6 7 8 9 10   25 24 23 22 21 20 19 18

CONTENTS

ACKNOWLEDGMENTS

I dedicate this book to my beautiful and patient wife, Andrea. Without you, this would not have been possible. Thank you to you and our sons, James and Wesley, for your love and support.

I would also like to thank my colleagues at Concordia University Irvine and the Pacific Southwest District for their encouragement, as well as my students in the DCE program for their feedback, especially Katrina Johns for her editorial assistance.

INTRODUCTION

The Word of God was a central part of my home life for as long as I can remember. Thus, I have always had a passion for learning about God and His Word. Both of my parents were Lutheran teachers, so I not only received instruction in the home, but I also went to church just about every week. From preschool through eighth grade, I attended Good Shepherd Lutheran School in Downey, California, where my father served as principal as well as the seventh and eighth grade teacher. You might think that after all that I might want less, not more, from confirmation. Yet when it came time for confirmation, I found myself seeking out more, not less, instruction. I did not want simple answers and at times may have pushed my pastor further than he was prepared to go in order to satisfy my own curiosity.

As a church with a parochial school, Good Shepherd offered confirmation instruction both in the classroom during the week as well as on Wednesday afternoons for church members who did not attend the Day School. Although my pastor meant well, he was neither well prepared to deal with the junior high mind nor was he very enthusiastic about attempting to do so. I will admit that I may have been a bit much of a child to deal with. My desire to dig further than the average student into catechesis may have presented a challenge alongside other students who were more interested in flirting with the girls or playing baseball with wads of paper and a baseball-bat shaped pen (true story—we did play a form of homerun derby while instruction continued).

As a father of two young boys, I spend a good deal of time thinking about how I can re-create in my own children the passion I had for learning the faith. My wife, Andrea, and I started reading the Bible to both James and Wesley since well before they were able to sit through story time before bed. We have attempted to live out our conviction that the Word of God ought to be a central shaping force for our lives. We have attempted to engage in spiritual conversations, explaining what takes place when we worship at church, as well as discussing the Trinity at bath time (yes, even at age 3, James had a fairly detailed discussion on the Trinity while playing with toys in the tub).

My sons have not always wanted to sit still while reading stories from their various children's Bibles. Like all kids, there are times when they would rather spend the time after Sunday School on the playground rather than go into church with us to worship. And if I am being honest, I will have to say that I still have Sunday mornings when I would rather sleep in than fight to get the family out of bed, fed, dressed, and on the road to church. However, the passion that moved me as a child to seek out more knowledge of my Savior and motivated me to enter ministry as a Director of Christian Education still moves me, despite my not being a morning person, to accomplish this feat.

Looking back through my years as a Director of Christian Education, and especially at all the confirmation classes I have taught, I really appreciate just how much my parents shaped my faith in Christ and desire to grow in that faith. Year in and year out, the start of confirmation instruction in the fall meant that families would begin to come out of the woodwork and sign up little Timmy and Suzie for class. As exciting as that has been over the years, I have also learned to anticipate that a good number of those students will return to the woodwork from whence they came, just as soon as instruction is completed and the Rite of Confirmation is performed. Even students who, by all appearances, were engaged and even quite inquisitive in class (as I was) never show up again after the celebratory cake is served with the requisite red punch.

Now, I do need to mention that I have seen exceptions to this trend and they bring me much joy. I have seen whole families begin to engage in the life of the congregation as a direct result of the connections formed during and through the confirmation instructional process. However, having seen so many depart just as swiftly as they arrived, I have found my heart heavy and questioning the effectiveness of what was being done under that name of confirmation.

I wanted to know more about what was happening. I wanted, and even still desire, to understand all that I can about confirmation and its impact on the youth and families in our churches. This led me to spend the last few years in doctoral study on the nature, history, and models of instruction for confirmation. Just as I was not satisfied as a student in eighth grade with the confirmation instruction that I was receiving during the school day, I was not satisfied with dismissing the question of how we might do confirmation better. As an eighth grade student, I spent time attending an extra confirmation class after school for the public school kids. In the past few years, I have continued to explore the topic, spending time reading a wide variety of books and articles on confirmation and related topics. I make no claims to have discovered the perfect program that will keep your kids from heading out the door following confirmation. Would you really believe me if I claimed that I did have such a program? Even so, I do believe that I have locked in on a philosophy of ministry that is essential to constructing a catechesis culture within the life of your church.

Whether you are a pastor, DCE, parent, or church leader with a desire to improve your congregation's approach to confirmation, I want to begin here and now to challenge you to think beyond confirmation and to start thinking in terms of catechesis. We do not use words like that in the church much, which is a shame. Words like *catechesis* just sound too "churchy." At times, we rightly shy away from "churchy" words that only manage to confuse folks in our age of lessening biblical literacy. Yet, I want to challenge you to reclaim the term *catechesis* with me and explore in these pages how catechesis is the key to maintaining a connection to the Church and the faith through childhood and into adulthood.

Part 1 of this book focuses on laying a foundation. In order to accomplish this, I will begin by first defining just what catechesis is in chapter 1. In doing so, I will walk through the history and development of catechesis from the ancient Early Church through to the development of what we have come to know as confirmation. I know that not everyone may be interested in history, but take the time to walk through the years with me and together we will see more clearly where we have come from and establish a foundation for where we might propose to go in the years and decades ahead.

In chapter 2, I will review and explore the theology behind catechetical instruction. Following this theological exploration, chapter 3 will provide an assessment of the state of confirmation, examining what has gone wrong with the Church's approach to confirmation in recent history. The historical development, theological foundation, and critical assessment of confirmation and catechesis will provide the starting point from which this book will attempt to point ahead to a new and improved approach that will seek to better connect youth and their families with the Church, both well before and for eternity following confirmation.

To explore and develop the philosophy of ministry that I believe is essential for quality catechesis, chapter 4 will tackle the application of developmental theory to catechetical process. Chapter 5 will then discuss the concept of a thinking climate in both the Church and the home. Chapter 6 will focus on the ministry of confirmation itself. This chapter will examine how families and church leaders can best establish the proper place of confirmation in the structure of the larger ministry of the Church and life of the family. From there, chapter 7 will explore specific needs that blended and single parent families face with regard to catechizing their children.

Part 2 will be more practical. Chapter 8 will provide strategies that can be employed in the local church to help make catechesis and confirmation instruction not merely a brief class that students take to graduate, but rather an introduction to a lifetime of learning and growth in Christ. Then chapter 9 will introduce how parents are able to equip themselves for the teaching of their own children with the content of Luther's Small Catechism. Finally, chapter 10 and following will explore each of the Six Chief Parts and the Table of Duties. I will share practical ideas that parents can use as their children grow up in the faith to prepare them not only for the Rite of Confirmation but also for a lifetime of catechesis. Christian Questions with their Answers (section 4 in the Small Catechism) will be covered as an appendix. Parents are encouraged to draw on the material included in chapters 10–17 as they teach the faith at home.

The life of faith in Christ is a journey of relationship. God gathers us—created as social beings—into families and churches, where we journey together, offering support, correction, guidance, and encouragement. Please join me on the journey as I explore what might be if we were to reexamine the nature of catechesis in a Lutheran context.

PART 1

UNDERSTANDING CATECHESIS AND CONFIRMATION

CHAPTER 1

WHAT IS CATECHESIS ANYWAY?

"Catechesis? Is it contagious?"

I love Hugh Laurie. His portrayal of Gregory House on the television show *House* was "Must See TV" for me for years. Each week, Dr. House and his team were presented with some rare condition to diagnose that no other group of doctors was able to figure out. In round table form they would run through a barrage of diagnostic possibilities with technical language that left me a bit confused (really, why was sarcoidosis mentioned in just about every episode?) and often caused me to watch the show with medical dictionary in hand.

Catechesis is one of those "churchy" kinds of words that we tend to stray away from to avoid unnecessary confusion not only for new believers but also for longtime members who may have never heard nor understood what it means. Making use of this term in a book such as this may seem to be similar to my armchair medical practice of watching *House*. Yet, I would argue that when we lose terms like *catechesis*, we run the risk of losing the essential core of the Church practice that the term defines. So what is catechesis anyway, and why is such a term worth explaining in a culture uninterested in tradition and traditional-sounding terms?

The Greek word *katacheo*, from which our term *catechesis* is derived, means "to sound again." Thus, the educational process of catechesis is the sounding again of the historic truths of the Christian faith from one generation to the next.[1] An elder generation presents the content of our

---

[1] John Bombaro, "A Catechetical Imitation of Christ," *Modern Reformation* (March–April 2009): 32.

7

common faith, and the younger generation echoes back what they have learned. Catechesis, then, in its simplest form is a sort of call and response of the truths of the Christian faith. Luther's Small Catechism exemplifies this in its structure and form. Although there already were catechisms available prior to Luther's work, his innovation in structuring the book in a question and answer format was new to the genre.

In the Preface of his Large Catechism, Luther states substantive reasons why the Christian faithful should continually use the catechism. Both the weighty reasons and the urgency remain today. Luther was concerned with the lack of teaching of the faith that he saw in the churches of his day. I believe that we face a similar crisis today. Churches are full of activity, but may often fail to ensure quality teaching, especially for the young. The Church continues to struggle against the prevailing winds of the culture that seek to instill in emerging generations what Christian Smith calls "Moralistic Therapeutic Deism."[2] While the culture pushes toward a conception of faith lacking in distinctions, faithful Lutheran pastors, DCEs, teachers, and, most importantly, parents seek with much prayer to impart the unique claims of the Christian faith into the hearts and minds of young people. As Paul teaches in Romans 6, while we are still dead in our sins and wholly incapable of reaching out to God, Christ reaches out to us, removes from us our sins, and restores us to life and a right relationship with the Father through the Holy Spirit.

Catechesis is an educational practice of the Church that provides a portion of the pushing back against the tide of our culture. Through the sounding again of the truths of Scripture, one generation bequeaths to the next the essential core of Christianity. The presentation of the essential core truths of the Christian faith has developed over time, but the foundational structures have been with us for many centuries. What we have in the Small Catechism includes what are known as the Six Chief Parts. They are the Ten Commandments, the Apostles' Creed, the Lord's Prayer, Holy Baptism, Confession, and finally Holy Communion. These, along with the Daily Prayers, Table of Duties, and Christian Questions with Their Answers, form the substance of Luther's Small Catechism.

---

[2] Christian Smith, *Soul Searching: The Religious and Spiritual Lives of American Teenagers* (New York: Oxford University Press, 2005), 118–71.

Much of the foundational teachings of the Church summarized and taught through Luther's Small Catechism were already essential to the catechetical teaching of the Church in the centuries prior to Luther. The earliest written document related to the Church's catechetical efforts is the *Didache* (first century AD). With the bulk of converts of the time coming from the Gentile community, the *Didache* was written to pass on what it means to live as people of The Way.[3] Whereas Lutheran catechesis focuses more on right understanding, the focus of the *Didache* was more on right living than on right learning.

The Church Fathers used this early work to develop the practices of and structures for catechesis. In the third century AD, *On the Apostolic Tradition* presented a practice that included a rigorous examination on the merits of one's claim of faith and an examination of the changes evident in one's life. The teaching provided in this early document focused on what we today might call "Christian living," and instruction in it could last upwards of three years. The catechumen (formal student of the Christian faith) was then instructed on the teachings of the Gospel in preparation for Baptism and finally instructed on the sacrament of Holy Communion.[4]

This early practice of the Church seems to be very different from the "Pastor's Class" concept of modern Lutheranism. Yet, it makes sense when you stop to consider the precarious situation the Early Church was in at that time. Prior to Constantine, the Church lived through periods of violent persecution. The Early Church leadership had to be certain that those claiming to be new converts were not in fact spies sent to identify the leadership of this new religious movement. Judaism was legal while Christianity was not. Initially, Roman officials seemed to allow that Christianity was merely a sect within Judaism, but with time, the Christian faith was seen as more distinct from Judaism than legally allowable. The Roman practice had been to allow conquered people to maintain their pre-existing religious beliefs and practices (within certain parameters). However, the development of new religious beliefs and practices

---

[3] The Way was another name used during the first century AD to describe the Christian movement. It referred to people who followed "the way" of living as taught by Jesus.

[4] John H. Westerhoff III and O. C. Edwards Jr., *A Faithful Church* (Wilton, CT: Morehouse-Barlow Co, 1981), 52.

was severely restricted. Thus, what seems like extreme measures to our modern ears were in fact reasonable precautions given the culture in which the Church first took root.

Following the conversion of Constantine, things radically changed. Rather than having to protect the Church from spies, the church leaders had to protect the integrity of the Church teachings from the massive influx of converts to the now trendy faith of the emperor. In order to handle the massive influx of converts, catechesis could no longer take place in smaller, more private settings. The more intimate discipling of converts conducted by the Early Church had to give way to larger scale presentations. Thus, the catechetical sermon, presented to larger audiences, ascended to the forefront of the Church's catechetical preparations.[5] Great figures in the history of the catechetical sermon included Cyril of Jerusalem, John Chrysostom, and Augustine of Hippo. Cyril firmly established the pattern of catechesis as a threefold framework with the Creed, Ten Commandments, and Lord's Prayer. John Chrysostom was known for the practical nature of his catechetical sermons. In his *Baptismal Instruction*,[6] he skillfully connected teaching the faith with cultural commentary, providing a context for comprehension of doctrinal exposition. Augustine explored a number of pedagogical techniques including the use of questions as well as the honing of rhetorical skills. This, in fact, made Augustine a rather popular catechist.

As the golden age of the catechetical sermon waned, the form remained beyond its true fruitfulness. Catechetical sermons were still preached, but no longer were converts moving through the catechetical process toward Baptism. As the Medieval Church developed, major changes in theology and practice reshaped catechesis. One of these changes was the development of a longer time period between Baptism and first Communion. Early Church conversions tended to focus on adult populations. As Christianity spread and new people groups were added, this trend continued. It was only once the majority of the people groups of Europe were Christianized that the trend changed and larger numbers of children were baptized. While there had been, and in fact

---

[5] Josef A. Jungmann, *Handing on the Faith: A Manual of Catechesis* (New York: Herder and Herder, 1959), 3.

[6] John Chrysostom, *Baptismal Instruction* (New York: Paulist Press, 1963), 36–40.

continues to be, a tradition of infant Communion in the Eastern or Orthodox Church, the Western or Roman Church did not follow suit. Thus, catechesis moved from a form of instruction provided prior to Baptism to a practice of educating those baptized as infants once they were able to reason well enough to comprehend the faith for themselves. In response to this development, the Church developed two tools that have become foundational for modern catechetical efforts: the catechism and confirmation.

DEVELOPMENT OF THE CATECHISM AND CONFIRMATION

Although the basic structure of the catechism was fairly well solidified by the thirteenth century AD,[7] the term *catechism* was not used in English until 1357, in reference to John Thoresby's *The Lay Folks' Catechism*. The development of *The Lay Folks' Catechism* was approached with a dual purpose in mind. The simultaneous issuing of the work in both Latin and the vernacular meant that both the laity and the priests were able to improve their understanding of the Christian faith. The catechism taught on six items: the fourteen points of the Creed, the Ten Commandments, seven sacraments, seven works of mercy, seven virtues, and seven deadly sins.[8] This set the standard by which catechisms would be developed and evolve in the coming years.

Another example of the further development of early catechisms can be seen in *Life of Soul*.[9] What is interesting to note when reviewing *Life of Soul* is the large number of scriptural references included. This contribution to the development of the catechism would become far more common in future catechisms, like those of Luther and the other reformers.

Of the seven Roman Catholic sacraments, confirmation remained one of the worst defined within the practice of the faith in Medieval Catholicism.[10] In some sense, it can be argued that its development was more of a reaction to shifting practices in Baptism, since more infants

---

[7] Berard L. Marthaler, *The Catechism Yesterday and Today* (Collegeville, MN: Liturgical Press, 1995), 9.

[8] Marthaler, *The Catechism Yesterday and Today*, 13.

[9] P. F. Schaffner, trans., "Life of Soul," in *Culture of Piety: Medieval English Devotional Literature in Translation* (Ithaca, NY: Cornell University Press, 1999).

[10] Jaroslav Pelikan, *The Growth of Medieval Theology (600–1300)* (Chicago: University of Chicago Press, 1978), 211.

than adults were baptized in the Middle Ages in Europe, as opposed to the larger numbers of adult Baptisms that marked the Early Church period. The catechism—Luther's and others (see *The Lay Folks' Catechism* and *Life of Soul* for precursors to Luther's)—became the instruction manual for catechesis within the structure of confirmation. Confirmation thus took shape as a way for the Church to instruct youth in the faith of their Baptism as they transitioned toward adulthood.[11] As this method of instruction was taking shape, the Roman Catholic Church was solidifying its teaching on the sacramental nature of confirmation itself.

When the reformers set out to reform the Church, they did not neglect the educational aspects of church life, and thus brought their own theological understanding to bear on the practice of catechesis and the development of catechisms. The connection between catechesis and the catechism is that of instructional method and instructional tool. Just as the catechetical sermon once performed the task as a guide through the Scriptures and foundational doctrines, the catechism developed as a manual for instruction of the unlearned. As the form of some indicates, instructors and parents quizzed students with questions directly out of the catechism. The emphasis was on memorization, as it was assumed that all students had already accepted the teachings of the Church. Thus both the reformers and Rome used these documents to distinguish students' understanding of the Ten Commandments, the Sacraments, and the rest of the core elements found in their pages.

Forming Luther's Theology of Catechesis

Confirmation nearly did not survive Luther's reforms. More than merely rejecting the sacramental aspects of confirmation, he initially considered leaving the practice entirely behind. However, despite his concerns, Luther concluded that if a form of confirmation could be instituted that did not supplant Baptism, he could support it as an educational effort.[12]

---

[11] Keep in mind that adolescence was not a stage of development in the Middle Ages. The transition to adulthood was more closely tied to physiological changes at the onset of puberty. Thus, our "traditional" junior high confirmation once marked a truer transition into adulthood than it does today.

[12] Arthur Repp, *Confirmation in the Lutheran Church* (St. Louis: Concordia, 1964), 16.

Luther came to this conclusion when he realized how much the German people of his day needed solid biblical instruction and that proper training and tools were lacking for local parish priests. He rightly maintained the distinction that confirmation was not to be viewed as a sacrament, but rather as a critically essential educational ministry of the Church. In this way, Luther sought to disconnect the catechetical nature of confirmation from the sacramental theology that grew up around it as developed by the Roman Catholic Church. Catechesis was once again adapted to respond to the shifting needs and theological reforms of the Church.

Just as it took Luther time to discover the value that catechesis and catechism might have for his reform movement, it also took time for him to develop his own work. His theology evolved as the answers to certain questions caused him to move on to other emerging questions. As he worked, he made use of a series of charts from which he would later develop both his Large and Small Catechisms. Through these charts, Luther developed what became known as the Six Chief Parts of the Small Catechism.[13]

Luther, though an educated man, possessed the ability to write to the uneducated. The success of the Small Catechism can be seen in the clarity with which it presents biblical material.[14] The logical flow that Luther developed aided in the use of the Small Catechism for study. This made his theology accessible to the growing number of Lutherans in Germany and across Europe. Luther's Small Catechism should be considered a text for the life of the Church, not merely used for a brief period of instruction, as is more common today.

Luther's work on the Small Catechism affected more than the churches that bear his name today. In many ways, Luther was really introducing catechesis in a modern sense. He sought to disconnect the catechetical nature of confirmation from the sacramental emphasis placed upon it by the Roman Catholic Church.

---

[13] Harold Grimm, "Luther's Catechism as Textbook," in *Teaching the Faith* (River Forest, IL: Lutheran Education Association, 1967), 34.

[14] Grimm, "Luther's Catechism as Textbook," 38.

Luther's Catechism Comes to America

When Lutherans came to America, they brought with them an assortment of catechisms from the various regional Lutheran churches to which they had belonged in Europe. Each regional exposition of the catechism lent its own interpretation of Luther to the theological discussion. As theological trends in Europe shaped these interpretations, the various groups of Lutherans who gathered together in America struggled to form a united voice. This resulted in the development of two main streams of Lutheranism: American Lutheranism and Confessional Lutheranism.

Lacking a central publishing house, dozens of variant catechisms were found within a single Lutheran congregation.[15] Compounding this confusion, the first edition of Luther's Small Catechism produced in America was published not by a Lutheran, but by a Moravian. As one might expect, this edition, published in 1744, was not well accepted or widely used. It was not until 1785 that a single unified catechism was officially recognized and printed for the Pennsylvania Ministerium. Thus, American Lutheranism took shape in an ambiguous approach to confessional standards and the influence of German Rationalism.

By way of contrast, the development of early Confessional Lutheranism offered a counter to the movement of American Lutheranism. Immigration played a key factor in the resurgence of confessionalism in America around the mid-nineteenth century.[16] As these more conservative immigrants arrived, they brought with them a desire to maintain the confessional standards that they held dear. Many, in fact, fled the Old World to avoid the Prussian Union that sought to merge Lutheran and Reformed churches in Germany.

This renewed confessionalism is evident from the inclusion of the Augsburg Confession in many editions of the catechism printed after 1840.[17] Clearly, this new wave of Lutheran immigrants approached their faith in a different way than their American Lutheran predecessors. Nevertheless, this does not mean that there had not been confessional Lutherans in America prior to this wave.

---

[15] Arthur Repp, *Luther's Catechism Comes to America* (Metuchen, NJ: The Scarecrow Press, 1982), 47.

[16] Repp, *Luther's Catechism Comes to America*, 178.

[17] Repp, *Luther's Catechism Comes to America*, 179.

In 1613, the more orthodox Johann Conrad Dietrich published a catechism that drew from the exposition of Luther's Small Catechism in a series of catechetical lectures.[18] It was this version that was selected to be the first official catechism of the newly forming confessional Lutheran Church body, the German Evangelical Lutheran Synod of Missouri, Ohio, and Other States, known since 1947 as the Lutheran Church—Missouri Synod (LCMS). The early founders of the LCMS saw in Dietrich a fellow brother who was as concerned as they were about the teaching of the pure doctrines of the Church.[19] Purity of doctrine and a strict adherence to the confessions marked and defined his catechism for Confessional Lutheranism.

Catechisms were used in the Christian home as well as in the local church. Luther taught that the teaching of the faith to the young was a duty of local government, the church, and the family.[20] Parents would spend time quizzing their children, perhaps at the dinner table, to assist them in memorization. Instruction focused around these quizzing interactions in a memorization/recitation model. Lutheran parish pastors made use of the Small and Large Catechisms in both their own learning and as instructional guides while teaching the children in their parish.

Luther's pedagogical model involved three basic stages:

1. Learn and remember the basics.[21]

2. Understand the basics.[22]

3. Make applying the fundamentals a lifelong practice.[23]

In stage 1, the catechist (the teacher or instructor) would present the material in the catechism, then the catechumen would recite what was just taught. In this manner, the students put the basics to memory.[24] Luther's

---

[18] S. Carter, "Catechisms in the Lutheran Church—Missouri Synod: An Historical Survey" in *Teaching the Faith* (River Forest, IL: Lutheran Education Association, 1967), 59.

[19] Carter, "Catechisms in the Lutheran Church—Missouri Synod," 59–60.

[20] Charles Arand, *That I May Be His Own: An Overview of Luther's Catechisms* (St. Louis: Concordia, 2000), 92.

[21] Arand, *That I May Be His Own*, 97.

[22] Arand, *That I May Be His Own*, 100.

[23] Arand, *That I May Be His Own*, 109.

[24] Arand, *That I May Be His Own*, 98.

question and answer method was used in stage 2, when the catechist moved from memorization to understanding as the famous Lutheran phrase "What does this mean?" was asked and Luther's explanations came into play. In stage 3, Luther stressed the need for ongoing study of the catechism, since it covers the very foundations of the faith.[25] The time of formal catechesis and the use of the catechism was only a beginning. Following confirmation, students were to continue to make use of the catechism as a form of daily meditation and guide to God's Word.

LUTHERAN CATECHESIS TODAY

Today we find the inheritance of both Confessional and American Lutheranism across Lutheran denominations. In general, the Evangelical Lutheran Church in America (ELCA) tends toward American Lutheranism, while the LCMS and Wisconsin Evangelical Lutheran Synod (WELS) are marked by Confessional Lutheranism. However, the streams of both approaches to confirmation have crossed to such an extent that one can find the influence of both within each of these three church bodies.

A diversity of forms and models mark the current practice of confirmation in Lutheran churches in America. What was once uniform and directed primarily through denominational publishing houses is now a multifaceted and creative mix of denominational, independent, and local church developed curriculums.

Each of the three largest Lutheran church bodies in America (ELCA, LCMS, and WELS) publishes its own confirmation materials with its own focus. The ELCA is currently promoting its Here We Stand[26] curriculum. With online content and customizable lessons, the focus is on flexible, contextual usage. The LCMS, through Concordia Publishing House (CPH), offers a subscription service called Confirmation Builder[27] that enables pastors and other instructors to customize lessons drawing from a number of sources in the CPH catalog. The Faith Foundations[28] curriculum of the WELS similarly remains strictly faithful to the Small Cate-

---

[25] Arand, *That I May Be His Own*, 110.

[26] See www.augsburgfortress.org/herewestand/.

[27] See www.confirmationbuilder.com.

[28] See online.nph.net/p-7713-faith-foundations-catechism-student-lessons-yr1.aspx.

chism for fifth and sixth graders. Their Luther's Catechism Lessons for seventh and eighth graders walk students through the original questions in the Small Catechism and provides additional instructional aides to better connect the content to students' lives.

The Concordia Catechetical Academy[29] is at the forefront of a movement within the LCMS to return to a more traditional model of catechesis in the style of the Small Catechism itself. To accomplish this, they have published the Lutheran Catechesis Series, as well as other publications, and have held conferences on catechesis. Moving beyond the practice of seventh and eighth grade confirmation instruction, the Academy's catechesis model begins far earlier. Students learn and memorize the Six Chief Parts in third grade and the Table of Duties in fourth grade. They then go on to learn the Old Testament in fourth grade and the New Testament in fifth grade, followed by instruction on the Large Catechism in sixth and seventh grade. In eighth grade, they study the Table of Duties at a greater depth, along with the Parables and Miracles of Jesus, the Smalcald Articles, and the Augsburg Confession.

In the new confessionalism of the Lutheran Catechesis Series, the question and answer structure of Luther's Small Catechism is reprised and expanded into the other teachings of the Church. The Lutheran Catechesis Series model seeks to incorporate additional material to respond to weaknesses seen in students' biblical literacy. The key difference, however, is its instructional approach. Whereas other curriculums have moved away from rote memorization, the Lutheran Catechesis Series stresses its usage as fundamental.

Supplementing the congregational instruction, the Lutheran Catechesis Series makes use of what it calls the Congregation at Prayer. Using a structured order of worship for the home, the Congregation at Prayer provides hymns, prayers, Bible readings, and elements from the Small Catechism for home study and reflection.

In addition to the resurgence of confessional approaches to confirmation, a number of innovative new models are being explored. These emerging models seek to strengthen the weaknesses that have crept into confirmation ministry since its inception in the Lutheran Church. Many seek to avoid the "graduation effect," in which students consider their

---

[29] An auxiliary organization of Peace Lutheran Church, Sussex, WI.

confirmation to be a graduation from church life. Others merely hope to improve the educational methodology used to convey traditional content. Some new models augment the content of Lutheran confirmation instruction to compensate for changes in culture, resulting in a larger focus on overall biblical understanding and literacy.

Rev. Dr. Kevin Wyssmann developed one such innovative approach when he served at Christ's Greenfield Lutheran Church in Gilbert, Arizona. In his "Systemic Catechesis,"[30] students are not required to begin or complete their studies at a single predetermined date. Instead, he allows for learning beginning in fifth grade with no set required completion date. In this manner, students can work at their own pace; they are not left to drop through the cracks, because they have the support of the ministry staff and elders.

This systemic model also throws into the mix a youth-oriented worship service to teach students the richness of weekly worship. It involves the students in parish service hours, through which they experience how the gifts God gives them can translate into service in the church. "Systemic Catechesis" offers a balanced approach that attempts to provide students of different learning styles time to consider their learning in a way more conducive to their needs.[31]

Wyssmann stresses that the church needs to be flexible as it works with individual students. He notes that all students bring with them their own unique prior knowledge of the Christian faith.[32] In some cases, our students need to unlearn false understandings of the faith before they are able to learn and build upon right understandings. One can see how, with a task such as this, flexibility in the time of instruction is essential.

Under the guidance of Dr. William Knippa, the confirmation program at Bethany Lutheran Church in Austin, Texas, delays instruction until students are in ninth and tenth grade. Basing this model on his Ph.D. work in psychology, Dr. Knippa seeks to work with students at a more advanced stage of concept abstraction. Students are expected to know the Ten Commandments, the Lord's Prayer, the Apostles' Creed,

---

[30] Kevin L. Wyssmann, "Systemic Catechesis" (Ph.D. diss., Concordia Seminary, 2002).

[31] Wyssmann, "Systemic Catechesis," 5.

[32] Wyssmann, "Systemic Catechesis," 51.

and the books of the Bible prior to the beginning of instruction. In this way, instruction time can focus on life application and a student's beliefs or questions regarding the doctrines of the Church.[33]

In 1993, Rev. Rich Melheim, a pastor in the ELCA, developed Faith Inkubators, which has reinvigorated confirmation across several denominations Melheim's model of confirmation involves both a large group time and small group discussions. The multi-media curriculum provides students with game-show style activities designed to engage the learner. The small group time encourages a more personal application of the large group learning.

Faith Inkubators has many features designed to keep students' attention, but it has been criticized for lacking depth of content. In addition to the traditional Six Chief Parts of Luther's Small Catechism, the curriculum includes sections on Martin Luther, an overview of both the Old and New Testaments, and the life of Jesus. Another section covers what they call "Hot Topics," such as Sex and Love; Drugs: Your Body is a Temple; Fast Cars and Other Risky Business; War and Peace; Suicide; and others.[34] With these additional topics as well as the overall structure of the program, church leaders are able to supplement where they find the need to add depth to the curriculum.

Faith Inkubators has added Living Faith Journals as a tool to take home the learning done in confirmation class. Just like in small group time, during which highs and lows (what went well and not so well in the past week), along with prayer requests, are discussed before reiterating the main teaching, the journals replicate small group time daily in the home. The overarching goal of the journals, as well as Faith Inkubators as a whole, is to resurrect confirmation from the previously mentioned "graduation effect."

CATECHESIS: MORE THAN JUST CONFIRMATION

In *What Does This Mean?: Catechesis in the Lutheran Congregation,* former LCMS president A. L. Barry defines catechesis as having everything to do with leading to faith in Christ and living the life of

---

[33] I experienced this practice firsthand when on my internship at Bethany.

[34] "Faith Inkubators: Head to the Heart," www.faithink.com/Inkubators/h2h_90_themes.asp (accessed October 27, 2008).

faith.[35] This implies that multiple strands of Christian education are at play in catechesis, including discipleship and spiritual formation.

Catechesis is a term that the Church does not use as often as it should. Catechesis is far larger than confirmation. While confirmation can be seen as either the Rite of Confirmation or a sequence of study leading to that rite, catechesis is the larger formation of core doctrinal understanding that begins far sooner and lasts far longer than even the most extensive confirmation program.

Christian education is broader than catechesis. Whereas catechesis focuses on core doctrines, Christian education seeks to teach the full content of the Bible. Looking at the relationship between catechesis and Christian education this way, we see that all of catechesis is Christian education, but not all of Christian education is catechesis.

The relationship between Christian education and discipleship is similar. Christian education is necessary, catechesis included, but it is not sufficient for discipleship to take place. Discipleship is the following of Christ in one's life. As Lutherans, we tend not to emphasize what it means to live out our Christian faith as much as our Evangelical brothers, which may, to a certain extent, be wise on our part. Our strength lies in teaching the doctrines of the Christian faith with clarity. The hope is that a clear understanding of the doctrines of the Christian faith will naturally result in individuals living out that faith in a Christlike manner. Nevertheless, I would suggest that, at times, our neglect to draw the connection between our rich doctrinal emphasis and our life in Christ hinders the spiritual maturity of our congregations—especially as it relates to teaching the faith to the young people in our church. This sets up a false distinction between the head and the heart as they relate to our faith.

In his book *Life Together*, Dietrich Bonhoeffer stresses that God is the one who has laid the foundation of our discipleship in the Christian life.[36] As thankful recipients of God's grace, we are less likely to fall into cheap grace.[37] Out of a sense of thanksgiving, we rejoice in the blessings

---

[35] A. L. Barry, *What Does This Mean?: Catechesis and the Lutheran Church* (St. Louis: Concordia, 1996), 9.

[36] Dietrich Bonhoeffer, *Life Together* (San Francisco: Harper Collins, 1954), 28.

[37] See Dietrich Bonhoeffer, *The Cost of Discipleship* (New York: Touchstone, 1995).

of forgiveness and seek to respond in joyful service of our Lord and King. As a community of faith, we gather for mutual support and growth, and each week we seek to grow in faith and in joy-filled service.

It is in this context that catechesis is righty placed. There is no catechesis apart from the community of faith. Within the community of the Church, that is, the Body of Christ, fellow sinners gather to receive forgiveness from and restoration with God along with their fellow members of humanity. For people to be led into the Christian faith and life, there must be someone doing the leading. Once they have been led into the faith, they also need someone to lead the growth and development of their faith. The Church is, by God's design, a place devoted to the teaching of the apostles, fellowship, prayers, and breaking bread together (Acts 2:42).[38]

Again, we see the strands of catechesis, Christian education, and discipleship come together. Thus, as a working definition of catechesis, I would suggest that we proceed with the following: Catechesis is the element of Christian education focused on understanding the essential doctrines of the Bible that form the foundation of the Christian faith and the adoption of those claims as central tenants of one's own faith and life leading toward richer discipleship.

In worship, the liturgy of the Church teaches believers, new and old, the language of our relationship with God and one another. Through our worship, we come to learn the story of the relationship between God and His creation, the fall and subsequent redemption through Christ. In worship, Christ comes to us through Word and Sacrament. God's grace restores us, bringing us into a right relationship with Him and one another.

Having heard from God's Word and responding in praise to Him, we naturally seek to grow in our knowledge of Him and all that He has and continues to do for us. Our instruction in the Christian faith, essentially what catechesis is all about, provides additional content to the faith we express and confess in worship. Steven P. Mueller notes that despite ongoing struggles to understand Christ's claims of divinity, His role as

---

[38] "The breaking of bread" may be a reference to Holy Communion. I tend to lean that direction, but others suggest that this was merely another aspect of fellowship through the practice of communal meals.

teacher was recognized.[39] The Great Commission charged Christ's disciples, and by extension their disciples, with continuing His teaching ministry. However, Jesus was no mere instructor, since we know Him to be God incarnate. Thus, the central content of the faith taught is Christ Himself. This is the core of our catechetical efforts.

Having been instructed in the faith, we are, in theory, equipped for service in the name of Christ. As Christians, we each take part in the ministry[40] of the Church, though through a wide variety of ways.[41] In our catechesis and spiritual growth, we learn about how we might seek to serve others within the Church and those outside the Body of Christ in need of the Gospel's saving message. Matthew 25:35–36 provides a view of how faithful Christians might serve their fellow man. In this way, we minister to the physical needs of those in our communities in need and through that service minister to Christ.

Thus, we see that catechesis ought to be a foundational element of our Christian education efforts in the local church. However, we also see that this is not done in isolation. It could be argued that catechesis is the foundational element of one's personal discipleship. Whether one becomes a part of the Body of Christ through Baptism as a child or is called into a relationship with Him later in life, a life of discipleship begins as God makes us His own. Infants who are not able to respond to the faith given them at their Baptism must rely for years upon the instruction and support of their parents, sponsors, and others in the family of faith.

Just over a month after he was born, our son James was baptized at Shepherd of the Hills Lutheran Church in Rancho Cucamonga, California. We have an absolutely classic photo of a rare occurrence. James was perfectly still! It's not just that he did not cry or cause some other typical

---

[39] Steven P. Mueller, "The Doctrine of God," in *Learning at the Foot of the Cross* (Austin, TX: Concordia University Press, 2011), 27.

[40] Ministry here is used in the broad sense—not ministry in the narrow sense as defined by the pastoral office. Steven P. Mueller clarifies the distinction in *Called to Believe, Teach, and Confess* (Wipf & Stock, 2005): "Ministry—from a Latin word meaning, 'service,' ministry is sometimes used as a synonym for any service done by a Christian. More narrowly, ministry refers to the work of specific Christians who are called to specific offices in the church. In its most proper sense, ministry refers to the ministry of word and sacrament, namely the pastoral office." It is the first sense, not the last, that is implied here.

[41] See Matthew 25:35–36 and 1 Corinthians 12:1–11.

fuss, it was that he was, in fact, fast asleep. James did exactly what he had to in order to be baptized—he fell asleep. There in the pastor's arms, James was adopted into the family of God, purely as an action of God. He did not even need to be awake for the experience. While we ought not to sleep throughout our life of faith, we are, in fact, in more than a state of spiritual sleep prior to Baptism—we are dead. We offer nothing. Catechesis, then, is a time in which we dig more deeply into the faith of our Baptism and come to terms with the specifics and implications of those beliefs. We are still led by the Holy Spirit, but we are actively growing and learning for ourselves.

In their book, *Grounded in the Gospel*, Packer and Parrett present catechesis as a part of building believers.[42] They emphasize quality in the workmanship in our approach to catechesis as well as the whole of discipleship.[43] They are speaking of the quality of the workmanship that we employ as we pour into the lives of young people and those young in the faith. In order to achieve this quality, I believe that we need to understand catechesis as a unified part of Christian education and our discipleship. The Early Church's emphasis on orthopraxis (right action) as well as orthodoxy (right belief) speaks to the historicity of this combined emphasis. Our efforts for catechesis very much should be an intentional part of our spiritual-formation efforts as a part of an overall discipleship plan. In the coming chapters we will discuss more about the theological approach to catechesis itself. Then we will get into the practical questions: How do we put catechesis into practice as the element of Christian education focused on understanding the essential doctrines of the Bible that form the foundation of the Christian faith? How do we adopt those claims as central tenants of our own faith and life leading toward richer discipleship?

---

[42] J. I. Packer and Gary A. Parrett, *Grounded in the Gospel: Building Believers the Old-Fashioned Way* (Grand Rapids: Baker Books, 2010), 16.

[43] Packer and Parrett, *Grounded in the Gospel*, 16.

CHAPTER 2

WHY CATECHESIS?

A THEOLOGY OF CATECHETICAL INSTRUCTION

Perhaps it ought to go without saying that in order for the faith of one generation to be passed along to another, some form of teaching has to take place. This passing on of the faith was a central feature of the formation of the nation of Israel, and since the time of Christ, each generation has taught the next generation the story of Jesus' life, ministry, death, and resurrection. Even though it may not always be referred to with this term, this teaching of the basics of the faith is catechesis. Lutheran pastor John Bombaro defines the process of catechesis as a sounding again between learner and master.[1] This sounding again encapsulates the process by which the faith of one generation is echoed back by succeeding generations.

Catechesis has come in many forms over the years. The Early Church Fathers gathered to themselves disciples, much like Jesus had done. They then taught the disciples the same teachings that Jesus had taught to them. The forming of new generations of disciples, as John did with Polycarp (who was the last living connection to the first disciples before his martyrdom), is both discipleship as well as catechesis. It is discipleship as it focuses on our sanctification and taking on of Christ-likeness. It is catechesis as a foundation to that discipleship as it focuses

---

[1] John Bombaro, "A Catechetical Imitation of Christ," *Modern Reformation* (March–April 2009): 32.

on our coming to understand the doctrinal content of the faith handed down from one generation to the next.

As the Church grew, more formal structures were developed to manage the effectiveness of catechesis as well as the strength and orthodoxy of the content transmitted. This in turn gave rise to various questions: Do our methods of teaching measure up to biblical standards for the passing of the faith from generation to generation? For that matter, what are the biblical standards for such instruction? Who is responsible for said teaching? Are all methods of instruction truly adiaphora, or are some, in fact, in violation of biblical standards of catechesis?

So how can we answer these questions? To begin with, we need to explore the appropriate place of both the Church and the Christian family in the catechesis of a student. Then we need to consider whether it is appropriate to view confirmation as merely a programmatic level or, as suggested above, whether a more organic, whole life, learning approach would serve the Church better.

There are practices of the Early Church that, though they are both good and biblical, ought not to be taken as universally applicable for the Church today. While the New Testament does describe some of the instruction that took place as the Early Church was forming, it does not prescribe a particular method of instruction as a singularly acceptable method of catechesis. Where Scripture provides direct instruction, the Church ought not to deviate from that instruction. On the other hand, where God through His Word has chosen to remain silent, the Church is at liberty to establish practices in line with other biblical prescriptions. Citing a particular method of teaching as prescriptive for all places and all times might not be wise, or an appropriate use of Scripture. For example, many are returning to the Early Church model of house churches, using the home for a place of worship. However, this practice occurred due to the circumstances of the time. It was not a prescription of what everyone in future generations must do, just simply a description of what the Early Church did.

Why make this point in a book on catechesis? Churches by their very nature are traditional; even non-traditional churches have their traditions. There is occasionally a tendency to conflate the traditions of a particular church or denomination with biblical prescription on the matter. We make sacred that which is not in and of itself sacred. There are traditions regarding the date for the Rite of Confirmation, which differ from church to church. Some use Pentecost, others Palm Sunday, still others have moved to the use of Reformation Sunday in October. All of these are great ideas. None of these are biblical in the sense that they are prescribed for our practice; but just try and make a change to one of these traditionally held dates in your local church, and be prepared for a fight!

SCRIPTURAL FOUNDATION

It is critically important to understand the distinction between those elements of Scripture that are descriptive and those that are prescriptive. The Bible describes a good many things that we ought not to emulate. Therefore, we should take care in our interpretation only to bind ourselves to those commands that God actually commands of us. God may have told certain individuals in Scripture to take a particular action, but that does not mean it was a command meant also for us. God told Hosea to marry a prostitute, but that does not mean God calls other workers of the church to do likewise. In this, we see a descriptive text. On the other hand, the issuing of the Ten Commandments stands in contrast as a clear prescriptive command, which holds for us today.

Although confirmation as we know it today does not appear in the New Testament or the Early Church, the practice of confirmation is rooted in the New Testament—Christ's command in the Great Commission (Matthew 28:19–20) to go into all the nations and make disciples. We can see a foundation for confirmation in Christ's instruction to make those disciples through Baptism and the teaching of the faith. In the Great Commission, there is one mission with two aspects: outreach and teaching. Confirmation in the Early Church, as it is today, is a response of the Church to Christ's command to teach and make disciples.

The practice of confirmation is grounded in the scriptural command to teach, but this does not imply that confirmation, as we understand it today, is strictly biblical in the sense that it is a direct command of God. This is a point with which Luther himself struggled greatly as he sought to determine what to do with the practice. Rather, the church is free to establish its confirmation practices along theological principles rather than prescriptive passages related to Early Church practice.

Theological Foundation

So what, then, is the theological place of catechesis in the life of the Church? For the Lutheran, catechesis has its beginning in Baptism. Through the waters of Baptism, we are welcomed into the family of God. We are adopted into His family. Thus, even infants are welcomed into faith through Baptism, as God is the prime mover and the giver of faith through the Holy Spirit in Baptism.

Although confirmation is often associated with the sacrament of Communion more than Baptism, Baptism is actually the focal point of confirmation—not the Lord's Supper. If we understand that faith is a gift of God given in the waters of Baptism (Acts 2:38), then further instruction in that faith for students coming to an age of greater reasoning ability should be seen as the natural continuation of its development, especially for those baptized as infants or young children.

Luther understood confirmation to be the teaching of the faith given in Baptism. He established the primacy of Baptism as the beginning of catechesis, and taught that the Lord's Supper in and with the regular worship life of the church is the sustaining power of God on one's spiritual journey of greater understanding and closer relationship with Christ.

There are certain essential practices that the church must make a part of its corporate life in order for the local church truly to be a church. Lutherans have traditionally defined these as the proper preaching/teaching of the Gospel and right administration of the Sacraments. Confirmation has held a place of high honor within the Lutheran Church. As a part of the teaching ministry of the Church, catechesis provides a structure through which the Church can instruct successive generations on the truths of the Christian faith as understood by Lutherans.

Right teaching of the Gospel cannot take place in a vacuum. We understand the Gospel through the work of the Holy Spirit—both through the writers of Holy Scripture and through the Spirit's work in our heart to comprehend and believe what the Scriptures have to say. While Baptism brings us into faith in Christ, it is the teaching of the Church as seen in catechesis that informs that faith. The teaching ministry of the Church supports and sustains the faith given to us by God. Therefore, catechesis lays a foundational knowledge of the faith in the heart and mind so that we can more fully live out that faith in the Church. And the Lord's Supper sustains and uplifts our faith as a sacramental Means of Grace.

The sacramental sequence, if you desire to use such language, places catechesis between Baptism and the Lord's Supper. Baptism provides the gift of faith, which is then explored in catechesis and sustained for a lifetime in the celebration and reception of God's grace in the Lord's Supper.

SCRIPTURAL PRACTICE

THE OLD TESTAMENT

Let's take a step back for a moment and consider catechesis historically in order to understand further how this sequence works. Ancient Israel was of necessity an oral culture. Unlike our modern culture, where books are not only plentiful but also relatively inexpensive, ancient Israelites did not personally possess copies of God's Word. Therefore, it was critical for them to develop oral methods for the transmission of the faith from one generation to another.

The Book of Deuteronomy contains a family-based model that may help us develop a fuller understanding of catechesis as established in the life of the nation of Israel. In the *Shema*, Deuteronomy 6:4–9, the newly formed nation of Israel receives instructions on how they are to teach their young about the faith. The family is placed at the center of the matter: parents are to tend to the teaching of the faith as a central part of their identity as a family and as part of the larger family of God's people. As God is establishing His people as a nation, he establishes the foundation of their faith and identity in Him through the charge to parents to take spiritual leadership within their own families and provide catechesis for their children.

Luther's emphasis on the family as the center for the teaching of the faith from one generation to the next is thus nothing new. God established this pattern from the start of the nation of Israel. Just as God called upon the family in ancient Israel to keep His teachings always before them, the Christian family is to keep Scripture, and therefore the content of the catechism, ever-present in daily life. What is interesting is both the emphasis on the day-to-day nature of catechesis as well as the depth of reflection and digestion of the content of the faith implied in the text of Deuteronomy. This already presents an interesting challenge for parents who seek to fulfill this biblical role as spiritual leaders in the home. It thus seems only natural that the history of catechesis reviewed above would be a movement from the home to the congregation and back to the home.

A simple way to understand how the Jewish culture understood their calling to pass on the faith can be seen in Deuteronomy 11:19, which instructs parents to teach their children at all times. The list detailing when they were to teach the faith (when lying down, sitting, walking, etc.) perhaps ought not to be seen as a complete list, but rather as a way for God to get the point across that faith in Him was to be an all-day everyday thing. Thus, the teaching of the faith to the young should also be an all-day everyday type of thing. Here we get a picture of the all-pervasive effort that was to be a part of the family life of the people of Israel. Parents were to instruct their children not just occasionally, but at all times.

We might be tempted to guess what is meant by "children" in Deuteronomy 11:19, but the context of the passage does not present us with a specific description or age. Yet, even though we do not receive a clear picture of the age of the children when they received instruction, we are able to discern a sense of the manner in which that instruction took place.

In this structure, we can see both the command of God as well as the love upon which He bases His commands. Consider the process as described. Instruction was to take place, principally by parents, at all times of the day. The description "when you sit at home and when you walk along the road, when you lie down and when you get up" suggests that parents are to find times throughout the entire day for the teaching of the faith. We are not talking about merely formal times for instruction (though there ought to be times for discussion and instruction that are more formal), but rather what you see here is a description of teaching that is naturally woven into the tapestry of everyday life.

This makes good sense. Children quite naturally will learn from their parents as they observe them living out their faith. They will at times ask questions that require parents to explain and provide context for the particular ways in which they and other adults make choices in life. The point here is not to merely wait until our children ask, but instead to seek out teachable moments and strategically use them in order to connect elements of what might be taught in a formal setting into the context of the Christian life.

Above, we looked at the *Shema* from Deuteronomy 6:4–9. In addition to reflecting a similar command for the family to teach the faith as we find in Deuteronomy 11:19, in Deuteronomy 6:4–9 we also see the context and the central content of the faith that God commands parents to teach to their children. Because the Ten Commandments were recorded in the preceding verses, we can conclude that the core content for this instruction was to be God's commandments. But, even more fundamental than the Ten Commandments, the *Shema* lays the foundation for the relationship between God and His chosen people.

With the repetition of the *Shema*, children learned the fundamental truth upon which the Jewish faith was and is founded. The *Shema* was never far from their lips. Repeated often, the words would begin to echo in the mind and ultimately in the heart of children brought up in the Jewish faith. Like slowly turning a diamond, the repetition of a statement as simple as this phrase over time continued to reveal ever-deeper elements of the relationship between God and His people. It was not optional for Jewish children to learn the basic teachings of the faith. Parents would be failing in their duty as parents if they were to neglect this practice. There were both cultural and religious pressures that motivated parents to fulfill this duty.

As Jewish religious traditions developed, they came to center around two connected institutions, the temple and the synagogue. The concept of the synagogue developed as early as the fifth or sixth century BC during the Babylonian captivity, due to the lack of the temple as the center of religious life. The temple of Christ's day was thus supported by local synagogues, with elements of instruction taking place in both.

THE NEW TESTAMENT AND THE EARLY CHURCH

The model of instruction in the local synagogue that we encounter in Luke 2:46 would likely have been in place as a traditional method of religious instruction for some time. The rabbi, either one who was regularly instructing the faithful or a traveling rabbi as was the case with Jesus, would read an appointed or selected text. Then the rabbi would provide commentary, attempting to provide application for those being instructed. An alternative approach that may well have been used would have interwoven the commentary into the reading of the text. The rabbi would teach from a seated position, while those there to learn would stand while being instructed. Thus, you note a similarity to catechesis in a portion, though not the whole, of the approach found in teaching within the synagogue.

Whereas culturally the people of the Old Testament appear far more distant to us as modern Christians, the Early Church found in the New

Testament more readily connects with the practices of the Church today. Our mutual faith in Christ and mission to preach and teach the Gospel to others provides a connection that continues to draw us back to the practices of the Early Church. These Early Church practices provide instruction on how to worship our Lord, celebrate with and minister to His people, and educate the Body of Christ on the teachings that Jesus left in the care of His disciples.

If one thing is constant, it is that everything in creation changes. In Acts 2:42, fellowship is set up as a central mark of the life of the Early Church along with the apostles' teaching and the breaking of bread. Three activities are interrelated with one another as a part of congregational life in the Early Church.[2] Fellowship in the New Testament involved teaching and correcting one another, as well as the mutual support of the faithful as they lived life together.[3] Thus, quality fellowship provides the necessary connections that allow for teaching and the breaking of bread to take place within the local church.

Jesus ministered to different sized groups and the group size related to what took place with the various groups.[4] There were times when Jesus taught large crowds. Other times, He provided private instruction only to the Twelve. Still other times, Jesus taught individuals or small groups (Peter, James, and John, for example). Thus, Jesus made use of a variety of settings in which to teach the Good News. He provided more in-depth training in smaller settings, and used small groups and one-on-one attention to better tailor the instruction to the needs of the learner.

Although the settings that Christ, and then His disciples, used for instruction varied, the message remained consistent. In Matthew 28:20, Jesus instructs His disciples to teach all of the commands that He taught them. Then, we see in Acts 2:42 that the disciples did indeed establish a community of believers who were devoted to Christ's teachings, which were passed on by the disciples. Therefore, it is clear that the teachings as handed down by Jesus remained central to the faith formation of members of the New Testament Church.

---

[2] Margaret Lawson, "The Church's Role in Teaching," in *The Teaching Ministry of the Church* (Nashville, TN: B & H Publishing Group, 2008), 131.

[3] Lawson, "The Church's Role in Teaching," 132.

[4] Lawson, "The Church's Role in Teaching," 133.

The question that remains, however, is whether current confirmation practice qualifies as a presentation of the apostles' teaching. Can a connection between the two be established? Marvin Bergman argues that though the word *confirmation* does not appear in Scripture, and by extension one could say the practice, as we know it, does not either, the foundation upon which the Early Church was instructed to teach is the very same foundation upon which confirmation instruction is to be structured. Bergman further argues that the connection between the Great Commission and confirmation extends beyond simply that call to continue to teach others the teachings of Jesus.[5]

WHO BEARS THE PRIMARY RESPONSIBILITY?

The debate over who bears the primary responsibility with respect to teaching children the faith has continued through the centuries of the life of the Church and into today. At times, the Church has made statements that indicate a desire for parents to take charge of such instruction, but then institutionally and programmatically undercut that effort by continuing to direct instructional efforts back to itself. Therefore, we will next examine this question in light of the practices of both the Old and New Testaments. Perhaps some light can be shed upon modern practices through such a consideration of biblically recorded practices.

As seen above, the religious life of ancient Israel focused around both the temple and the synagogue. Although rabbis did not expressly teach children, there would have been an element of instruction provided through their involvement in the religious life of the temple and synagogue. The experience of corporate worship[6] in which Jesus took part, as recorded in Luke 2:41–51, would have included some form of instruction on matters of faith.

The practice of daily meeting in the temple courts for instruction (used only until AD 70 when the temple was destroyed) as noted in Acts 2:46 suggests continuity with practices held during their time as

---

[5] Marvin Bergman, "What Is Confirmation? A Brief History," in *Confirmation Basics* (St. Louis: Concordia, 2009), 8.

[6] Corporate worship is what takes place on Sunday or at other times, when the local church gathers together to hear the Word of God, receive God's grace through the Sacraments, and respond in worship to Him.

observant Jews. Seeing their faith in Christ not as a break with their Jewish faith, but rather the fulfillment thereof, they would have retained such a practice. Thus, they retained corporately at least some basic elements of faith formation and instruction. If this Early Church teaching is logically and foundationally connected with modern confirmation and catechetical instructional practices, this establishes the place in the corporate life of the church for said instruction to take place.

It is not a matter of asking whether the church or the family is to be the focal point of catechesis. Rather, it is essential that both take on that critical role, though each in their own way. God charges both the Church in an institutional sense and the family in an individual sense to step fully into the center of the catechesis of its members.

Because cultural and religious identity were so critically important in ancient Israel, this task of teaching the faith within the family would likely have been viewed as the most important role for parents right after providing for shelter and food. God's instruction for parents to teach their children takes place in Deuteronomy 4 in the context of His establishment of a covenant with His people. This places their teaching of the faith as a core part of this covenantal connection between the people and their God.

We also can see this faith formation in action in Paul's New Testament description of the faith-forming work in the life of Timothy. Paul stresses the strength that the ministry of Timothy's mother and grandmother provided him in teaching him the faith (2 Timothy 1:5; 3:14–15).

The biblical record provides for both corporate and family catechesis. Neither institution is eligible to forego its part in teaching the faith to succeeding generations. The family cannot claim that this role is for the professionals of the church to handle, nor can the church simply leave families to their own resources to teach their children. Catechesis is thus a team effort in which the church and the family must play their part. What parts each must play is a topic with which many involved in the planning of confirmation wrestle. Thus, we will next consider the nature and structure of instruction.

NATURE AND STRUCTURE OF INSTRUCTION

In order to get a handle on the question of biblically appropriate instructional methodology, one must first ascertain the full nature of what distinguishes Christian education from education in general. As Michael Anthony points out, Christian education is about more than content; it is rather about the transformation of individual believers to be more like Christ.[7] Christian education is thus no mere content-oriented endeavor. Knowledge of the Gospel cannot be equated with faith in the Savior. The devil is fully aware of the content of the Gospel, better than most, but without faith, this mere knowledge fails to restore a right relationship between the devil and God. This distinction between education in a general sense and Christian education does not negate the need to understand and make quality use of structured educational methodologies. Quality education is still quality education. However, spiritual transformation is not the result of educational technique. It is rather solely the work of the Holy Spirit.

Having the end clearly in mind, which is where general education and Christian education find their distinction, does not negate the use of proper educational methods.[8] Rather, because of the critical nature of the message of Christian education and the urgent desire for spiritual transformation to result from said instruction, it would seem more natural to stress methods toward effective communication of the Gospel message even more.

The use of the right methods in Christian education is critical when teaching the faith to our children.[9] Teaching the faith to children must rely upon age-appropriate instructional methods. Abstract concepts beyond their reasoning abilities are of no benefit to younger children. The field of education offers the church much in the way of understanding age-appropriate instruction. Pastors must bring highly complicated theological concepts down to the level of their students in order for the truth that they intend to communicate to mean anything in their lives.

This does not deny the power that is inherent in the Word of God (Ephesians 1:19). On the contrary, it recognizes that individuals are by nature distinct from one another in matters of personality, learning style, and developmental abilities. Similarly, Paul in 1 Corinthians 9:22 talks

---

[7] Michael Anthony, "The Nature of Theology and Education," in *A Theology for Christian Education* (Nashville: B & H Publishing Group, 2008), 21.

[8] Anthony, "The Nature of Theology and Education," 22.

[9] Lawson, "The Church's Role in Teaching," 154.

about how we ought to adjust our approach depending upon those to whom we are called to witness. Christian educators are called to adapt and adopt educational methods that, if used well, would best communicate the timeless truths of the Gospel in such a way as to assist the hearer in understanding and accepting those truths.

Much can be said in favor of structured instruction that relies on course plans and detailed curricula. However, the Church has always been a place for a more organic approach to learning within its faith-formation efforts. By organic, I intend to convey the idea of a lack of a pre-planned structure for curricula. Organic instruction tends to form around current needs of students as they present themselves at the time instead of a systematically prior-organized plan. As noted above, faith formation is no mere passing of a set content from teacher to student. Confirmation instruction as a part of faith formation is thus not merely about its content, though content is critical. Confirmation is also about forming a lifelong relationship between the student and God Almighty. This relational aspect of Confirmation implies a more organic (whole-life) approach to learning.

There might be instructional elements that are best suited for formal educational methods, but the overall process is more organic and naturally arising than planned and structured. When confirmation becomes merely the structured instruction, the bigger picture can get lost.

How easily Lutherans forget that what God, through His Word and Spirit, does in the Rite of Confirmation is primary. The public act of confession and other significant human actions in the rite derive their significance from God's action through Baptism, the Word, and the Lord's Supper. Something has gone terribly awry when confirmation overshadows its own source—Baptism. When one sees confirmation in the context of a lifelong process of catechesis, then confirmation is set within a proper framework in relation to the Word and the Means of Grace.[10]

Wrapped in a sacramental understanding of the Christian life, confirmation is viewed as part of an organic whole, beginning with Baptism as one's entry into the Body of Christ and thus the Christian faith. Confirmation is not an educational prerequisite for participation in the

---

[10] Kent Berreson, "What is Confirmation? Shaping a Word-Filled, Sacramental Life," in *Confirmation Basics* (St. Louis: Concordia, 2009), 24.

Lord's Supper, though it both functions and is viewed as such in many congregations. Thus, Kent Berreson suggests that it would be better to separate the Rite of Confirmation from first Communion.[11]

Rather than functioning as a special one-time instructional program, confirmation instruction should prepare youth for not merely the Confirmation Rite, but rather their entire life in Christ.[12] Berreson warns that an emphasis on grade level instruction reinforces a graduation mentality in confirmation.[13] Thus, if the church adopts too much from general educational methodologies, the distinctive nature of Christian education is lost in the process. Students who move through the system with a mind toward passing a class may fail to prepare for a further lifetime of growth in the faith. This may be a reality that is hard to avoid for churches whose Lutheran Day Schools house some, if not most or all, of their confirmation instruction. In some way, however, church leaders should attempt to distinguish between the academic aspect of a junior high theology class that teaches the catechism, and catechesis in preparation for the Rite of Confirmation.

Keeping this in mind, the Lutheran catechist ought to be mindful of novelty for the sake of being innovative. One must remain faithful in presenting ancient, unchanging truth to succeeding generations. There may well be a need to examine instructional models, as they may have been forms of novelty falsely accepted as good and right methods in their time and may not convey these ancient truths with appropriate clarity for postmodern learners. One should not make changes simply blowing along with the winds of change, nor should one remain conformed to past instructional patterns that have in fact outlived their usefulness.

While catechists should take great care when changing instructional methods, they should also always be mindful of the change that they desire in their students. We know and believe that there is power in the Word to effect change. Through confirmation instruction, the Word of God shapes or transforms students into the likeness of Christ. In Romans, Paul speaks of this change in two ways. First in Romans 8:1–11, Paul talks about having our minds guided by the Spirit (v. 6). Luther

---

[11] Berreson, "What is Confirmation?," 24.

[12] Berreson, "What is Confirmation?," 30.

[13] Berreson, "What is Confirmation?," 30.

stresses that we are not to live as the old man, but as one in relationship with the Father through the Spirit.[14] Richard Lenski suggests that our new nature is rooted in our justification.[15] Justification as understood theologically in Lutheranism is a one-time declaration of righteousness. According to this understanding of transformation, Paul is speaking of what has already occurred to bring one to faith in Christ.

Then in Romans 12:2, Paul discusses the connection between that transformation and the renewing of the mind. Although God declares us righteous when we come to faith in Christ, the full nature of transformation into Christlikeness has only just begun. Paul is here discussing our continuing sanctification—that process by which we are made into that which we were declared to be when we were justified. Luther discusses this further transformation by teaching that God so transforms our will that we willingly do that which we previously would least desire to do.[16] Here Luther is perhaps connecting Paul's struggles in Romans 7, as he discusses how God transforms us, causing us to desire to do that which by our sinful nature we would least like to do.

Students enter into this process as a part of their confirmation instruction. The assumption going in (though at times this is not entirely accurate) is that the students in confirmation classes are already justified through Baptism and have been in some measure taught the faith at a basic childlike level. The question then becomes how we understand the content of our instruction in light of God's transformative power.

There are times when we might desire that our teaching be made acceptable to our students and the world at large. However, just as Luther noted above, God calls us to act in ways that run counter to our natural understanding. In 1 Corinthians 1:18–25, Paul compares the world's wisdom with God's. Paul teaches that our human thinking sees the cross of Christ as foolishness.[17]

---

[14] Martin Luther, *Commentary on the Epistle to the Romans* (Grand Rapids: Zondervan, 1954), 104.

[15] Richard Lenski, *The Interpretation of St. Paul's Epistle to the Romans* (Columbus, OH: Wartburg Press, 1945), 505.

[16] Luther, *Commentary on the Epistle to the Romans*, 493.

[17] Gregory Lockwood, *1 Corinthians*. Concordia Commentary (St. Louis: Concordia, 2000), 68–69.

There is a distinct difference between the way Christians and non-Christians receive the Gospel. The Gentile focus on power and success could make little sense of a crucified God.[18] Despite their believing the cross to be foolishness, God outsmarted humanity and their claims to wisdom.[19] If that is where we left the story, we all would be greatly pitied, for by our own power, we cannot come to understand the things of God. Thus we return to Paul's theme of transformation and rejoice in the work that Christ through the Holy Spirit has worked in us, giving us faith and sustaining us as we grow in that faith.

Whether a particular church emphasizes a more organic or a more structured approach to confirmation instruction, what is most important is the intent to convey a Christian lifestyle[20] more than a mere set of content goals. The purpose of confirmation is not to merely pass on a set of facts, but to pass along a vibrantly living faith capable of being sustained by the Holy Spirit through all adversity.

I have concluded that a healthy balance of both structured and organic instruction is necessary. Students need the structure to ensure that the entire panoply of the Christian Gospel message is presented and understood. Students also need to see their faith in daily practice as modeled and lived by those mentoring them in the faith.

The apostle Paul emphasized modeling of the faith when he affirmed Timothy's father/son relationship with him in Philippians 2:22 and 2 Timothy 3:10. Whereas Paul speaks *about* Timothy to the Philippians, in 2 Timothy 3:10–14 he speaks directly *to* Timothy about his continued maturation toward Christlikeness. Timothy followed the example of Paul as he lived out the content of what he taught (v. 10), while Paul further encouraged him to remain true and firm in his beliefs (v. 14). Then later in 2 Timothy 4:2–5, he instructed Timothy to teach others the same truths Paul taught him. This is a fine example of organic instruction in that the faith taught is the faith learned from one mentor-mentee relationship to the next.

---

[18] Lockwood, *1 Corinthians*, 70.

[19] Lockwood, *1 Corinthians*, 72.

[20] By Christian lifestyle, I am not here talking about morality per se, but more the life of the faithful in Christ. This naturally involves moral behavior, but ought not be reduced solely to it.

In Philippians 2:22, the father-son relationship mentioned by Paul with respect to Timothy may well be connected to not only the taking on of disciples as the apostles did, but also the rabbinic tradition of gathering students to study with a particular rabbi. This interpretation implies a relationship of a voluntary nature. There is no compulsion. When the mentor takes on a mentee, the relationship might imply authority, but the mentee enters that relationship of his own free will and volition.

What does Philippians 2:22 teach us about catechesis? Paul here instructs us on the nature of the learner who willingly enters into a mentoring relationship with the instructor in order to grow in Christlikeness. Think of this as a posture one takes or an attitude one adopts while learning. Timothy is heralded as an example because he learned from Paul with the willingness one might otherwise expect to find in a son learning from a father. Just as Paul taught Timothy and Timothy was held up by Paul as a model for the Church at Philippi, we are to draw upon the example of Christ (as well as the imitation of Christ as seen in Paul, Timothy, and others) as we instruct others in the faith in preparation for the Rite of Confirmation.

Thus, in confirmation instruction there is a necessary place for modeling in order to illustrate for the students the connection between doctrinal faith and daily faith life. As a rite, there are certain standard preparatory features that confirmation instruction must possess (the Six Chief Parts of Luther's Small Catechism). As a catechetical process, instruction must not be limited to merely the transmission of content, but must move into the realm of faith formation and Christian life formation, thus setting confirmation in the context of the entire Christian life.

In many ways, the tension between organic instruction and programmatic approaches relates to how one understands the relationship between learning orthodox doctrinal content and being conformed to the image of Christ. The emphasis on orthodox understanding of the doctrines of the faith and the life changing power the Gospel of Jesus Christ exerts on believers creates a delicate tension that needs attention in each generation. Thus, we see that there is no break between doctrinal content and Christlike conformity, rather that doctrinal content is derived from a faithful understanding of faith in Christ and not prior to the working of Christ in our lives. One cannot have conformity with the image of Christ without proper doctrinal content, but doctrinal content presented in the absence of faith working toward such conformity is likely to be received as utter foolishness (1 Corinthians 1:23).

Putting together the big picture for confirmation ministry is important, just as such bigger picture thinking is essential for all aspects of a church's ministry. Christ called us to make disciples through the power of Baptism and the teaching of His Word (Matthew 28:19–20). We can look back to the pattern of life in the Early Church in Acts 2:42. The disciples sounded again the teachings of Jesus, and successive generations have sounded again on down through the ages.

The case has here been made that the Bible does not offer a single prescriptive model for ministry that ought to be held up as the single model for confirmation practice. The Lutheran understanding of adiaphora allows for certain latitude (though not without purposeful intention and faithful theological reflection) to explore new models and instructional methods. Just as in Jewish culture, we are called upon to teach our children at all times and in all places (Deuteronomy 11:19). Just as Jesus used both larger and smaller groups and taught in a variety of settings, we may employ a variety of instructional models. And, finally, just as catechesis in the family was supported through the modeling of other adults and religious leaders in a local faith community in ancient Israel, so, too, should the church today support families as they take primary responsibility for the catechesis of the family.

CHAPTER 3

WHAT WENT WRONG?

ASSESSMENT OF WHY THE CHURCH
STRUGGLES WITH CONFIRMATION

If there is one thing I have learned in my years of ministry, it is that just when you think you have a handle on the nature of some aspect of your ministry, things will change. This is especially true when it comes to teaching children and youth. While there is great truth in knowing that in the big picture there is nothing new under the sun (Ecclesiastes 1:9), it is just as true that in ministry there is a season for everything (Ecclesiastes 3:1). When assessing the changes and challenges that have taken place in the recent history of catechesis in the Church, it is essential that we keep this tension in mind. God's Word never changes, but we do need to reassess how we teach that Word if we find that our methods are less than helpful.

While it is a rather tricky thing to attempt to assess the nature and cause of systemic change, it is critical to do so in order to get a handle on the reality facing our young people as it relates to their time of study in confirmation. This chapter will attempt to paint a picture of the societal landscape in which many of our youth find themselves immersed. Please note the qualification "many." Whenever one attempts to assess one's own culture and the subcultures within, or to assess the impact of cultural shifts on emerging generations, one is of necessity going to paint a picture that while hopefully an accurate generalization, is nonetheless a generalization and must be understood within its inherent limitations. Thus, the youth that you encounter may be radically different from the trends described here. Please take from this chapter that which you can apply to the reality of the culture in your part of the country or corner of the globe and the reality of the culture of the youth in your congregation.

The Influence of Postmodernism

To begin this assessment, I believe that we need to come to terms with the ways in which postmodernism has influenced and, in places, radically reshaped how people view and interact with matters of religion and spirituality. Notice right from the start my choice to distinguish religion and spirituality. I have done so with deliberate intent. Postmodernism has created in the minds of many a separation of religious faith and spiritual faith. You have perhaps encountered a young person who has said something along the lines of, "I'm spiritual, not religious." This simple statement encapsulates a good deal of the spirit (to abuse a pun here) of the age formed through postmodern philosophy. For some years now, there has been a growing interest in all things spiritual. This emphasis on the spiritual, however, resists the structure of the traditional form of a specific religion. The structures of religion are seen as restrictions to the freedom of individuals to follow their own spiritual path and encounter God or some other higher power, as they desire it to be.

There is a lot going on here. Fundamentally, there is growing distrust of organized religion (however "organized" religion actually is) and an insistence on the right of individuals to define the terms of their spirituality on their own. This seemingly radical departure from the way in which religious truth claims were viewed in the past has been a part of the culture in which our young people have been marinating since they were very young. Consequently, what are we to do?

Well, actually, I would suggest that we first ask from where this philosophy came so that we might then know how to respond. In short, postmodernism is a sign of the failure of the Age of Enlightenment. The belief that humanity was capable of answering all questions through the might of our own reason proved to be a task we were not able to achieve.

The postmodernity influenced young person has grown up with what has become a seemingly natural distrust in the power of human reason to grasp real universally applicable truth. Thus, you end up with arguments against "Western logic" as if the law of contradiction, for example, is an invention of the Greek philosophical tradition, rather than the discovery and codification of a universal law that does, in fact, govern the way in which the world does and must work. In a false attempt to be open to anything, the postmodern mind is closed to truly knowing much with any certainty.

I have noticed that people now talk about what they *feel* about a subject rather than what they *think* about it. This subtle shift, I believe, is actually seismic in its impact on the way in which we see the world. Rather than thinking and applying our minds rationally to reach a conclusion or position, we are encouraged to *feel* our way to what is "right." Thus, our emotions supplant the life of the mind. Rather than thinking through the moral implications of a position, young people have grown up learning to empathize and formulate their positions on that basis. So for example, it becomes increasingly hard to talk through confessional doctrinal positions on the role of women in the Church or any number of topics related to sexual ethics. Rather than discussing the factual effects that such actions might have and pairing that with God's establishment of laws that conform to the realities of the world He created, we instead work with students who are more inclined to take positions based on a desire to see all people feel affirmed, regardless of the personal choices of those individuals. Thus, they end up accepting only the teachings of Jesus that they are comfortable with, rather than relying on His full counsel, especially the counsel in which He condemns sinners who forsake His efforts to rescue them from bondage to sin.

Now let me be more precise than that. There is still truth, and most people in some way or another believe that certain things are true and others are false. What changed in our understanding of truth? Rather than holding to a correspondence view of truth in which the veracity of a claim was determined by testing it against observable evidence or other forms of verification, a move toward a coherence view of truth took place. In a coherence view of truth, individuals must only be consistent within their own system of thinking for truth to be truth for them. The key here is the "for them" part. Truth has increasingly moved out of the realm of universal applicability and into a more self-referential construct.

A shift has taken place between what is known as a fact and what is an interpretation of a known fact. When the line between facts and interpretations blur, there is a natural weakening of understanding facts as anything more than mere personal interpretations.[1] Thus especially in the case of religious beliefs, we have reached a point in which people view doctrinal positions as preferences or opinions more so than attempts at understanding universally applicable truth. Instead, we are left with the mere competition of the ideas of individuals that are valid only to those individuals who choose to believe them valid.

The natural outgrowth of this form of thinking is a weakening of our ability to understand the nature of the self. Value has become a social construct. Thus, the value of the individual is itself contingent upon the value a given society chooses to place upon the individual.[2] Rather than knowing ourselves to be valued creations of a God who loves us and dies for us, we are forming a society in which we select to whom we apply value. One could almost say that there is no "there" there. By this, I mean that there is not enough substance left upon which to truly establish such value standards. The value of the individual is merely left to the collective desires of a given society. There is no way to appeal to a higher or universal standard. This has real implications for the faith lives or potential thereof for the postmodern.

What are the implications of such a change? If we are not of value by an objective godly standard, then the influences we subject ourselves to are merely of our own choosing. There is no higher standard to violate. Rather than maintaining an ethical standard that is universally applicable, we find ourselves talking about right and wrong based on whether there is a harmed party. This implies that an action cannot be morally wrong if there is no individual or group harmed in the process. Conversely, otherwise free actions are restricted by individuals or groups who perceive that they have been in some way emotionally harmed by those who merely hold publicly to a particular position.

This clouded thinking has wreaked havoc on the discourse surrounding same-sex marriage. Moral standards, long-term and nearly universally held, are overturned in favor of the emotional affirmation of individuals who desire that their relationship be equivocated with

---

[1] Heath White, *Postmodernism 101: A First Course for the Curious Christian* (Grand Rapids: Brazos Press, 2006), 97–98.

[2] White, *Postmodernism 101*, 73.

marriage. Conscientious Christians and others who object are fair game to vilify, as they are deemed guilty of causing emotional harm by the merely holding and professing of their differing beliefs. It is into this type of emotional "logic" that we must lead our students in our teaching.

It is no wonder that the youth we encounter in our confirmation classes struggle with what to do with the truth claims of Christianity. Some may not even know enough even to begin to evaluate such truth claims. They may view life as a series of isolated and unrelated experiences rather than a coherent whole bound together by a loving God.

We must teach in this context. There are implications for how we should approach our teaching, and a distinct deficit can be found in much of the way we have traditionally approached Sunday School teaching. Presenting often-isolated biblical stories without much in the way of drawing the whole into a larger metanarrative, many of our churches play further into this disjointed understanding of the world and the place of faith within it. This additionally plays into other aspects of the postmodern view of Scripture.

First, there is a tendency to believe that there is really no ability to draw together a metanarrative that binds together all of human history. Traditionally this is what Christianity has claimed the Bible does. If in our presentation of the Bible to children we are not consistent in providing for them the structure in which to put together a metanarrative for the Bible itself, how then are we to hope to instruct them in a metanarrative that binds together the larger story of humanity?

Second, while the Reformation rightly placed the Bible in the hands of the laity, the implication that is often drawn from this in postmodern thinking is that the very interpretation of Scripture is left up to the individual. The postmodern thinker sees no authority in the Bible, since the individual is the only authority to which one is responsible.[3] Thus, many students seek primarily to understand each passage by what it means to them, rather than finding the meaning of the text as defined by the authors (human and divine). Unlike the reformers who placed the Bible into the hands of the laity, trusting in the work of the Holy Spirit to reveal the truth claims contained within to all, the postmodern thinker is more interested in his or her own perspective. He or she ends up

---

[3] White, *Postmodernism 101*, 117.

performing an eisegesis of the text (reading one's own meaning into the text), rather than performing an exegesis of the text (drawing the original meaning out of the text). In so doing, the postmodern approach to Scripture allows one to draw together interpretations from across theological and even religious traditions. Claims that were seen as inherent contradictions a generation ago are held out as novel and perfectly acceptable viewpoints.

Therefore, we end up with a sort of spiritual stew in which each individual feels free to adapt the recipe, tossing in ingredients as he or she sees fit. I personally enjoy the mash-up of music genres (at least when well done) as well as the mash-up of foods (a pastrami pizza that I get in Long Beach, California, is a fantastic case in point). However, if we perform a theological mash-up, we end up constructing a belief system that might suit our personal tastes, but may well be rife with logical inconsistencies making evangelism and apologetics all the more difficult to present to our unbelieving neighbors. Why would they wish to buy into a system of beliefs that we put together, when they can simply construct their own variation to suit their own tastes? This is unfortunately the false message received by our culture in response to the proliferation of denominations. They wrongly draw the conclusion that theological disputation implies the lack of universal truth, when in fact it merely implies the sinful inability of individuals and churches to agree upon what is true on all counts. We do not separate due to a low view of truth, but the opposite. We maintain distinctive beliefs in a quest to adhere as strictly as possible to the truths of Scripture; we simply lack the capacity to ensure that we will always reach the same conclusions as other truth-seeking followers of Christ. Thus, we are left with students who are instructed by the larger culture to view spirituality as so very personal that holding to a confession is seen as antiquated and very much against the spirit of the age.

What this means is that we are and have been raising generations who are no longer able to connect with the convictions and values of their parents. They may simply lack the learned capacity to conceptualize in consistent moral categories. This in turn influences what our youth believe they can really "know." With truth so elusive, the hope of forming improvements in society from one generation to the next is discarded. In part due to the economy, but also in part due to a lack of vision for the nature of truth to impact our world holistically, youth no longer tend toward optimism that they will have improved lives over against the lives their parents had. With the individual as the sole arbiter of truth, post-moderns approach the development of their belief systems in such a way as one might approach a dining experience at a Las Vegas buffet. They sample a variety of beliefs, seeing no contractions, even when they should be obvious.[4]

Teens have seen the negative effects of what they might term the failed experiment of reason and humanity's attempt to master all matter and all knowledge. This has led to a questioning of the nature of truth, and whether one can know it by rational means.[5] Rather than merely temper the over-ambitiousness of the Enlightenment, postmoderns have seen the failure of reason and have rejected the universal nature of truth. While there is valid grounding within the Christian faith for a critic of modernism's claims to understanding truth, postmodernism rejects the whole of the Enlightenment project. Where modern and Enlightenment thinkers placed the quest for universal truth, seeing the apparent failure of this project, postmodern thinkers reject the very notion of universally applied truth. Rather than accept the truth of the fallibility of the human mind as evidence for a mind far beyond our own, postmoderns reject the notion that there even is such a thing as universal truth out there to be found, or from a more theologically minded perspective, revealed.

There seems to be a current of both optimism and yet pessimism with regard to emerging generations. There had been some hope that the millennial generation would be more service-oriented than prior genera-tions. However, this seems to have been short lived, as recent data has been trending back toward a less optimistic view.[6] What I think is going on is a reflection of a both/and within the culture. For those who still maintain a hope and a center founded on something beyond their own opinions, there is indeed a drive to accomplish and to change the world for the better. However, for those who have rejected the very notion of universal truth, there is a tendency to seek to influence only the immedi-ate with the belief that any loftier of a goal would be futile.

---

[4] White, *Postmodernism 101*, 130.

[5] Stanley Grenz, *A Primer on Postmodernism* (Grand Rapids: Eerdmans), 14.

[6] See Tim Elmore's *Generation iY: Our Last Chance to Save Their Future* (Atlanta: Poet Gardener Publishing, 2010).

Thus, the quest for truth becomes a personal journey to construct a "reality" that works for the individual. Sound familiar? In Judges 21:25, we learn that without a king, the people each did what they believed to be right by their own definition, rather than follow the leadership of God and His judges. Solomon rightly noted that there is nothing new under the sun. What seems novel in our day is merely a reshaped version of ancient heresy. Having rejected God, and having failed to replace His wisdom with our own, we reject truth rather than humbly return to its source. There is no longer a center to hold the whole together.

The center once founded upon the eternal now rests upon the truly temporal. We have put ourselves in the place of God. Thus, the metanarrative is unnecessary; only the story of reality as it is shaped around us is of true personal import. This is the thinking that we may encounter in our congregations and in the students presented to us for instruction in the faith. Therefore, we must adjust our approach. We can no longer assume that the assertion of a truth claim will be examined on its merits. We may encounter teens who will agree that our claim makes sense and cannot counter the argument. Yet, they may still reject the adoption of the truth claim and refuse to make any sort of corresponding adjustment in their life or belief system merely because they don't believe that they really have to if they don't really want to. Teaching doctrinal truths changes if there is no longer even a concern with whether they are right or not, but only whether one likes what they say or not.

In an ideal world, one would posit that you ought to be able to argue your way through this haze of sloppy thinking. However, this might not be pragmatically possible. If that is how students think when we confront them with the Gospel, then as a point of fact, that is how they think, or more accurately *feel* their way through an issue. This means that my initial approach in persuading a teen about the truth of the Gospel may not strategically be through the head, but rather through the heart. Once the heart is engaged, naturally my goal would be to get the mind engaged, and in fact retrained to think properly. However, if my initial goal is that Christ be a part of this youth's life, I cannot merely bemoan his lack of critical thinking skills and be done with him. I am called to do more.

The movement to incorporate more story (Christ's story and our entering into that story) into catechesis may be a wise response to postmodern thinking. Ultimately, we know that truth has not changed, merely that the way in which people assess their acceptance of truth has changed.

While truth itself has not changed, the approach taken to understanding and appropriating it certainly has. Having been raised by educational processes in which children are encouraged to explore and discover truth, young people naturally resist the idea that any type of authority might attempt to impose truth upon them.

We are a society fascinated with the new and novel. Teens and preteens are no different. Just as soon as you think you have a handle on where to find teens on social media, they have already migrated on to something else. There has developed in our culture little patience for the formal. E-mail made us all more accessible to one another and now social media has pushed that even further. Young people have access to leaders in ways that many of prior generations would never have dreamed. This access does bring leaders closer to us, but at the same time can erode the natural respect that being in a leadership position used to carry. This leaves teens with very little interest in stiff or restrictive structures. They believe that the world is to be flexible and accessible, as much of it has been for them. When they find that the Church fails on either or both accounts, they have little willingness to stick it through and make a change. They would rather move along to find those who are open to their contribution and influence.

Consequently, this disconnects youth from the mentorship that comes from being around those more seasoned in the faith and in life generally. Unfettered from a foundation of historically accepted standards by which to analyze the veracity of a truth claim, young people instead set out to explore truth as though they were on an adventure for its own sake rather than a quest for ultimate truth. The process has become the focus rather than the seeking of truth itself.

MORALISTIC THERAPEUTIC DEISM

Christian Smith has been conducting research since 2002 on the impact that current trends in our culture have had on the religious lives and outlook of American teens and young adults. The results of this study (National Study of Youth and Religion) have received mixed reviews. Some find much to be optimistic about within its pages. Others find only further despair in regards to their ministry and work with young people. In my own research on confirmation, I examined the work of Christian Smith and his team and found a degree of hope, though only a degree.

The positive element from Smith's work that should bring hope lies in the reality that the hostility so often thought to exist in the unchurched or non-Christian is by and large just not there. Teens tend to have a neutral to generally positive feeling toward all things religious.[7] An element of a blank slate exists upon which we may be able to imprint a new vision of faith in Christ. Further, most teens in the United States still identify themselves as Christians or some variety thereof (Mormons are included here), with more than half of that number relatively active in the practice of their faith. However, the other side of this research comes with the realization that for both Christians and non-Christians, faith is not a part of life as it once was, or as it might be envisioned by those of us in ministry to young people.[8]

The main learning that one can take away from the research of Smith and his team is that parental influence is still king, for good or for ill. In this case, perhaps this is more for ill than for good. You see, the faith legacy being handed down is what Smith calls Moralistic Therapeutic Deism. It is not the faith of a community that knows what it believes and why it believes as it does. Rather, it is a pragmatic faith that seeks from the spiritual that which is of personal benefit. Those things that do not fit such a category are discarded as faulty relics from the past, no longer relevant for modern times. There seems to be a tendency to view matters of faith as options from which we might choose rather than realities we must confront. The skeletal frame of Christianity remains, but the core essentials have often been hollowed out.[9]

In order to understand this, we must examine what Moral Therapeutic Deism (MTD) means. Taking each element in turn:

- Therapeutic deals with a tendency of the individual to be most concerned about his own emotional and psychological well-being;

- Moralistic deals with a definition of ethics or morality based on individual responsibility; and

---

[7] Christian Smith, *Soul Searching* (New York: Oxford University Press, 2005), 70.

[8] Smith, *Soul Searching*, 68.

[9] Smith, *Soul Searching*, 171.

- Deism refers to a belief system in which God as creator wound up the universe and has simply left it to wind down throughout history without any guidance or supervision on His part.

Thus, MTD is about the individual and fits nicely into our discussion of postmodernism.

Americans love the idea of the individual. We love individual freedoms and individual rights. However, the pervasiveness of MTD reveals the dark side of this individualism that has taken shape in our approach to religion and metastasized into a cancer eating way at the very soul of our faith.

At times, parts of MTD may seem relatively innocuous. I recall a question-and-answer session at a conference at which Christian Smith presented, during which time someone commented that the real concern one should have with MTD is the increased influence of deism. I contended then, and still do today, that the real concern should be the moralistic and therapeutic "packaging" in which this deism is wrapped. As I see it, the MT in MTD makes the D all the more acceptable. One might otherwise reject outright deism's ideas that God has formed creation and now is no longer actively involved sustaining or interacting with creation, except for the influence of the moralistic and therapeutic presentation of this incarnation of deism.

MTD is individualism gone to seed. Moral decision-making becomes all about the individual. Moral decision-making comes to focus on the therapeutic improvement of the individual rather than attaching itself to a system of ethics with a reference point beyond the individual. Religious traditions and teachings, the idea of some kind of natural law, and other cultural traditions no longer hold the same binding strength as they once did. The individual is encouraged by the philosophy of MTD to seek what works for him or her alone.[10] This pushes past the concept of Rousseau's social contract, though it is a natural outgrowth of the belief that groups of individuals determine their own system of ethics along with their own system of governance when forming societies. Now, rather than forming societies around a unique set of morals, each family, and in fact each individual, to some degree has taken responsibility for its own moral system formation.

---

[10] Smith, *Soul Searching*, 173.

Naturally, each individual is willing to push this only so far. This does not mean that MTD and postmodernism have entirely unleashed the individual to the complete detriment of the concept of a society. We do still tend toward acceptance of cultural or societal standards; however, there is no longer an understanding that these standards are universally applicable to us, even within our own cultural context. Rather, those influenced by MTD and postmodernism accept the ethical concepts that they find personally appealing and reject those that they do not. That leaves still a good deal of commonality, as an individual raised within a culture, especially a culture with a rich heritage of Christian teaching, will be shaped to accept a certain degree of moral concepts that are in line with the true Christian faith. What it does mean, however, is that as a society we have become far more suspicious of organizations and far less willing to submit to the guidance of authority. In a culture that prizes our own individual rights to determine what we believe and how we live our lives, MTD offers just the right mix of Christian-like structures without the obligation to participate in any way in the transformation that comes as one is sanctified in Christ.

As children, we are shaped by our parents. Although it may come as a surprise to those who have teenagers, parents are still the single biggest influencers of their children. The way in which we speak and think is shaped by what we see modeled in our parents. Thus, despite the tendency for teens to rebel against their parents, especially as it relates to religious beliefs and practice, their core belief systems are still largely the product of their home environment. Therefore, one may argue that what was merely the practice of previous generations has become the core tenants of the faith for many of those whom we are seeking to catechize. The message is getting through. However, what is the message? Put another way, what kind of a spiritual legacy is being left?

Recent trends point to a legacy in which religion is that which encourages followers to do good, care for the poor, love your neighbor, and such; but very little emphasis on doctrinal content seems to be getting through. For years, I have interacted with parents who bring their children to church so that we can teach them how to be good little boys and girls. "Sure, you can teach them about Jesus, and all that, but really just keep them safe and keep them around good influences so that they won't get into too much trouble in high school and college." Thus, the core delivered content of the "Christian" faith received by many by the time they are teenagers is devoid of true theological content. In the place of Christ and Him crucified is a therapeutic message of self-help founded on personal moral piety. Is it any wonder why the core contents of Luther's Small Catechism seem so foreign to ears who have not heard a message of Christ as Redeemer consistently in their lives?

Rather than providing teaching of substance, too often the instruction that teens receive is shallow at best. Responding to the parental cry for help, pastors, DCEs, and youth leaders have spent too much time focusing on shaping the moral behaviors of the teens in their ministries rather that passing along the true substance of the Christian faith. Concerned with making sure not to run off the few teenagers who remain connected to church and involved in youth ministry, there is a tendency to lower that bar and seek to provide the most agreeable version of Christian teaching possible, while remaining within the bounds of orthodox teaching. Notice that I am not suggesting that the vast majority of youth leaders are intentionally offering false teaching. It is my observation that the dumbing down of the content of the faith presented to teens is done out of a fear that we might say too much in too strong a manner. We may be concerned that if we push too hard, we will not only lose those youth to whom we are called to minister, but we might lose our ministry positions as well.

There is no meat coming for so many of our young people. It is not a case wherein milk is provided in the place of solid food, as Paul notes in 1 Corinthians. Instead, they receive filler in the form of moralism and therapeutic teachings, rather than a life-transforming presentation of God's Law and Gospel. This form of teaching goes down easy but lacks enough substantive content to truly nourish the faith as teens enter emerging adulthood.

The porridge of MTD teaching is a concoction of the following guiding beliefs:

1. A god exists who created and orders the world and watches over life on earth.

2. God wants people to be good, nice, and fair to each other, as taught in the Bible and by most world religions.

3. The central goal of life is to be happy and to feel good about oneself.

4. God is not involved in my life except when I need Him to resolve a problem.

5. Good people go to heaven when they die.[11]

Did you see what was left out? There was no cross. There was no Christ. The central teachings of Christianity that otherwise distinguish it from other world religions are entirely lacking.

Given this kind of instruction in the faith, is it any wonder why what might have been deemed as foundational beliefs a generation ago are now viewed in a more fluid and hazy manner? The message our young people are hearing is that moral norms are matters for individual opinion. Furthermore, they are taught that one ought not pass judgment on each individual's moral understanding, because that would be like condemning someone else's feelings or the central core of their being. I, as a worker in the church, am being judgmental when I attempt to offer a critique of rival ethical systems. Instead, I am expected to offer my opinion and respect the opinions of others. The problem naturally is that morality is not founded on opinion, as so many today seem to believe.

While from a theological standpoint we know that we lack the ability to save ourselves through moral living, it is still troubling that teens view morality in such a fluid and self-constructed manner. Rather than objective standards to be measured against and found wanting, God's laws are reduced to mere suggestions that we can accept or reject in the process of constructing our own self-referential moral system.

However, this statement in and of itself implies something with which emerging adults seem less than comfortable. The very notion of there being a moral system tends not to sit comfortably in their mind. Just like with the move from modernity in the Enlightenment to postmodernity, emerging adults influenced by MTD appear to have a difficult time believing that it is even possible to sort out challenging moral issues. They see the proliferation of viewpoints as evidence that there is no ultimate morality, and thus resist those who attempt to teach based upon a universal moral system as hopelessly foolish and outdated thinkers. Thus, morality for emerging adults becomes simply a matter of

---

[11] Kenda Creasy Dean, *Almost Christian* (Oxford University Press: New York, 2010), 14.

personal preference.[12] As challenging as it is for emerging adults to sort out moral actions on an individual basis, it strikes them as hopeless ever to achieve an understanding of morality as a holistic system.[13]

There is a very pragmatic ring to this argument. Working through moral issues is truly a difficult task. How can one be expected to assemble a consistent system by which to live? When attempting to put together such a system, one is likely to encounter the disagreement of others, which in today's society has become disproportionately uncomfortable. By focusing on the individual, the challenging task of reaching societal agreement is set aside.[14] Rather than seek a universal system, the very concept of such a moral system is rejected outright, allowing all an equal right to be "right." How very egalitarian! How very irrational! Refusing to do the heavy lifting intellectually does not eliminate the moral standards God has imprinted upon His creation. We do not get a pass because we are trying to be nice rather than seek what is morally upright.

Further complicating matters, our increasingly global culture pushes back against the classic position of C. S. Lewis in *Mere Christianity* in which he attempted to demonstrate the moral universals found across cultures. Rather, emerging adults tend to view morality not as something of a universal nature, applicable to all of humanity, but rather as something more of an opinion. Thus, morality is seen as subjective and a matter for individuals, groups, and cultures to assent to at any given time. Morality is merely a social construct with no value beyond conceptualizations. There is no ultimate reality to morality in any real lasting or permanent sense.[15] Further, this provides the lack of secure moral footing that can be seen bearing fruit in the shifting sands of opinion as it relates, for example, to homosexuality and gay marriage.

Our increasingly globally minded youth will resist attempts to apply "Christian" morality, possibly seeing this as something exclusively Western or solely applying to those who are a part of the Christian faith community (notice how we got back to postmodernism there). Through this, we end up with a Christianity of practical atheists. We might believe

---

[12] Christian Smith, *Lost in Transition* (New York: Oxford University Press, 2011), 21.

[13] Smith, *Lost in Transition*, 22.

[14] Smith, *Lost in Transition*, 22.

[15] Smith, *Lost in Transition*, 27.

in God, but functionally we do not act as though He truly exists.[16] MTD posits a God who does not make demands upon us, which is seen worked out in such free form attempts at morality.

The very way in which the postmodern mind approaches the written word in general has had an impact on the respect granted to *the* Word, the Bible. Once revered as the Word of God, the Bible now seems to be viewed as a set of optional guidelines that may or may not apply in our given context. Postmodernism has gone to seed, even within the Church. Postmodern textual criticism has retrained the reader of Scripture to find in the text what he desires rather than seek within the text the message of the original author. Further, this philosophy is being applied beyond the text itself and to the very world that the written Word has attempted to describe. All is now a matter of individual interpretation. Thus, just as a text is in need of interpretation, so, too, is life and all things.

There is no longer an objective standard by which to evaluate truth claims. As expressed in the philosophical work of Derrida, there is not only nothing more than the text, but in fact, everything is context. Thus, context becomes the foundation upon which to construct or reconstruct morality and belief itself. Granted, in educational theory there is much made of understanding the context in which one is teaching. Specifically within Christian educational practice, context is critical to learning. However, that is not what we are evaluating here. We are confronted not with a message in need of clear explication within a given context, but rather a context that reshapes the very meaning of the message itself. What is needed is a very delicate balance indeed.

FINDING THE RIGHT BALANCE

While there are reasons for legitimate concern, given the tendency to reduce truth claims to the context in which they are placed, there is some room for hope that an emphasis on community will provide the necessary context in which to explore truth claims and ultimately find a way out of an overemphasis on the individual and his or her interpretive prerogative. Perhaps the concerns from the time of the Reformation will reverse course. Rather than unleashing radical individualism, postmodernism may instruct the Church on how to form an interpretive

---

[16] Craig Groeschel, *The Christian Atheist* (Grand Rapids: Zondervan, 2010), 14.

community around the text of Scripture. Rather than weakening the standing of the Bible, this may strengthen its position within the community of faith. However, that trade-off might well remain as this process will likely leave little room for interpretive work across traditions and communities. While there is strength in a renewed attention to the theological contours of theological traditions such as Lutheranism, what may be lost is the ability to speak to the nature of truth that transcends traditions and particular communities of faith. However, the very manner in which the Christian faith has traditionally been tied to history and specific revelation might well reteach the larger culture how to assess reality in a manner that could prove to be more satisfying than the interpretive sands that postmodernity provides. Thus, in the midst of postmodern thinking that lacks sure footing, the Church can provide a foundational type of thinking, believing, and likely most importantly living that will attract attention due to its distinct nature in the surrounding culture.

Rev. Robert Newton, President of the California-Nevada-Hawaii (CNH) District of the LCMS, often talks about the nature of the post-Church context in which we live. Comparing our current context with the area that was pre-Church and that which was known as Christendom, Newton writes about how both Christians and non-Christians in our society claim the position of the insider. Taking this approach, each fails to reach the other, instead creating boundaries between one another in order to protect their own inside status.[17]

This is the point of contact at which our young people struggle. They are often taught by leaders whose frame of reference is more Christendom oriented. This creates a confused approach for a teen fully immersed in a post-Church cultural context. Although their parents might have existed in both eras, that time is past. Thus, we nearly can create a point of apologetic tension within the context of our own catechesis. Attempting to instruct our students in a Christendom-type of mindset rings hollow, even if our students are not able to identify what is at work. The lower level of spiritual commitment of the prior generations

---

[17] Robert Newton, "The Church in a Post-Church Culture," *The Lutheran Witness* (January 2010): 10.

is forming in emerging generations belief systems without the structural integrity to withstand serious questioning.

At times, however, the church attempts to propagate the faith merely through socialization. Although there are individual cases in which youth reconnect to the church through confirmation (I have had the privilege to witness this a few times), this is statistically not the norm. My own research into the congregational connectedness of teens before and after confirmation pointed to their connection to the church prior to confirmation instruction as the single biggest influence on their level of connection following confirmation. Thus, the habits formed through the influence of the family are critical. As parents model faith life for their children, their children notice what is of value to their parents and largely incorporate those behaviors into their lives. If parents are regular in worship, then teens will more likely be regular in worship. If Bible study is important to parents, then their teens will be more likely to place a similar importance on Bible study as well. However, doesn't this cut against the anecdotal evidence that we have all seen in our ministries of youth rejecting the influence of their parents for that of their peers? Is it no longer the case that teens need youth workers as intermediaries between them and their parents? In truth, was that to be our role in the first place?

Rather than rejecting their parents outright, teens put up a sort of "macho" facade, projecting the image that they no longer need their parents. In reality, they continue to both desire, and in fact need, positive affirmations in order to continue to develop a healthy sense of self. Despite media portrayals to the contrary, teens need and desire their parents in their lives. They do not always know how to show it (I believe due in part to negative media pressure to at least act as if there is no desire for parental approval or life involvement), but they desire to feel loved and accepted nonetheless, even more so than they desire love and acceptance from their peers. The influence of peers may well increase, but it does not typically supplant that of parents who remain actively engaged in the lives of their teens.[18]

---

[18] To examine this issue, see Mark Regnerus and Jeremy Uecker, "Finding Faith, Losing Faith: The Prevalence and Context of Religious Transformations during Adolescence," *Review of Religious Research* 47, no. 3 (2006): 220; Christian Smith and Patricia Snell, *Souls in Transition: The Religious and Spiritual Lives of Emerging*

POSITIVE OR NEUTRAL VIEWS OF THE CHURCH

Thus, we must wrestle with a pair of competing views of how to understand teens today. Smith and his research team tend to find little reason to believe that teens harbor a genuinely negative view of the Church. Kenda Creasy Dean builds off their findings, positing that:

1. Most American teenagers have a positive view of religion but otherwise don't give it much thought.

2. Most U.S. teenagers mirror their parents' religious faith.

3. Teenagers lack a theological language with which to express their faith or interpret their experience of the world.

4. A minority of American teenagers—but a significant minority— say religious faith is important, and that it makes a difference in their lives. These teenagers are doing better in life on a number of scales, compared to their less religious peers.

5. Many teenagers enact and espouse a religious outlook that is distinct from traditional teachings of most world religions.[19]

One might argue that due to the influence of MTD on pop-Christianity, it is only natural for there to be a positive or at least neutral outlook on the Church. After all, without much substance with which to interact and potentially find disagreement, what point of conflict with the Church remains with which emerging adults can contend?

NEGATIVE VIEWS OF THE CHURCH

The counterpoint to this assessment comes through the work of David Kinnaman and Gabe Lyons. Attempting to gauge the view of Christianity from the outside, Kinnaman and Lyons do not find nearly the potentially positive picture as found by Smith and the NSYR research team. Instead, they find that despite possible good intentions, many of the teachings of the Church project a message rejected as immoral by the

---

Adults (New York: Oxford University Press, 2009), 26; and Vern L. Bengtson, Norella M. Putney, and Susan Harris, *Families and Faith: How Religion Is Passed Down across Generations* (New York: Oxford University Press, 2013), 195–98.

[19] Kenda Creasy Dean, *Almost Christian* (New York: Oxford University Press, 2010), 17–21.

culture at large. They found that as younger adults grew up with less of a direct exposure to the teachings of the Christian faith, the only images from which they have been able to construct a view of the faith is through media news and pop culture. Thus, they reject Christ's followers without hearing from Christ directly.[20]

What has instilled this sense of distrust in an institution that should be noted as the ultimate in trustworthiness? Kinnaman and Lyons suggest six themes offered by skeptics that ground the negative impression of the Church in our culture. Christians are seen as

1. hypocritical,

2. focused on conversion rather than people,

3. anti-homosexual,

4. sheltered,

5. overly political, and

6. judgmental.[21]

Unpacking each of these in great detail, Kinnaman and Lyons paint a picture of a church out of touch with the hearts and minds of the people whom its mission is to reach with the saving Gospel of Jesus Christ. Reading their analysis, one may find oneself ready to argue away the perceptions, confident that these misunderstandings would all go away if only people would hear a better and more accurate presentation of Christian beliefs from actual Christians, rather than strawman caricatures. Yet, we ought not to be tempted to deny away reality in this manner. If, as Kinnaman and Lyons find, the popular understanding of Christianity is this decidedly negative, protesting may only serve to reinforce the misperceptions. After all, perception is reality; at least in as far as perception shapes the hearts of those we in the Church are called to serve.

Hitting closer to home, Kinnaman continued his research and found a picture of Christians from young people in the church that doesn't look any better. Kinnaman found that young people are leaving churches in

---

[20] David Kinnaman and Gabe Lyons, *unChristian* (Grand Rapids: Baker Book House, 2007), 11.

[21] Kinnaman and Lyons, *unChristian*, 29–30.

part because they see their church as overprotective, shallow, anti-science, repressive, exclusive, and closed to potential doubts.[22] Again, one might be tempted to despair. However, we know that our God is far larger than the very doubts that obscure the sight of those who fair to see His handiwork. Knowing the areas in which we need to work to present the Gospel in a freshly orthodox manner should give us hope that the guiding wisdom of the Holy Spirit will empower current and future church leaders to provide training in the faith that will correct misperceptions through presenting the Gospel with clarity and love.

Our task in catechesis is to enter into relationship with those whom we seek to catechize. More to the point, it is critical that we forge a relationship with the family unit as a whole, and the sooner the better. Through deep relational formation, discipleship can penetrate the cultural barriers that exist even in the lives of the students whom we have known since the time of their Baptism, not that many years ago. Our culture is filled with challenges that push our buttons and might cause us at times to despair. Challenging as these intellectual movements might be, and as powerless as we may feel to contend with their effects in the lives of the young people we serve, we must remember that we serve a God far bigger than any current trend.

Having reviewed the impact that postmodern culture has on our youth, we now turn to examine the very nature of how they learn and grow developmentally in the faith and how that has bearing on our task.

---

[22] David Kinnaman, *You Lost Me* (Grand Rapids: Baker Book House, 2011).

CHAPTER 4

HOW WE GROW AND HOW WE KNOW

REVIEW OF HOW CHILDREN DEVELOP AND LEARN

Excellence in teaching is far more than the mere transmission of content from the instructor to the learner. We must take the capacity of the student into account if we are to be at all effective in our teaching. It does no good to claim faithfulness to our calling to teach if we claim success for simply presenting the material. We must rather attempt to understand those whom we teach on an individual basis and tailor our instruction accordingly. This is true for parents, as we teach the faith in the home, as well as for pastors, DCEs, and others who seek to pass on the treasure that is the Christian faith from one generation to another.

This is especially relevant when considering how we teach the Christian faith to the young people in our congregations. If your confirmation program is like the majority of Lutheran confirmation programs, you have seventh and eighth graders (perhaps sixth or ninth graders if you do three years of instruction) walking with you through the historic faith presented in Luther's Small Catechism. Dealing with junior high youth can be rather challenging. Even if you have not studied and do not know all the developmental changes going on in those years, you are still likely to instinctively know that there is something unique taking place in those years.

In many ways, junior high youth are on the edge between two worlds. They have a growing awareness that things are no longer what they once were. They desire to relate more to older teens whom they may idolize and emulate, and yet there is a continued need for the nurturing from childhood years recently past. They are entering into a time of great transition, right at the time many of our churches begin to ask them deeper questions related to their faith. As faithful parents and catechists, we need to apprise ourselves of the developmental nature of our students at this age, and may need to assess the developmental appropriateness of the questions we are asking of the youth in our congregation as they progress through confirmation.

To begin, I want to be clear about what I mean by a developmental appropriateness of confirmation. I mean to query the appropriateness of the questions we ask of young people during confirmation instruction with respect to their current psychological and spiritual development. What will be under examination is the manner in which doctrinal content is communicated to and understood by early teens in the traditional seventh and eighth grade levels.[1]

There are three critical questions to consider when approaching confirmation instruction. Those questions are:

1. What outcomes do we desire from confirmation instruction?

2. Where are our students developmentally?

3. Are the outcomes we desire developmentally appropriate for our students?

You will notice that these three critical questions build upon each other in sort of a natural progression. Once one has been able to articulate the outcomes desired of students in confirmation, then an assessment of their development will confirm if the outcomes chosen are appropriate for the students.

DEVELOPMENTAL PSYCHOLOGY

Integrating Christian educational practices with research from developmental psychology ought to take place with a certain amount of caution. The presuppositions typically part of the framework from which developmental psychologists conduct their research are at times

---

[1] For broadest application, I will set aside the argument made by some that confirmation instruction would be more beneficial if it were offered at another age. This I will take up later, but will establish a foundation for such an argument in the following pages.

diametrically opposed to a theistic worldview, let alone a specifically Christian worldview. These are helpful to have and keep in mind so that we understand those areas in which our Christian faith does and does not comfortably intersect with these developmental theories. A few of the more common presuppositions of developmental psychology are:

1. Atheistic rather than theistic

2. Reductionism rather than constructivism (religious inclinations are reduced to being based on very base inclinations)

3. Determinism rather than freedom

4. Individualism rather than interdependence

5. Self-centered rather than God-centered morality

6. Subjectivism rather than realism

This is not to say that we cannot synthesize any useful information from the theorists discussed below. Instead, when considering the whole of their work, we ought to do so with some caution, and an understanding of the presuppositions from which they conducted their work can provide just that.

Jean Piaget (1896–1980)

The Swiss psychologist Jean Piaget's theory of children's intellectual development places the traditional[2] confirmation student in what he called the formal operational stage.[3] He posited that starting around age 11, children begin to think logically and develop the ability to reason abstractly. In this way, they begin to be able to form generalizations based on prior experience. Prior to this development, children in the concrete operational stage have begun to think logically, though only with respect to objects and events.[4] The ages related to this transition are not nearly as fixed as Piaget supposed, yet, the question posed from his research can help us in understanding our approach with our students.

---

[2] This assumes a "normal" development and the instruction of seventh and eighth grade youth. No theory fully captures the reality of the development of individuals with complete accuracy.

[3] Dorothy Singer and Tracy Revenson, *A Piaget Primer: How a Child Thinks* (Madison, CT: International Universities Press, 1997), 26.

[4] Singer and Revenson, *A Piaget Primer*, 22.

For example, we can introduce God as Father, Son, and Holy Spirit sooner than the traditional confirmation age. Students might recognize that Jesus is God, but not be able to unpack the nuances of the Trinity until they are in confirmation or beyond. However, introducing the divinity of Christ along with the Father and Holy Spirit provide the necessary underpinning to consider the more abstract nature of the Trinity as a whole. In this way, students know the general concept earlier, even before abstraction is possible.

A further example can be found in the recitation of the Lord's Prayer. There is simply no reason to believe that children must wait until seventh grade to consider the use of this prayer. In both ministry settings and at home with my children, I have used a form of repetition to instruct children as young as three or four in the Lord's Prayer. Speaking a few words, then pausing for the children to repeat in kind, provides a basic structure by which they are able to learn the prayer. Some kids, like my own four-year-old son, engage further by asking questions related to parts of the prayer. This form of corporate prayer thus becomes an active part of their young lives.

At this age, in Piaget's pre-operational stage, the student is not yet ready to make too much application of this prayer. Nevertheless, the general form of the prayer acts as a spiritual imprint on a young mind and spirit so that when older, further deepening considerations of the contours and context of the prayer's petitions will have richer meaning due to familiarity and comfort with its language. While in the concrete operational stage, students will begin to connect this prayer with prayer in general using it as a model prayer for their own prayers. Once in confirmation, that continued use of the Lord's Prayer will aid in their abstract application of the individual petitions, understanding what God gives to us and what we need from God.

ERIK ERIKSON (1902–94)

According to the work of Erik Erikson, the teenage years that most confirmation students enter into during their course of study is marked by the struggle between Identity versus Role Confusion.[5] It is during this

---

[5] Erik Erikson, *Identity and the Life Cycle* (New York: W. W. Norton & Company, 1980), 94.

time that students seek a sense of belonging.[6] At the time in which we engage our students in study and questions related to their future in the Body of Christ, they are working out issues related to fidelity and loyalty. These internal struggles match well with the typical stated outcomes of confirmation instruction. However, since this stage, as defined by Erikson, lasts from approximately age 12 to age 18, seeking a conclusion at 14 years of age might be premature. Recent research on the transition to adulthood and what has become known as emerging adulthood only further underscores the developmental challenge of a 14-year-old making adult decisions, when individuals may not truly feel like adults until they are nearly age 30.[7]

As witnessed in youth ministries across the country, adolescence is a time when students try on a variety of identities before settling upon one that they believe most resonates with their core being. Erikson recognized that our culture facilitates many opportunities to hide in multiple identities that fail to reach an authentic true self. To counter this, Erikson believed in the power of education to transmit values and goals from which to aspire to heights beyond merely getting by.[8] Although Erikson intended this as a recommendation for traditional school education, the educational processes of confirmation do provide for the formation of such values. The challenge remains, however, that by prematurely drawing the educational process to a conclusion in eighth grade, the actual developmental process of identity formation is left unguided by the best educational process that the church brings to bear on this issue.

LAWRENCE KOHLBERG (1927–87)

In the matrix of the six stages of moral judgment developed by Lawrence Kohlberg, confirmation students are generally found in Stage 3.[9] It is during this stage that students find themselves very concerned with the expectations of others and conformity with the group of which they desire to be a part. A part of this conformity concerns conformity to

---

[6] Erikson, *Identity and the Life Cycle*, 95.

[7] See Jeffery Arnett, *Emerging Adulthood: The Winding Road from the Late Teens Through the Twenties* (New York: Oxford University Press, 2014).

[8] Arnett, *Emerging Adulthood*, 100.

[9] Clark Powers, Ann Higgins, and Lawrence Kohlberg, *Lawrence Kohlberg's Approach to Moral Education* (New York: Columbia University Press, 1989), 8.

authority figures. The good boy/good girl attitude involves the desire to be a good person and to be known as a good person. This involves both caring for others as well as an emphasis on obeying rules and authority.[10] While in this stage, it can be relatively simple to encourage right behavior in a manner that fails to provide time to reflect upon the purposes behind such right behavior. As Christian leaders engaging in confirmation instruction, we can confuse a lack of deep questioning with assent to what is being taught, rather than a lack of deeper reflection upon the content that we have presented.

Upon entering Kohlberg's Stage 4, students move beyond mere good/bad thinking toward a more nuanced understanding of how to answer moral questions. They move beyond a black and white understanding of the world and begin to uncover the various shades of grey that make understanding the Ten Commandments, for example, far more complicated. For some confirmation students, these grey shaded questions begin to surface especially in eighth grade. They are beginning the process of applying the definitions of moral imperatives to their own lives. As students are at various points in this transition, not everyone in a given class will be engaged by the more advanced questions with which some students might be wrestling. Understanding this, the use of small groups in confirmation instruction can provide the necessary space and time during which these grey area questions can be unpacked with those students who desire such engagement, while those students less interested and less prepared to deal with such questions can be engaged in other matters.

JAMES FOWLER (1940–2015)

Connecting child development with faith development, James Fowler concluded that students in confirmation classes generally have what he calls "Synthetic-Conventional" faith.[11] It is during this time of instruction

---

[10] Powers, Higgins, and Kohlberg, *Lawrence Kohlberg's Approach to Moral Education*, 8.

[11] While Fowler's work is a helpful framework to understand faith development, a few cautions should be noted from the outset. (1) Fowler discusses faith from a purely humanistic perspective and thus leaves the dimension of faith founded on the work of God in the believer's life relatively unexamined. (2) Although general stages of faith can be identified to some degree, faith development in individuals is more unique than implied in Fowler's framework. See A. Coyle, "Critical Responses to Faith

in the faith that they move from "Mythic-Literal" faith into a more abstract conception of faith as they enter into early adolescence. This stage is characterized by conformity. As we teach the contents of the faith to our students, we apply our own pressure upon that concern with conformity.

In this stage, a person begins to consider why he or she believes as he or she does. One pulls together various parts of faith and tends to conform to the majority, and students perceive that they are rewarded or punished for following rules laid down by the proper authority (the Church or the Bible). As noted above, we as catechists exert a pressure on our students toward conformity.[12] Their peers exert an even greater pressure in this regard. We are able to reflect deeply upon the methods by which we attempt to exert a positive pressure. Their peers tend not to be nearly as reflective or deliberate. The much discussed additional shaping that pop culture provides in concert with their peers sets a potential tone that runs counter to that of our own.

What gets interesting is when students begin to move deeper into this stage. The influence of peers increases while the influence of other more traditional authority figures declines, at least as seen in the immediate circumstances of life. If confirmation instructors exert this formative pressure in such a way that the later rejection of this influence is not overly reactionary, there is a greater potential for a return to the appreciation of this wisdom by the student. What I believe makes the difference is to avoid abuse of the conforming influence when we have it, considering that influence to be a precious gift from God for proper stewardship and care just as all other such gifts of God are treated. The difficulty of this situation is that all too often we do not recognize this fact and proceed under the false assumption that merely presenting the material and receiving affirmative responses to that presentation is enough. Students at this age are likely simply to acquiesce without much depth of understanding or personal integration of the contents of the Christian faith. If we take this defensive posture as true understanding and true faith, we fail in our calling. This may well be a better time to

---

Development Theory: A Useful Agenda for Change?" *Archive for the Psychology of Religion* 33, no. 3 (2011): 281–98.

[12] James Fowler, *Stages of Faith* (San Francisco: HarperCollins, 1981), 75.

introduce content for discussion and dissection rather than a time for the presentation of closed doctrines to which students should subscribe. More on this thought to come.

BALSWICK, KING, AND REIMER

In an attempt to provide a conception of human development that does not rely upon neo-orthodoxy as heavily as James Fowler's work, Jack Balswick, Pamela King, and Kevin Reimer published *The Reciprocating Self* in 2005. The concept of "the reciprocating self," as defined by their work, is the self that, in all its uniqueness and fullness of being, engages fully in relationship with another in all its particularity.[13] Similar to the concept of self-differentiation, the reciprocating self is fully relationally connected while remaining psychologically distinct from those around him or her. The authors assert that the reciprocating self is cultivated by unconditional love, grace, empowerment, and intimacy.[14] They envision the interplay of these four components as a cyclical exchange where the increase in each component provides the impetus for an increase in other areas, thus spiraling toward mature reciprocating self.

Within the framework of the reciprocating self, confirmation students confront emerging particularity, emerging relationality, and the thriving self.[15] What is meant by emerging particularity can be seen in the interplay between identity and differentiation. It is during this time that our students are distinguishing themselves from the identity of their families. They explore the beliefs that have been handed to them and come to terms with what it will mean for them to retain or reject those beliefs. Thus, students wrestle with the development of a self that can remain in relationship with his or her own parents while renegotiating the terms by which this relationship will take place. Youth may explore alternate identities and belief systems at this time of their lives. In a way, they try on different selves through this exploration of worldviews and belief systems.[16] They seek to assent to their own belief system on their

---

[13] Jack Balswick, Pamela Ebstyne King, and Kevin Reimer, *The Reciprocating Self* (Downers Grove, IL: InterVarsity Press, 2005), 21.

[14] Balswick, King, and Reimer, *The Reciprocating Self*, 51.

[15] Balswick, King, and Reimer, *The Reciprocating Self*, 178–82.

[16] Balswick, King, and Reimer, *The Reciprocating Self*, 179.

own terms rather than inherit a worldview from their parents or other authority figures.

Once again, a word of caution is necessary for those who tend to be less than comfortable with watching their students question the very foundation of the Christian faith. Disturbing as it might be to watch, this exploration is a part of the process of the development of the adult reciprocating self. This does not mean that we are left with nothing to do, rather, we are to remain faithful in a supportive role, providing guidance and answers as our students' questions surface and are explored. While there is a need for this exploration to reach maturity in faith and belief, we are able to, and, more to the point, ought to walk right beside youth as they try on these new identities. We must reserve judgment, offering key questions to help them evaluate their emotional, relational, and rational attachment to each taken identity. In this way, we help them learn the skills needed to understand more deeply the contours of not only the Christian faith, but also alternate and opposing faiths and worldviews.

Emerging relationality entails an understanding that relationships are everything to an adolescent.[17] Anyone in youth ministry knows this by the ever-repeated question, "Who is going to be there?" Our students are motivated not nearly as much by what activities are programmed or what lessons are taught as they are by the peers with whom they will engage in the activities we offer. Although at times this concern might appear self-important, Balswick, King, and Reimer stress that rather than being self-absorbed, adolescents are deeply concerned with the plight of others, both those with whom they are in direct relationship and those whose concerns are known to them in a more global manner.

All of this coalesces into a thriving self. Youths who thrive are able to make the most out of their lives and the circumstances in which they find themselves. They are able to find meaning in life and are generally satisfied. A thriving self in teenagers can be seen in their commitment to the community in which they live, which includes the faith community that nurtures their faith.[18]

Could this not serve as a partial goal for our confirmation instruction? Without foregoing the doctrinal imperatives of our instruction, the

---

[17] Balswick, King, and Reimer, *The Reciprocating Self*, 180.
[18] Balswick, King, and Reimer, *The Reciprocating Self*, 181.

formation of a student who functions as a reciprocating self—engaged in care of those around him or her—would be a student fully connected to the heart of Christ. One of the key things to remember regarding the development of the reciprocating self in adolescence is that it is a process.[19] Our confirmation students may be on their way through this process, but clearly, they are far from their destination. With this in mind, a few recommendations for the practice of confirmation can be postulated.

RECOMMENDATIONS FOR PRACTICE

Walt Mueller asserts that the task of adolescence is self-discovery. A disconnect between who God has created a student to be and the person the student may feel pressured to be may cause great stress.[20] To this end, we have explored what developmental theorists have found with regard to the development of our students in this very critical and challenging developmental task. The goal in this endeavor has not been to establish what we ought to teach to our young people. The course of study for Lutheran youth in confirmation is well established and truly has a good foundation. Rather, the purpose here is to explore exactly how we can best teach the content of our faith to our students so that they can discover their identity in Christ.

Richard Osmer suggests that students should not have mandated starting times but should be allowed to work their way through confirmation instruction as they are developmentally ready for it.[21] Along a similar line, I would like to offer the following four recommendations for a practice of confirmation that is in line with what we know about our students' development at this age.

1. Introduce the content of the Small Catechism at a younger age.

2. Provide greater depth over time in catechesis.

3. Mentor children and youth in the faith longer.

4. Ask youth to confirm their faith later in their personal development.

---

[19] Balswick, King, and Reimer, *The Reciprocating Self*, 183.

[20] Walt Mueller, *Youth Culture 101* (Grand Rapids: Zondervan, 2007), 266.

[21] Richard Osmer, *Confirmation: Presbyterian Practices in Ecumenical Perspective* (Louisville, KY: Geneva Press, 1996), 195.

Children begin to develop "procedural memory" when they are old enough to go to school.[22] It is at this time that they are able not only to place events in their own lives in order, but they are also able to place other lists, such as the alphabet and basic math tables, in their memory for later usage. Thus, I would suggest that the Six Chief Parts should be introduced into Sunday School starting in first grade, beginning with the Lord's Prayer, which will already be familiar if the child has regularly attended worship with his or her parents. The students will also be capable of learning the list of the Ten Commandments. Abstract content such as the Sacraments and Apostles' Creed should be held in reserve until fourth grade, when they enter Fowler's mythic-literal stage of faith. It is at this time that the use of story helps teach the Apostles' Creed as the story of our creation, salvation, and faith in God.[23]

One point of caution should be noted here. Children in the mythic-literal stage can at times lack the ability to distinguish between the concept of a superhero and God. It may be hard to completely avoid a natural blending of these concepts, so care should be taken to limit this potential confusion where possible. Curriculum themed after superheroes for Vacation Bible School or Sunday School may add to this conflation. Where possible, make sure to distinguish deliberately the difference between the mythology of Batman from the historical reality of Jesus (as well as Jonah, Joshua, the Judges, etc.).

I had the privilege of seeing this process in action when serving as the DCE for Family Ministry at Shepherd of the Hills Lutheran Church in Rancho Cucamonga, California. For years, the church had a pair of Sunday School sessions due to the large number of services (at one point, it was six) and the large number of families in the congregation and community. Shortly after I began to serve there, I discovered that the students who went through that system did not have an adequate understanding of worship and thus found assignments in confirmation, such as sermon reports, more daunting. The children had been going to Sunday School, but not church. This was the same even for many of the children of Sunday School teachers, who sent their kids to Sunday School twice in order to both volunteer and attend worship. Imagine being a teacher in that

---

[22] Balswick, King, and Reimer, *The Reciprocating Self*, 150.

[23] James Fowler, *Stages of Faith* (San Francisco: HarperCollins, 1981), 136.

second hour when you have students who already know the answers. A solution was very much needed to address both short-term discipline issues as well as long-term discipleship and catechetical issues related to teaching the faith in a more comprehensive manner.

The solution we developed was the introduction of a children's church. Now I will stress at this point that I am more a fan of children being in worship with their families than I am of children's church. However, having assessed the situation, we concluded that this was a necessary step to correct the issues created by the lack of time spent in worship by the children of that congregation. While I loved the emphasis on the family that was a part of the DNA of the church, it was time to make a change, and a transitional move to children's church was the right fit.

I began by laying out a basic liturgical structure based on the structure of the services the children's parents would attend. Then I spent additional time each week teaching through aspects of the service. I talked about prayer when we prayed. I talked about the importance of the Bible when the Scripture lessons were read. More central to this process and relevant to this book was the way in which I taught my way through the Lord's Prayer and Apostles' Creed. Each week I would have the children, ranging from four-year-olds through sixth grade students, repeat back to me lines from both the Lord's Prayer and Apostles' Creed. Every week an additional line was included in each and then explained. For example, I began by having the children repeat "Our Father" when we began the Lord's Prayer. Then I went into some detail, asking them questions about who it is we pray to and why we pray to God as our Father. Some questions were specific for the younger children, while others were designed to include and challenge older children who would demonstrate their knowledge and in turn provide learning for the younger kids. The next week, we would continue to include "who art in heaven" and then discuss our relationship to God in heaven.

Through this process, children learned to pray the Lord's Prayer and recite the Apostles' Creed, while also learning what they were praying and reciting meant. The goal was to train them to understand worship better, preparing them for a lifetime of worshiping the Creator of the universe, as well as laying a foundation for their understanding of the basic tenants of the Christian faith. The net result was children who had a better familiarity with the content of their faith and a better preparation for the instruction they would receive in confirmation.

In the years to come, it would have been possible to spend more time digging into the most abstract nature of the Christian faith, rather than focusing on the memorization of the Six Chief Parts as would normally be necessary. By introducing the content of the faith that makes up traditional instruction prior to the formal start of confirmation, students' time in confirmation can be used to increase their depth of understanding of that content. The ability to think abstractly along with the desire to explore and understand for themselves the faith of their families should be taken into account as an asset for a quality confirmation program, rather than be seen as something to work against. One method that can be used to accomplish this would be to offer shorter courses for seventh through tenth graders on each of the Six Chief Parts. Courses should be no longer than four to eight weeks at a stretch, but can be two to three hours in length if a variety of teaching methods is used to help students move from surface level inquiry toward a deeper exploration. Rather than spending time drilling students on what the Ten Commandments are, instructional time should be used to inquire along with students as to the nature and nuance of each commandment and its impact as a whole on our lives. The Sacraments can be unpacked not as doctrinal points only, but rather as a functioning part of church life.

An added feature of these courses as well as a way to offer support between sessions and courses can include the use of mentors. Upon entering seventh grade, students are provided with a mentor, someone with a prior connection to the student or the student's family if possible, but certainly one with a personal deepening and growing walk with Christ. Students have time during each session of the short courses to discuss with the mentor what the larger group has been learning. In this way, the instructional methods are varied while a spiritual-direction type relationship is fostered that will help guide the student through the entire process. This also helps to ensure that students do not progress too fast nor too slowly through the courses.

Students take the courses on the Six Chief Parts in a self-paced format and make their confirmation by tenth grade, or sooner if ready. In this way, students are not rushed, nor are they allowed to get stuck in the program, failing to progress or be challenged to really consider the claims of the faith. The traditional seventh grade start for this work is appropriate, as students are moving into a stage in their development when they are able to consider abstract issues related to faith. However, rather than mandating a particular start, students who are not yet ready upon entering the seventh grade should be encouraged to wait until they and their mentor believe that they are sufficiently ready.

Readiness on both the front and back ends is the key. We must remember that the Holy Spirit works the individual desire to make such a commitment to study and to adhere to the promises expressed in the Rite of Confirmation. We must also keep in mind that each student has a unique developmental timeline, which God, who controls all things, also established.

Arthur Repp notes that throughout the history of confirmation in Lutheranism, there has never been a single, uniformly accepted model of instruction.[24] Although we in the Lutheran Church have been solid on our understanding of what we are to teach to our children, we have wrestled with the open question of how best to provide that instruction since the time of Luther. What I have suggested is but one approach. This approach attempts to take into account the learning found in the work of developmental theorists. The hope is that by applying such knowledge, our children will not merely retain the facts of the faith with greater efficiency, but that also through our instruction and the work of the Holy Spirit our youth will build the foundation for a lifelong growing and vibrant faith in God. We hope that they will remain an active part of the Body of Christ rather than making a quick exit from church life immediately after they are confirmed. Isn't that what confirmation is really all about?

---

[24] Arthur Repp, *Confirmation in the Lutheran Church* (St. Louis: Concordia, 1964), 155.

CHAPTER 5

DEEP IN MY HEART

HOW THE DEVELOPMENT
OF A THINKING CLIMATE ENCOURAGES LEARNING

"Why?" Depending on your perspective or perhaps the current state of your stamina, the simple question "Why?" can represent the beginning of something wonderful, an exploration of the greater depth of a subject or a rabbit hole down which you may find no escape. In the hands of both teens and toddlers, "Why?" is a potent question. As the father of two boys and a DCE with nearly twenty years of experience ministering to teenagers, I am well acquainted with the power of "Why?" At times, when my sons ask "Why?" questions, they are trying to assess just how much their mother and I are on the same page. They are trying to find out if there is any way they can change our minds or cause us to doubt our course of action. They are also very much trying to dig in deeper to discover just how it is that our decision-making works. From this understanding, they develop their own ability to assess the world around them and draw a wise conclusion on what course of action to take, or at least to assess if the thrill of the potential fun they might have outweighs the potential for the trouble they might get in. Though with a much higher level of sophistication, the "Why?" questions of early adolescents push boundaries in a similar manner.

In each instance, the child has reached a developmental transitional stage in which individuation becomes more important; thus, the idea of merely accepting the answer of a parent or other authority at face value is less of a readily accepted option. While the questioning occurs at dramatically different levels, the motivation is strikingly similar. In each case, an enlarging world presents more information that needs to be assessed and evaluated.

THE QUESTIONS OF CHILDREN

As children grow and develop psychologically and intellectually, the manner in which they learn about the world around them changes. What stays constant is the need to know "Why?" At times, this process can be frustrating. At other times, this process is a wonder to behold. My sons are still young. As I write, the oldest is six and in first grade. His "Why?" questions can truly be exhausting.[1] This is due in part to a lack of background information or mental structures with which to make sense of the answers to the questions he is asking. There are natural periods in a child's life when he or she tends toward the asking of more questions. Often enough, these questions are on subjects well beyond the child's ability to comprehend. This is both natural and good for children to do. It may well be frustrating for parents or teachers attempting to provide clarity in the barrage of inquiries, but the alternative is to squelch their inquisitiveness.

My older son is, I believe, somewhat above average in his question asking. While I enjoy his desire to understand, at times neither my wife nor I have the patience needed to help him understand. I may lack the patience to really dig in and try to comprehend the nature of what he is asking, and he may lack the patience to make sense out of my answers. At six years old, my son is still quite literal in his thinking. Thus, when he asks questions that require abstract concepts to answer him, we start to enter challenging waters. My job in formulating answers for him is not merely to attempt to provide an expedient answer to get him back to whatever we were doing prior to his question(s). It is, rather, to take the time to really listen to what he wants to know through his question and to provide not just an answer to that question, but perhaps also the framework that he needs in order to understand the answer. Still further,

---

[1] Compounding this, he is by nature a highly verbal child, not merely verbal for a boy, but also in comparison to girls his age. He is also a morning person, which I am not. The number of questions prior to 6:00 a.m. is staggering at times. I love it, but it is a bit much to take in before adequate caffeine.

I need to take the time to make things as concrete as I possibly can. This is challenging when the topic is by nature more abstract than concrete.

For example, consider a child raised in a Christian home who attends church regularly and is exposed to the socialization side of the church (whether that is through a circle of Christian families with kids the child's age or through parochial Christian schooling). This child may experience a sort of crisis to discover that not everyone knows about Christ or even cares to know about God generally. The concept of God has, for this child, been previously defined in strictly Christian terms. Therefore, exposure to new concepts of divinity requires new mental structures in which to organize the information.

One summer, while on vacation visiting friends and family in Colorado, my family drove through St. George, Utah, and visited the local Mormon temple. Naturally, this created a situation in which to discuss the distinctions between the Mormon faith and Christianity. Fortunately, we had in recent months been visited by Mormon missionaries, with whom I enjoyed engaging on theological topics, so my son was already generally familiar with the concept that Mormons, though they might claim to be Christians, do not believe that Jesus is God in the same way that we as Christians do. However, when at the visitor's center at the temple, there was a need to sort through the projected message of the Mormon faith as a restoration of Christianity. On a basic level, we were able to do this and build upon the mental structures of true and false concepts of the nature and identity of God. As both our sons grow and mature in their understanding of the world, there will be many more conversations to fill in blanks that cannot be dealt with currently.

There are great parallels between the questions asked in my home and the questions that I have encountered in my ministry to youth and their families. What I love the most about youth ministry are the great questions that young people ask. At the same time, what makes me most exasperated about youth ministry are the questions that young people ask. Youth asking questions is a double-edged sword. Their naturally inquisitive minds seek out the world around them, sometimes desperately trying to make sense of it all. Yet, their minds lack the conceptual categories in which to place much of what they encounter. Youth tend to present their parents and other adults with a blizzard of sometimes seemingly disconnected questions. This is a part of the nature of what it means to be a teenager. What it means to be a leader of youth, especially in the Church, is to be responsive to their questions. This art requires a combination of patience and wisdom. You will need patience in order to listen actively to the question that is actually being asked and because responding to one question may well lead to many more questions. Patience with yourself is also necessary, as you will need to do additional research at times in order to respond. You will also need wisdom in order to best present what you have learned throughout your lifetime in a way that is accessible to the child.

CULTIVATING A THINKING CLIMATE

Eugene Roehlkepartain's article *The Thinking Climate: A Missing Ingredient in Youth Ministry*[2] has greatly influenced my thinking related to some of the ways in which we approach not only youth ministry, but confirmation instruction as well. My concern is that if we make the memorization of a certain set of theological facts the main focus in confirmation instruction, we will end up missing a great opportunity to minister to the young people in our midst. Hear me on this—I am not at all suggesting that we downgrade or give a lesser standing to the content of our faith. Rather, I would suggest that the educational process of catechesis that takes place in confirmation is more than the sum total of the content taught. It is about that content at its foundation, but the full transmission of that content is a far deeper project that involves addressing affective and behavioral aspects. Therefore, whether you are a parent, pastor, DCE, or youth leader, the establishment of an open thinking climate in your home and church is critical.

So what is a thinking climate? Based on Roehlkepartain's work, I would define a thinking climate as one marked by a pervading acceptance of deep thinking and questioning rather than a particular programmatic approach. Let me repeat a part of that—a thinking climate is not a program or curricular approach. You do not have to change your curriculum in order to establish a thinking climate, though at times such a change might be helpful. Rather, a thinking climate has more of an impact on how through teaching methods, students are able to enter into

---

[2] Eugene Roehlkepartain, "The Thinking Climate: A Missing Ingredient in Youth Ministry?," *Christian Education Journal* 15, no. 1 (1994): 53–63.

a space in which deep thinking and questioning is not merely accepted, but encouraged.

A thinking climate in confirmation instruction begins with meeting your students where they are in terms of their knowledge of the faith. They may not have come to you with a wealth of biblical knowledge. They may not have been in worship much, if at all, prior to beginning instruction. They might have little to no idea what it means to be Lutheran as opposed to Catholic or Baptist. They may very well be the epitome of biblical illiteracy. A thinking climate allows engagement where they are in their understanding of the Lutheran faith as it relates to their own life and faith.

Roehlkepartain points out that in passing on our faith to the next generation, there is a distinction between spoon-feeding youth answers to questions and encouraging them to think through these same questions so that they can attempt to reach answers for themselves.[3] By providing youth with the answers that we as adults have already worked out for ourselves, we short circuit the learning process. Rather than encouraging them to learn to think through tough issues for themselves, we jump to the end and present youth with our thoughts. This may negatively impact their faith as they may find the issues we resolved for them resurfacing in college, where they will finally have to confront them on their own without any guidance from a trusted Christian adult. We cannot expect youth to handle tough challenges to their faith if they have not personally wrestled with the questions of faith. When we provide answers to which we have arrived, they will perhaps nod in agreement, but they may not really have learned much from us.

Youth don't just need time to hear about the faith; they need time to dig in and wrestle with the content of the faith as it is presented. They need space so that they can bring to the surface questions that may passingly occur to them but do not otherwise see the light of day in discussion. They need to be able to take apart their faith in order to put it back together again.

The reason that there is so much value in allowing youth to do this wrestling in the context of the church is that they will naturally do so at some point anyway. Therefore, why not provide opportunity for this

---

[3] Roehlkepartain, "The Thinking Climate," 53.

wrestling when they are in a community of faith that allows such exploration in a supportive rather than a hostile environment? Allowing youth to wrestle with deep questions related to their faith will not necessarily cause them to further doubt their faith. Instead, this process allows them freedom to examine their faith and seek the Lord's aid in strengthening their faith.[4] Youth will ask the questions that are on their hearts and minds. The question is whether our churches will be the welcome place they need to be for those questions to be asked and answered, or whether we will instead leave the youth of the church to seek the wisdom of the world.

For children, faith is more naturally something associated with the family. You might not speak of faith as inherited, but children developmentally draw their understanding of faith directly from their parents. They pray like their parents pray. They worship like their parents worship. They formulate concepts about the nature of God consistent with the expressions of that nature that they glean from conversations over time with their parents.

I recently experienced a Sunday when I had to take our boys to church alone. My wife was unable to join us, and—I have to be honest—I was a bit nervous about what would take place. We had been struggling to keep the boys engaged and down to a dull roar in the service. Now I was going to be there with the both of them, but without my wife. I was going to be outnumbered.

Having had struggles with them handling the kids' bags in the recent past, I somewhat bravely chose to bring no toys in with me. In previous weeks, I tried to get my six-year-old to stand and sit with the congregation, hoping to teach him about the liturgy through the process of participation, even at his more basic level. That Sunday, I was not sure if I was going to push that, but to my surprise, I did not have to do anything. He willingly stood with the congregation and me when we stood. He attempted to sing the songs for worship that he knew. His younger brother even did his preschool best to participate. Toward the end of the service, he stood with his brother and me, trying to figure out if he wanted to stand with his hands behind his back or in front. He seemed to be trying

---

[4] Roehlkepartain, "The Thinking Climate," 53.

to assess if we were in fact praying and to assume a posture appropriate for that. Early learning is imitative and at times, very cute.

As children grow toward adolescence, the questioning stage that parents seemingly forget from when their kids were in the preschool and early elementary years returns with a vengeance. At a more sophisticated level, the emerging intellect of children as they transition through adolescence toward adulthood offers a barrage of questions that at times causes parents and church leaders alike some concern over their spiritual standing before their Maker.

In our pluralistic society, we cannot keep our young people from encountering a world full of belief systems that compete with and contradict our own. The influence of pop culture will push our youth to coexist with others of diverse backgrounds in a manner in which they are not merely agreeing to disagree, but rather in a way that accepts a sort of "truth" (if you can call it that) for all offered religious, spiritual, or philosophical positions. Rather than attempting to offer a shelter in this storm, the argument behind the establishment of a thinking climate would be that we embrace the changes inherent to the intellectual and spiritual development of our young people rather than fight over the influences upon them. We are called to enter into their lives and establish a supporting community in which questions are valued and not shunned.

However, the research Roehlkepartain conducted for the publication of his article led him to state that, sadly, far too few youth reap the benefits of a thinking climate in their local church.[5] When they need the space to explore their questions and discover answers, they find that the church is not the place where they are free to do so. Roehlkepartain goes on to estimate that half of Protestant youth are not exposed to environments in their churches that are conducive to the development of a thinking climate.[6] While this research is nearly twenty years old, I have found no new research demonstrating that the situation in the church is any different today. There are individual churches and leaders who create this space, but the church at large is anything but known for openness to the free discussion of difficult or even controversial topics. Rather, it is

---

[5] Roehlkepartain, "The Thinking Climate," 54.
[6] Roehlkepartain, "The Thinking Climate," 54.

known as a closed institution, asserting truth claims rather than engaging in respectful debate.

YOUNG ADULTS LEAVING THE CHURCH

Young adults dropping out of the church today often find the church to be controlling, surface level in its thinking and discussions, anti-science, repressive of disagreements, exclusive, and anything but open to doubt.[7] Let us explore each of these to see how the church can hinder its own cause due to poor public perception.

CONTROLLING

The Church has a tendency to like to control its own message. There is a propensity toward overprotection, manifesting itself in a restrictive internal climate that is at odds with the larger culture. For a generation with such an affinity for the arts and creativity as the Mosaics,[8] this can be a serious issue. Through creative expression, young people may well work out the meaning of their faith. As they do so, they may express less than orthodox beliefs as they seek to make heads or tails of life. Rather than view this as a part of their development and help them work toward a more mature faith or a clearer understanding of the Christian faith, churches all too often attempt to cut off the artistic expression, somehow hoping that the doubt, as might be expressed on canvas, might not be entertained at all. The problem with this line of thinking is that what is expressed is not necessarily an issue created by expression in the creative process, but rather the reality of a young person's faith as he or she moves from a childlike faith to a more well thought through adult faith.

Rather than attempting to control how youth express their faith, the church should take the task of creating creative space for young people to explore expressions of their faith. Yes, they will get things wrong on a regular basis. A young songwriter hoping to express his faith through music will err theologically and will need to be corrected. But rather than fully stifle the impulse to express his heart of faith in song, the church

---

[7] David Kinnaman, *You Lost Me* (Grand Rapids: Baker Books, 2011), 92.

[8] Mosaic is the term coined by researcher George Barna to describe what is more widely known as Generation Y or the Millennials. Barna preferred this term as he used it to emphasis the creative side that he saw as a distinguishing feature of the generation.

should offer a sounding board and a place of sharpening and learning. In this way, the church can bring artistic expression back into the church in a new and reinvigorated way and dispel the belief that the church seeks merely to control. We need to teach the Gospel and trust that in time its truth will come into full bloom in our youth.

SURFACE LEVEL

When I say that youth find the church to be surface level, I mean that they view the church as lacking the deep thinking and reflection necessary to handle today's complex faith-related questions. Too often, people falsely see the church as solely offering proof texts, at times out of context, instead of actually engaging with the culture to ascertain the true and full nature of the questions at hand. It is like the husband who answers his wife based upon what he thinks she is asking about only to find her frustrated at him for not listening.

Rather than equipping youth with the critical thinking skills needed to assess and evaluate faith challenges for themselves, too often apologetics is degraded into the provision of preset answers, often not even relevant to the questions at hand. This happens when youth are trained to memorize facts but are not taught to really listen to the concerns and objections of others. There seems to be a concern that if we discuss questions with our youth related to the faith, then this will in and of itself undermine their faith. I would argue that if we are creating a thinking climate well, we will tap into questions that teens already have, whether on the surface or not, and offer a safer place in which to ask and to explore the implications of answers to those questions. We are not creating the questions so much as being far better attuned to the reality that those questions exist and are in need of a substantive response on the part of the church.

By not allowing full, deep, and penetrating questions to be asked, churches have given the impression that they lack depth and certainly have ill-equipped their young people with shallow understandings of the Christian faith. The world presents youth with real and challenging questions. Youth who head off to college with the faith maturity of a child often find their faith unraveling. Some may return with questions about their faith that we did not prepare them to deal with. Others will seek answers from local churches or campus ministries, many of which are non-Lutheran, where they may find the willingness to facilitate the critical thinking that they need while at the same time offering fellowship that includes encouragement and support. Still others forsake their faith entirely, lacking the confidence that the church has any answers to offer.

We need to be intentionally pro-active. To think that our "church kids" should not be asking these questions in church is foolish. When they avoid or don't answer these questions, churches may end up leaving the impression that there may not really be any good answers. Once again, this can cause a weakening of faith as youth encounter challenges to their faith for which they are not prepared to respond.

While trying to avoid unnecessary doubt by staving off challenging issues, parents and church leaders may unintentionally set their youth up for future faith quakes. For many of our youth, it is not so much a question of if they will be forced to deal with challenges to their faith, but rather when and how forceful the challenges will be. We do a disservice to our youth when families and churches fail to prepare students so that they can provide well thought out and deeply reflective responses. The church is full of great thinkers. It is a fallacy to believe that being a person of faith somehow means that one is of lesser intelligence. Both historically and today, many of the greatest minds place their faith and trust in Christ. To leave youth with any other impression is to fail them radically. If we do not connect youth with those great thinkers, both from today and from history, we leave them with the impression that we do not have thinkers capable of offering deeply considered answers. In this way, the church is seen as a place for simpler minds to hide from the fearfulness of the world.

ANTI-SCIENCE

One of the areas in which youth receive the greatest challenges to their faith is the field of science. There is a widespread belief among young people that faith and science are incompatible. Bill Nye and Neil deGrasse Tyson have made it a recent mission to prove that science is incompatible with and intellectually superior to religion. Postmodernism has succeeded in asserting that since the scientific method seeks the verifiable, science therefore deals with the facts and faith deals with unverifiable superstitions. Where the two have no conflict, there is no need for one to win out over the other. However, in areas of perceived conflict, science is alleged to have the higher intellectual ground. Historically, this has not always been the case, as there was a time when theology held the high ground and people of faith (both Christianity and Islam) were responsible for laying the foundations for science as an academic discipline. Ironically, postmodernism, which has had such a negative effect on universal truth, has not managed to do the same to truth as established by science. Rather, religious truth is viewed as subjective, while scientific truth is held as objective. This is an interesting claim considering the postmodern assertion that there is no universal truth and the processes of the scientific method that have time and again led to the overturning of one theory in favor of a new theory that better comports with the evidence.

Dovetailing back to our discussion on the perception of a controlling church, it is important to note that science is not viewed as being nearly so stringent of a controlling agent. Science is seen as open to new knowledge in a way that religion is not. It is seen as open to the testing of truth claims, whereas religion, and specifically Christianity, is not.

In reality, the beloved disciple John instructs followers of Christ to test the spirits for truthfulness in 1 John 4:1. It is patently false to assert that Christianity is not open to verification. Rather, of all world religions, the Christian faith is the one that is most open to verification. We have gone out of our way to explore how we might as tangibly as possible establish demonstrable evidence for the claims of our faith. It is more a case of science overreaching in its claims to discover and verify truth than the faithful resisting deep explorations of our world and universe.

Some would point out that science, when it takes on the form of scientism, falls prey to the same trap in which religious people all too often find themselves. Both science and faith have the tendency to see their own categories of knowledge as superior. In so doing, they fail to take seriously the arguments and the evidence behind the arguments presented by the other side. There are those in science who seem to reject the supernatural out of hand due to a subscription to materialism. At the same time, the Church is seen as antagonistic to the free exploration of the truth in science. Yet, faith and science are not antithetical to one another. Again, not only is history replete with examples of scholarly scientists who were also upstanding and faithful churchmen, but there also remains today a goodly number of scientists who are men and women of faith seeking to understand God's creation and the Creator through their vocation of scientific inquiry.

REPRESSIVE

Going back to the list of why youth leave the Church, another reason is that they see the Church as being repressive of disagreements. When it comes to matters of sexuality, the Church does not have the greatest record in this regard. The Church is seen as repressive for being so far out of step with the larger society on a range of sex-related issues. From contraception to homosexuality to pre-marital sex, the message of the Church is a repressive litany of "NO!"

The Church has sadly become known more for what it stands against than what it stands for. Young people, even those in the Church, might have a hard time expressing a clear understanding of what the Church teaches on salvation, but they "know" we "hate" homosexuals. Casting Crowns, in their song "Jesus, Friend of Sinners," points the Church and more specifically individual Christians toward relational connections of healing and care as a way in which to respond to this challenge.[9]

When we fail to be relational in our confirmation instruction with our own youth, how well can we prepare them to respond out of love when presented with the accusation that the Church just wants to repress people and the freedom that they should be able to enjoy with their bodies? When we fail to help our young people who are wrestling with their own understanding of God's design for sex, we falsely give the impression that sex is something dirty that we cannot discuss in church. This leaves them to have their view of sexuality shaped by pop culture, complete with a view that the Christian faith and parents are repressive for not wanting their children to enjoy sex with anyone they might desire.

EXCLUSIVE

In John 14:6, Christ makes it clear that He is the only way to the Father. To the sensibilities of postmodern youth, making such a claim screams of intolerance. Young people see Christianity as exclusive, and exclusivity is something with which they don't want to be associated. Even youth growing up in the church struggle with such strong claims to the exclusivity of faith in Christ. Our culture has been so deeply

---

[9] See David Kinnaman and Gabe Lyons, *unChristian* (Grand Rapids: Baker Book House, 2007) for a similar analysis.

influenced by Eastern religious philosophy that having a single path to heaven no longer seems very loving.

In this exclusivity, youth see a God who rejects rather than a God who loves and seeks the lost to make them His own. This perception is a major stumbling block for teens to overcome. They do not want to be seen as intolerant. They have grown up in a pluralistic world and have a hard time understanding religious claims that exclude the majority of the world's population.

NOT OPEN TO DOUBT

Finally, young people see the Church as a place where doubt is unwelcome instead of a safe place in which to express and explore the doubt so many of them experience either periodically or chronically. In an effort to help project confidence, the Church seemingly fails to allow youth to see doubt as a natural part of faith. In Mark 9, a father, whose son Jesus was about to cast a demon out of, makes a truly classic statement on the nature of faith when he says, "I believe; help my unbelief!" (v. 24). The Christian faith is not without its challenges, and to pretend otherwise is to engage in a life of denial. When parents or churches fail to create a space in which doubt can be expressed, youth fail to be comfortable expressing their doubts.

HOW CAN A THINKING CLIMATE HELP?

Moving back to Roehlkepartain's work, he asserts that quality Christian education is among a number of essential elements for nurturing a thinking climate.[10] Each of these factors touches on how we ought to approach catechesis through our confirmation programs. Catechesis by its very nature is Christian education. There is and must be teaching that takes place. The emphasis here is the effective nature of that teaching. Presenting material is not equivalent to effective teaching. Understanding your learners is required for teaching to be effective (more on that later). Pastors, DCEs, and others serving the role of catechist should be well-versed in creative educational methodologies in order to engage the heart as well as the mind of their students.

---

[10] Roehlkepartain, "The Thinking Climate," 54.

The thinking climate must be such that questions are encouraged rather than discouraged. The simplest way to discourage free inquiry into the beliefs of our faith is to make students feel as though their questions are somehow foolish, wrong, or simply unwelcome. As your students are just entering into adolescence, their world is beginning to change radically. They are no longer as certain of themselves or their own identity as they once were. The views of their peers are beginning to hold enormous sway.[11] Your opinion of them still matters a great deal, but the extent to which you allow room for their free exploration of the questions that they have, serious or not in your mind, lays a foundation for the way in which they will interact with the faith in years to come.

Some of the most energizing times I have had in ministry, as well as some of the more memorable lessons I have taught, have taken place on youth group nights without specific agendas. In each church I have served, I have developed the habit of offering open question nights. These nights are designed to be totally free form discussions in which I am put on the spot to address as best as I can the questions most pressing on the hearts of the youth there that night.

As I said, this really puts me on the spot. In preparation for those nights, I have to brush up a bit on the questions that I might anticipate. I also have to be willing to offer a humble "I don't know" for questions that I am not equipped to handle. Matters of complex philosophy or science that I have not yet pondered are not areas in which to bluff my way through. There may be times when I begin to explore possible answers with the youth and even involve them in the process of seeking an answer. However, when I reach a point at which I know that I cannot offer a solid answer, I let that be known. I make a note of the topic and question, offering to do my work to develop a more complete response. I make sure to do that work and to find a time to communicate what I found back to the group and the specific youth asking the question. This last step is critical. I cannot forget to return to the topic and address it. The work to establish a thinking climate relies greatly upon the follow through.

---

[11] The foundation of parental influence remains the largest influencer, but the influence gap radically shrinks during this time.

The youth in all the churches where I have done this have loved it. It takes time to get them used to and, more to the point, comfortable with asking real and truly deep, heartfelt questions, but once that climate is established, watch out. Initially, the room is quiet. As a leader, this can be a bit uncomfortable. A rookie mistake would be to keep talking in the silence. Even if the silence makes you uncomfortable, you need to leave the space in which youth can take the risk to start asking questions.

The questions will eventually begin to flow. As youth begin to offer initial, less personal questions, they will learn that their questions are valid and worth seeking an answer. They will additionally learn that the Church is a place in which such deeper reflection is encouraged. They will learn that having doubts is not an end to faith, but an invitation to develop an even deeper faith. "I believe; help my unbelief!" (Mark 9:24b).

I really cannot say this too strongly: give serious consideration to the questions that your students ask. Establish for them a judgment-free zone in your class. You should show no signs of shock at the twelve-year-old you have known since Baptism who asks if there really is a God, or if the crucifixion was an act of evil on God's part against His Son. These are questions with which they might be wrestling on their own or perhaps issues their parents wrestle with as well. Perhaps they have a teacher who is pushing them to reject Christianity.[12] Taking their concerns seriously, even when they struggle to express them seriously (you know those junior high boys who can't do much of anything seriously), is the key to keeping them engaged and thinking through their faith.

Let me take a moment to mention that I firmly believe that this is a good thing. Having young people seriously and critically thinking through their faith, scary as it is for their leaders and parents, is an essential part of their maturation. Life will hit them with deep questions. The real question is whether they are prepared to think through and respond faithfully. By establishing a thinking climate in which students are able to ask their own questions, we establish in them thinking skills that will allow them to know how to evaluate arguments and reach biblically founded, well-reasoned conclusions. Although it might at times seem that their questions reveal a lack of faith, we can in fact move them

---

[12] See the movie *God Is Not Dead* for an example.

toward a renewed and stronger faith by aiding them in their ability to understand the intellectual underpinnings of our faith.

The next few factors that Roehlkepartain notes speak to how we can establish that thinking climate. The climate of your teaching must be both warm and caring. By how you respond to questions, you can demonstrate that you greatly care for each student and the state of his or her faith; you can show that you care about their understanding of that faith and are not simply concerned that they know the right answers. Students get enough class time that teaches them to merely seek the right answer rather than to learn to think critically. If the Church can be the place that instills a love and openness for critical thinking as it approaches matters of faith, the very faith of emerging generations will be uplifted and strengthened. Indeed, if we view questions as opportunities for the strengthening of our students' faith—through both the work of the Holy Spirit (something critically essential) and sound reason (something with which God has gifted us but society often seems to neglect)—then indeed their faith may grow far deeper for having been through the process.

Finally, expressing the faith in worship and service to others has become a more pronounced part of many confirmation programs. I would suggest that establishing a thinking climate means that even in worship and service our young people need to see an openness to meaningful reflection on the truths of Scripture and the questions that go along with the reflection. Our worship should engage students in an encounter with God that demonstrates to them the reality of His presence in this world and in their lives. Through worship, they should be encouraged to develop a prayer life that might help sustain them as they wrestle with questions of faith. As they serve others, they should see Christ's love in action and be able to connect that service and love back to the very character of the God whom they serve.

Roehlkepartain offers a series of questions with which I would like to close this section. I suggest their use as a sort of diagnostic tool for evaluating the thinking climate of your catechesis:

1. Are questions encouraged or discouraged?

2. How does the congregation deal with diverse opinions?

3. Are members challenged to examine their faith and everyday life?

4. How do leaders model a thinking faith?

5. Are youth given answers, or are they led to discover answers?[13]

Deep in the heart of all teens, there are questions. That goes with the territory. You cannot enter into a ministry relationship with a group of teens and not expect at some point to have to deal with their questions. The question for you as a leader, however, is whether you will proactively solicit those questions or merely allow them to surface as they come naturally. Granted, one could systematically stifle questions, but for now let us assume that we all understand the folly of attempting such a pointless exercise. If we set out in ministry to proactively seek out questions, we will establish a thinking climate that will encourage deep consideration of the faith in our youth and allow them to be tested within the church in preparation for the testing of their faith that they will undoubtedly face in high school, college, and beyond.

Confirmation is just one such area of educational ministry in which the development of a thinking climate is critical. Children entering into this stage in their lives have a great many questions. A confirmation ministry designed to allow for the exploration of these questions can go a long way toward establishing the foundation of faith for which those of us who have poured much time and effort into teaching have hoped and prayed. It is that to which we now turn as we explore the place of confirmation ministry in the life of teens and the Church.

---

[13] Roehlkepartain, "The Thinking Climate," 61–62.

CHAPTER 6

CONFIRMATION MINISTRY

THE PLACE OF CONFIRMATION IN THE CHURCH AND THE FAMILY

Luther begins the preface to his Large Catechism discussing the duty of the head of the family to examine his children in the doctrines of the Church discussed in the catechism.[1] Luther's comment stresses the importance of ongoing instruction in the home. The concept of graduating from confirmation would be foreign to Luther. The home was to be the center of learning for the young. Fathers were to daily take up the catechism and instruct their children. The role of the church was to examine and confirm the learning that had already taken place in the home. Today these roles have been reversed. From the perspective of church leaders, little learning takes place in the home. Parents feel ill equipped to teach their children. Thus, pastors, DCEs, and others have taken up the slack and the role of primary faith teachers.

FALSE ASSUMPTIONS

A few years ago, I published a brief guide for parents on how to evaluate if they should take their children to see the movie *The Passion of the Christ*, as well as to help them prepare to talk through the events portrayed in the film. I mentioned that it might be a good idea to read the Gospel accounts both before and after viewing the movie so that they have some basis of comparison. However, in my naiveté, I failed to spell

---

[1] Martin Luther, *Luther's Large Catechism* (St. Louis: Concordia, 1978), 10.

out just where in Scripture these accounts can be found. Shortly after publishing this guide, I had a conversation with the parent of one of my confirmation students about it. This sweet, well-meaning mother of three was rather embarrassed to admit that she was not only unsure of where to find the Gospel accounts of Christ's crucifixion, but she also was not entirely sure she could tell me what a Gospel was. She was embarrassed, but I was the fool.

All too often in the church we assume a standard of knowledge that cannot and should not be relied upon. I had assumed that this mom, a lifelong Lutheran, would have the required background to understand what I meant in my article. She, and sadly many others who were not brave enough to ask, was ill equipped for the task. Many parents like her simply had not taken part in any form of serious study of God's Word since their own confirmation. As parents, they may mean well, as they do honestly have the best in mind for their children. However, we as a church have failed to equip them with the resources needed to walk through the Scriptures with their children.

As noted above, Luther's vision for confirmation was not the establishment of an educational program. He did not have in mind a one-year, two-year, or even three-year process during which youth would be dropped off at church for instruction by their pastor. Rather, Luther placed the responsibility of this teaching on fathers. Fathers (or mothers when the father is absent) are called to serve as the spiritual heads of their families and as such are to instruct their children in the basics of the faith. The struggle, as noted, is that far too many parents are not equipped well enough to understand the basics of the faith in order to take on that instruction.

A further complication results when families make little effort either to instruct at home or to send their children through Sunday School or Vacation Bible School (VBS). Youth then tend to view confirmation as a stand-alone program rather than a part of an ongoing process of education in the faith.

We cannot prepare our youth for lifelong participation in the church if they view confirmation as a one-time program to attend rather than a small part of the larger educational process. More importantly, we cannot equip our young people to face the challenges that modern (or post-modern, if you'd like) life will throw at their faith if they do not view confirmation as an ongoing part of their faith education.

Whether we intend to or not, practically speaking we send the message on a far too regular basis that confirmation is a two- to three-year program followed by a graduation of sorts at the completion of the time of study. Perhaps it is because of the way in which we present confirmation instruction. Perhaps it is because we have so closely mirrored the way education is conducted in our local schools. Perhaps it is because we have all too often adopted programing organized by grade level, without seriously considering how the individual programs connect to one another and truly form individual children who receive instruction in the faith. Likely, it is a combination of these and many other factors that has brought us to this point of concern (or, one might argue, crisis).

For those churches who include confirmation as a part of the ministry of their Lutheran school along with instruction as a ministry of the congregation, the question of age-level instruction may get tricky. While there may be a very good rationale for the inclusion of confirmation instruction in the Lutheran school, the church would be wise not to adopt in total an age-level approach to instruction.

A WAY FORWARD

So what can we do to restore confirmation to its proper place within the life of the Church? For that matter, *should* confirmation still have a similar place in the life of the Church that it once had? Are we in need of something different in its place? If you have read the book this far, you likely know that I by no means intend to suggest that confirmation has lost its purpose in the Church. I do believe that there is a proper place for it. However, I also believe that our approach to the practice of confirmation is in need of a serious refocusing. In order to address this concern, this chapter will present and discuss foundational terminology that will seek to orient our thinking about what we should hope to accomplish through confirmation so that we can establish that ministry's place in the large flow of church life.

We have already discussed the connection between faith and the development of young people as seen through theorists like Piaget, Kohlberg, Fowler, and others. We also spent time in chapters 1 and 2 exploring the nature and development of catechesis. After all, understanding the historic foundation for confirmation and catechesis is essential to our task of assessing the place for current practice in the Church today. We will not revisit those topics here. Instead, we will explore the conceptual categories of Christian education in order to map out the place of confirmation.

Christ provides instructions to His disciples on how to spread the Gospel just prior to departing this earth after His resurrection. In Acts, Luke records Jesus instructing the disciples to begin in Jerusalem, then to move on to Samaria, and finally out to the larger world (Acts 1:8b). Mark relays Jesus' instructions more directly, instructing them to go to all of creation (Mark 16:15b). Thus as disciples following a line of disciples dating back to Christ's own original band of followers, we are called to: (1) Go; (2) Proclaim; (3) Witness; (4) Make Disciples; (5) Baptize; and (6) Teach.

For the present task, let us focus on the making of disciples and teaching. These two aspects of the Great Commission can be distinguished from the others in that their focus is not exclusively on the initial connection of individuals or families to Christ, but on their ongoing growth in that faith. The sequence as presented in Matthew 28:19 implies as much, for the making of disciples is presented as a two-part task of Baptism and teaching. In this way, we see that discipleship is grounded in the sacramental adoption into the family of God that comes through Baptism and then is further developed through ongoing teaching.

I would suggest that what is meant here by teaching is not what we might associate with teaching in a technical, classroom-oriented sense. This is where I believe we have gotten off track in our approach to confirmation. If we see this teaching exclusively in the form of structured doctrinal learning, then we miss a fuller understanding of what it means to be made a disciple.

Gerhard Forde argued that through sanctification, we get used to our justification.[2] We do not add to our faith, but rather grow in our understanding of the faith with which God has already gifted us. We are freely justified by Christ through the waters of Baptism. We receive faith as a gift from God, something to which we cannot in or of ourselves lay claim. However, we are not to quit there, which we might be tempted to do.

---

[2] Gerhard Forde, "The Lutheran View" in *Christian Spirituality: Five Views of Sanctification* (Downers Grove, IL: InterVarsity Press, 1988), 13–14.

That would be to rest upon what Bonhoeffer referred to as cheap grace.[3] Having been justified by faith alone, we remain sinners. As Luther famously described our condition, we are *simul justus et peccator*, meaning that we are simultaneously just and sinners. Although we have been made right with God and can now live in a right relationship with Him, we continue to struggle as our old sinful nature fights back against that change to behave as one who is just and holy. Thus, speaking theologically, as we are made disciples, we are first justified and then embark on that lifelong process known as sanctification.

DISCIPLESHIP

Under that umbrella of sanctification, then, we live out lives of discipleship. Robert Hoerber points out that discipleship is more than mere learning. As disciples of our Lord Jesus Christ, we grow in our submission to His will. We then are able to live out that faith through our service.[4] Both sanctification and discipleship can be described as a process. This is critically important as we reflect upon the nature of confirmation. When presented as a program, confirmation implies something other than process. When we associate confirmation with instruction in the same way we might talk about math class or eighth grade, we connect confirmation to something through which one passes. True enough, a great deal of learning can and has taken place through such programmatic approaches, but this structure for confirmation likely disconnects students from the flow of their discipleship and perhaps is a part of the larger failure on the part of the Church to convey to our youth that they are forming as disciples.

When the church fails to integrate its discipleship approach in a more holistic manner across the breadth of the congregation, a stunted method of discipleship is often created that is potentially attritional and not truly connective. People may well be encouraged to be a disciple for a time, but they fail to see that this is more than a program or seasonal emphasis. They fail to recognize it as a central feature of an ongoing life in Christ. We create a revolving door attitude rather than a Christlike lifestyle. This is an all too familiar concern for our churches. Ask nearly any

---

[3] See Dietrich Bonhoeffer, *The Cost of Discipleship* (New York: Touchstone, 1995).

[4] Robert Hoerber, "Mathetes," *Concordia Journal* 6, no. 5 (Spring 1980): 181.

church leader about what takes place following confirmation and you will hear stories of heartbreak as youth and their families slowly fade away or simply never step foot in church again. We manage to attract students through the pressures of tradition and family members' expectations, but we do not instill a lifelong habit of worship and growth in Christ.

Discipleship can be defined as meeting people at their personal level of faith and equipping them to grow closer to Christ and more integrated in and with the Body of Christ. This does not just apply to confirmation, but to the entirety of discipleship in congregations' Christian education efforts. We should meet people where they are spiritually and doctrinally through educational processes that instruct and form them over time. By speaking the truth in love, we should seek to walk with families as they learn and grow in their understanding of how they are to walk together in Christ.[5] Those of us who grew up in the Church and make assumptions like I illustrated previously about parents knowing where the Gospels could be found, must instead take time to consider where we might be skipping ahead, leaving our students and their families so far behind that they get lost and give up trying to understand.

THE FAMILY AND CHURCH TOGETHER

This is a whole family issue. Approaching catechesis one student at a time is essential, but we must simultaneously provide discipleship training for parents and families as a whole. Parents need training in order to grow confident enough to take their God-given roles of spiritual leadership. Fathers especially need to be equipped not only to understand the Word of God at a deeper level, but also to see the connection between it and the daily lives of their family members. Thus, our approach to discipleship ought to focus as much on discipling families as it does on the discipling of their children before, during, and after confirmation. Laying a foundation for confirmation through family-based discipleship means that we seek to create within the family a place in which faith development is intentionally supported, spiritual formation is emphasized, and spiritual direction takes place.

---

[5] Gary Parrett and Steve Kang, *Teaching the Faith, Forming the Faithful* (Downers Grove, IL: InterVarsity Press, 2009), 136.

To begin laying this foundation, the church must walk alongside parents from the time that they first become parents. As simple as it is to become a parent (generally speaking), the act of parenting is substantially more complex and overwhelming. The church can walk alongside new and expecting parents to help them begin to think ahead about their growing family and the spiritual tasks that come with that growth. *Shaping Your Family's Future*[6] provides a method for exploring the spiritual history of parents in anticipation of the birth of their children. This is important since the spiritual heritage of parents greatly influences the manner in which they parent their children, including how and what they teach of the Christian faith. Walking with parents as they explore their spiritual roots sets the stage for how they might develop an intentional plan for including matters of faith in their family life.

In this process, pastors, DCEs, and other church leaders can help parents grow in their understanding of how their children develop as it relates to matters of faith. This was discussed in more detail in a prior chapter; however, I would like to suggest that we make use of resources such as Becky Peters' book *Building Faith One Child at a Time*[7] or the Faith Legacy Series[8] by Kids Kount Publishing, a ministry of King of Kings Lutheran Church in Omaha, Nebraska. Peters' book enables parents to better understand what to expect and how to teach their children at different stages in their development. The Faith Legacy Series provides teaching DVDs that can be used in classes for parents. Designed to have parents take a new course every two years from the birth of their child through their teenage years, the series provides a solid structure to walk with families all the way up to and beyond their children's time in confirmation.

The goal is to help parents feel comfortable discussing matters of faith and to help children feel comfortable asking the questions that they have about faith and life. Through tools such as these, we engage the larger team of a church (whether it is made of professionals or volun-

---

[6] See Carla Barnhill, *Shaping Your Family's Future* (Mount Gretna, PA: Philhaven, 2007).

[7] See Becky Peters, *Building Faith One Child at a Time* (St. Louis: Concordia, 1997).

[8] See www.kidskountpublishing.com/free-curriculum/family-ministry/

teers) in collaborating with parents to support their efforts toward the faith development of their children in the home and community.

COORDINATING MINISTRY EFFORTS

The growth of specializations in larger church ministries, while a much needed development, has come with collateral costs. When there is no one overseeing the whole of ministry—from birth, to children's ministry, to youth ministry, to college ministry, to family ministry—there may be no regular consideration of how each component of the larger church ministry affects the others. With no one ensuring that the fullness of the Gospel story is conveyed, children might grow up with a fragmented understanding of the Bible. Some Bible stories may be taught redundantly, while other stories and the full context into which all the stories fit remains unaddressed.

Therefore, whether you are involved in Sunday School, VBS, youth ministry, or a Lutheran Day School or high school; whether you are a pastor, DCE, Lutheran teacher, or are involved or responsible for any part of a ministry for, to, or with children, youth, or adults; you are on the same team. Rather than running the church as a series of loosely affiliated ministry silos, coordination is essential. Whether you do this through regular meetings, the mutual review of Christian educational materials, or the development of a master scope and sequence, it is critical for all church ministries to function on the same page. We are talking about coordinating ministry efforts for all family members, and not arbitrarily focusing efforts on the individuals we encounter in our assigned ministry age group.

ACTIVE LISTENING

Another way we can equip the parents in our congregations to be attuned to the developing spiritual needs of their children as they grow is to train them in their listening skills. It is unbelievably important to really listen to what our children have to say. It is through attentive listening that we are able to develop a relational connection and discern their educational and spiritual needs.[9] However, it is not always easy to listen

---

[9] Catherine Stonehouse and Scottie May, *Listening to Children on the Spiritual Journey* (Grand Rapids: Baker Academic, 2010), 11.

actively. Life is busy for all of us. American society rewards over-commitment, which contributes to parents' inability to focus on those to whom we ought to give our full focus and attention, our families.

It is truly only through good listening that we are able to hear the heart of our children. By listening, we get to know their hopes and dreams, as well as their fears and struggles. Through active listening to the children in our ministries and in our families, we can learn to assess where they are both spiritually and in regards to their understanding of the nature of God and His role in their lives. So how do we actively listen to our children? Active listening implies at least two activities.

First, be attuned to when children speak about God in the course of their daily life. My oldest son is an interesting case in point. Due to his exposure to the various churches that I have served and attended, he has developed an understanding of what takes place in the Sunday morning worship service. As a preschooler, he demonstrated his understanding in the form of play-acting. Thus, there were times when he role-played as though he were a pastor distributing the Lord's Supper in Costco, right there with all the samples of cheese and microwave snack foods. Rather than being embarrassed by the behavior, active listening meant that I needed to pay attention to what he had learned with regard to the practice of Communion. Due to his age, there was little point in focusing on why the play-acting was taking place in Costco; rather, it was important to listen to what he said as he recited parts of the liturgy.

The second activity of active listening involves intentional follow-up on what you have observed. When you have noted your child engaged in play-acting or other faith talk, inquire about it when they are done and talk through what they believe with them. The goal here is to reinforce as well as reshape their understanding. Another example from my son's life might help illustrate this method. While I was giving him a bath (yes, we do seem to get into matters of faith at interesting times), my son mentioned to me that Jesus was God. I followed up with him, noting that this was a simple statement rather than some larger play-acting, to ask if the Father is God, to which he replied, "Yes." Then I asked if he thought that the Holy Spirit was God. Again, he answered, "Yes." Drawing this all together, I asked him, based on what he had just mentioned about the Father being God, the Son being God, and the Spirit being God, how many gods he believed there are, to which he replied, "One, of course."

There it was—a simple conversation with a three-year-old on the Trinity. The purpose of the follow-up questions was to explore additional factors not presented in his original statement to see if his understanding was complete (at least as complete as realistically possible for a three-year-old) or if further exploration of the subject was necessary. These are just some of the approaches that can be taught to parents to aid them in supporting their children's faith development.

FAITH VS. SPIRITUAL DEVELOPMENT

I would like to take a moment to explain why I use the term *faith development* rather than *spiritual development,* and the importance of that distinction. On the surface, the two terms might appear similar or even synonymous. Whereas faith development is, to at least some extent, a natural process similar to a child's physical and psychological development, spiritual formation is more of an intentional process in which the influence of another is felt in the spiritual life of an individual. Through our formation, we are, as Paul says in Romans 8:29, being conformed into the likeness of Christ.[10]

Spiritual formation is that process of conforming to the likeness of Christ. Dallas Willard talks about spiritual formation as a process of transformation.[11] Tom Schwanda discusses spiritual formation as a shaping that is constant, with the potential for both positive and negative shaping to take place.[12] Taken together, we see that spiritual formation is a process in which both God and humanity struggle together to form the very image of our Savior in individual followers of Christ. Schwanda's willingness to concede the potential negative formation that can take place suggests an understanding of not only our own sinful natures, but also that of others around us.

Thus, spiritual formation must be an intentional process. In order for one to be shaped into the likeness of Christ, one needs to know what that likeness is. There is a clear need to provide those being discipled with

---

[10] Parrett and Kang, *Teaching the Faith, Forming the Faithful,* 33.

[11] Dallas Willard, "Spiritual Formation: What it is, and How it is Done," www.dwillard.org/articles/artview.asp?artID=58 (accessed November 12, 2015).

[12] Tom Schwanda, "Formation, Spiritual," in *Dictionary of Christian Spirituality,* ed. Glen Scorgie (Grand Rapids: Zondervan, 2011), 452.

doctrinal propositions on the nature and work of Christ, but there is an inherent limitation to relying solely on propositional content. While the content is critical, it must also be lived out through the power of the Holy Spirit.

In order to make this assessment and to begin to live out the likeness of Christ in one's life, the disciple must see Christlikeness in action. Jesus' disciples spent three years struggling to understand what it might mean to live as their Master lived. We, as descendent disciples, must witness others in order to fully assess how we can live out the Christlikeness that we find in the pages of Scripture. In like manner, students in our confirmation classes need to see and experience what it means to live in conformity to Christ and in so doing live as one who has been redeemed and justified.

The goal in spiritual formation specifically, and discipleship in general, is to move our students out of a state of complacent self-reliance into a dependent reliance upon Christ. Peter Nelson discusses this as discipleship dissonance. We are living in a state of the already and the not yet. We are being formed, but are not yet fully formed. We make progress in our spiritual growth, but we are still growing.[13] Upon entering into active discipleship through spiritual formation processes, our youth should not merely find that they gain confidence in their own spirituality, but that they begin to see more clearly and understand the sinfulness that remains a part of their lives. Rather than seeking quick successes, spiritual formation quickly becomes a lifelong process of gradual shaping. Spiritual formation is a marathon and not a sprint.

A couple of years ago, my wife ran the Nike Women's Marathon in San Francisco. She trained for that marathon with Team in Training, an organization that raises funds for cancer research. I can safely say that had she not had a team around her for training and for the marathon itself, she would not likely have completed her goal. Running 26.2 miles takes hours, not just on the day of the race, but in training and recovery from training as well. Spiritual formation is similar. We cannot be formed by reading only. God gave us His Word as a guide to show us the

---

[13] Peter K. Nelson, "Discipleship Dissonance: Toward a Theology of Imperfection Amidst the Pursuit of Holiness," *Journal of Spiritual Formation & Soul Care* 4, no. 1 (2011): 82.

path to salvation walked by Christ as well as the path to walk in life as a redeemed child of God following our being joined to Him in Baptism. God has also established His Church as a nurturing support community in which we rely on others for mutual support and correction. This is what we provide when we spiritually form our confirmation students. They need that support to see them through the long haul. When they reach the point when they are better able to assess just how much they have accomplished and how far from holy they truly are (foothills to mountains), we stand by them showing them the way forward. We walk with them pointing them back to Christ, who carries them through and powers their ascent.

As Nelson notes, this process implies a certain amount of trauma.[14] This is the natural effect of the saint warring with the sinner within each of us. This is not a peaceful process. Our youth struggle to live out their lives as disciples of Christ. Spiritual formation is the process by which we work with our students to aid them in forming or reforming themselves in the likeness of Christ. In this process, we take on the role of spiritual director. Generally speaking, as Lutherans, we do not tend to use this terminology. For that matter, much of the previous discussion is lacking in our circles. However, even though we might tend to avoid thinking of ourselves as spiritual directors, there is an element of spiritual direction taking place as we disciple our young people through spiritual formation practices.

Spiritual direction tends to need to be conducted in more of a one-on-one manner than most of us are able to accomplish during confirmation class time. However, I believe it would be wise to incorporate some element of this activity into the flow of our praxis of catechesis. We need to attend to the desires that we each have, even those resulting from our sinful nature. Through spiritual direction grounded in the teachings of Christ and the Word, we seek to combat our sinful yearnings, put on the fullness of Christ, and live in accordance with His example.[15] This is our calling, which is, however, well beyond our ability. Therefore, it is not merely the guidance of Christ that we need in His Word, but the strength

---

[14] Nelson, "Discipleship Dissonance," 82.

[15] Kim Olstad, "Direction, Spiritual," in *Dictionary of Christian Spirituality*, ed. Glen Scorgie (Grand Rapids: Zondervan, 2011), 402.

accorded to us through the Holy Spirit to accomplish even minor growth in sanctification.

LOCATING THE PLACE FOR CATECHESIS

So where does this leave us as we consider how to place catechesis into the bigger context of the church's ministry? How do we draw these various strands that have been discussed together with reflection upon our theology and practice in the Lutheran Church and find a place where catechesis might be done and done well?

To answer those questions, it is essential first to recognize the tension in which we find ourselves as justified believers in Christ. Having been declared righteous through the redemption won for us by Christ on the cross, we remain fallen sinners struggling to actualize said righteousness in our lives. We are, as Luther put it, *simul justus et peccator*. We are both justified and sinners. We are both saint and sinner. In that tension we work out our sanctification through the ministry and strength of the Holy Spirit, seeking to become Christlike, at least in so far as we are able this side of eternity.

In this state of between-ness, we seek to provide instruction and guidance to our students. We begin our ministry where they are moving toward and where we are all called to be in Christ. We begin assessing their state as disciples. Thus, foundationally, our task is that of discipleship. All that we do, whether that is catechesis, spiritual formation, or spiritual direction, must be founded upon an effort to disciple our young people in the life of the faith. As I see discipleship, these three component parts form the whole from which we are able to ground our ministry.

In catechesis, we present the content of the faith. Our catechetical work instructs young disciples in the Six Chief Parts of Luther's Small Catechism as well as the foundational structure and story of the Gospel. This content-oriented aspect of discipleship is critical, and fortunately has been an area of emphasis and strength within the Lutheran Church. Parrett, in personal correspondence with Richard Osmer, discussed their mutual concern regarding an over-emphasis on relational approaches to discipling that may undercut knowledge of scriptural content.[16] Osmer expressed his concerns that in focusing our efforts on the relational

---

[16] Parrett and Kang, *Teaching the Faith, Forming the Faithful*, 75.

aspect of discipleship, we fail to provide adequate focus on the very content of our faith. Lutherans, in my experience, have historically erred on the other side, emphasizing content to the potential exclusion of the relational aspects of catechesis.

Parrett argues for an approach to catechesis that is relational between catechist and catechumen; is liturgical and grounded in the worship life of the church; holistically seeks to reach the heart, mind, and body of those we teach; seeks to understand the background of those we teach in a culturally responsive way; is pedagogically sound; and is rich in biblical content and the essentials of the historic faith.[17] Thus in Parrett's view, catechesis must convey the subject matter in a manner that emphasizes neither content nor relationships over one another. Although he sweeps many aspects of discipleship into catechesis in a helpful manner, I am not convinced it is entirely warranted.

The approach that I am taking here provides a distinction between catechesis, spiritual formation, and spiritual direction. Although I would agree with Parrett that these are related terms and that each must be present for catechesis to be effective, I would maintain a greater distinction between each, which his comments do not suggest. In order to understand why I am stressing these distinctions, let us now explore spiritual formation and spiritual direction.

Spiritual formation is not to be understood as moving beyond the Gospel into the "meat" of the "Christian life." As Parrett rightly points out, the Gospel is not milk from which to move on to meatier material. Rather, the Gospel is that which is unfathomable in its depth for teaching and the formation of our lives.[18]

Spiritual formation, then, is not about a graduation beyond the Gospel, but rather the application of that Gospel in the daily lives of disciples. While catechesis spends its time on comprehension of content, spiritual formation takes place as we walk with our students, seeking to aid them as they re-form their lives after the model of Christ. Through spiritual formation, the application of Law and Gospel as taught in catechesis is fleshed out, reshaping the spirit of the individual into greater conformity

---

[17] Parrett and Kang, *Teaching the Faith, Forming the Faithful*, 89.

[18] Parrett and Kang, *Teaching the Faith, Forming the Faithful*, 99.

and communion with the Body of Christ and the Head of that Body, Christ Himself.

Through this emphasis on Law and Gospel, a Lutheran approach to spiritual formation prevents such formation from degenerating into moralism.[19] This Lutheran form of spiritual formation avoids a shallow approach to life as a redeemed follower of Christ. As Walther's sixteenth thesis points out, right dividing of Law and Gospel does not mean that merely discarding a set of vices or adopting a more moral lifestyle is evidence of conversion.[20] This approach to spiritual formation avoids whitewashing the exterior and instead allows the Law to work in the sinner's heart to a necessary degree, truly causing healthy despair that removes all hope of standing before God Almighty on our own merits.

Spiritual direction, finally, is an intentional process into which we enter with select students. I suggest only select students for two principal reasons. First, not all of our students are prepared for a more individually directed approach. Second, the number of individuals with whom we can engage in such a process has an inherent limit. It is in this intentional relationship that discipleship can be most fully experienced. The content of catechesis meets the formative nature of spiritual formation under the individual direction of a mentor. Bonhoeffer talks about the spiritual care that is a part of spiritual direction. He points out the connection between spiritual care and *diakonia*, or the ministry of service of others in the church. This ministry of service, Bonhoeffer believes, involves helping those whom we disciple to confront and confess their sin and seek to grow in obedience to Christ.[21] Thus in a spiritual direction relationship, the director seeks to truly know the one being directed and to provide challenge (Law) and comfort (Gospel) as necessary while living life together under Christ. This deeply personal exploration of the individual seeks to push past surface behavior and moralism to core character issues. These relationships with students in confirmation might be rare, but they are a true blessing for both parties when they are able to be formed.

---

[19] John Oberdeck, *Eutychus Youth* (St. Louis: Concordia, 2010), 27.

[20] C. F. W. Walther, *Law & Gospel: How to Read and Apply the Bible* (St. Louis: Concordia, 2010), 333.

[21] Dietrich Bonhoeffer, *Spiritual Care* (Minneapolis: Fortress Press, 1985), 35.

LUTHERAN SCHOOLS

Coming back to the place of the Lutheran school and the use of age-level instruction, we need to make sure to understand clearly how our practice of confirmation can hold captive our philosophy of confirmation. If, rather than considering confirmation as an element of discipleship, churches persist in treating confirmation as a program on its own, then there will be little to wrestle with here. If, however, the local congregation forms a philosophy that views confirmation as indeed part of a larger and longer ministry of the church, then they will need to consider what this means for the upper grade religion classes in the Lutheran school.

Pragmatically, it would not be wise to disregard the wonderful ministry that takes place through confirmation instruction as it has been done in Lutheran schools. A good number of students, who otherwise might not have been catechized at all, have encountered the rich heritage of Lutheran theology through this practice. Not wishing to jettison this beneficial area of ministry, we need to consider an appropriate way to connect catechesis with the ministry of the Lutheran school. Rather than setting aside all or a portion of a religion class for confirmation instruction in seventh and eighth grade, schools would be wise to create a structure woven throughout the whole of their curriculum to reflect a lifespan approach to catechesis from the start. Conversation should be encouraged between the church and school staff to coordinate instruction as appropriate. They will need to balance out academic goals at the school with discipleship and catechetical goals for the church, but these goals need not be mutually exclusive. Both church and school should develop a single philosophical approach and spend time communicating this approach to families connected to each.

In summary, the place of confirmation in the context of the church and the family is to be an educational process that is structurally linked to all aspects of Christian discipleship of a congregation. As a holistic ministry, its programmatic aspects must take into account the realities of family life as they present themselves for each individual. Thus, confirmation ministry is a part of a larger effort of discipleship begun when our students were baptized and continuing throughout their entire lives. Confirmation is discipleship in that it catechizes students in the critical content of the Christian faith, seeks to form them spiritually more and more into the image of Christ, and directs them toward their own growth in Christ.

Our confirmation ministries ought to connect conceptually and practically with our church's efforts in children's ministry and youth ministry as well as ministry to the entire family. Both through coordination of curriculum and the scheduling of events, confirmation should exist in fluid harmony with the ministry of the church as a whole. If this chapter convinces you of nothing else, let it convince you that confirmation is not a stand-alone program or ministry, but rather a stage of a larger discipleship through which we, as leaders, walk with and guide our young people.

CHAPTER 7

TEACHING THE FAITH IN BLENDED AND SINGLE-PARENT FAMILIES

Family life in American society is arguably marked more by a plurality of family types than the existence of any ideal concept of the family. Secularizing forces have moved society far enough on the nature of the family that one might be accused of being hopelessly out of touch to even suggest that there might be any definition of family that might be considered ideal. Yet, when God's Word places catechesis within the context of the family, our Creator had a very specific concept of family in mind.

That said, what is the local church to do given the reality that many of the families in their fellowship are blended from previously broken families? It is both wise and in accord with the counsel of the Bible to uplift a biblical concept of the family, which is founded upon the marriage of one man to one woman for a lifetime. But the church cannot stop there. Rather, we must both provide an affirmation of God's design for the family as well as encourage a vision of God's design for faithfulness within blended families.

All too often, the conflict that began as a fracture within the marriage of two parents spills over and affects their children in the divorce. Therefore, as much as possible, parents should attempt to keep the struggles that they have with one another out of their relationship with their children. A parent should not speak negatively about a former spouse, especially with the intent of altering their children's relationship with him or her. It takes personal maturity to handle this, but children should be encouraged to love and respect both their parents. Depending on how old children are when their parents divorce, they will already be well aware of at least some level of the conflict. However, they should not be made privy to the inner workings of their parents' relational struggles.

God's grace is still able to work in the lives of those parents who have already had a difficult divorce and have struggled in this area. They should seek to put past struggles in the past if for no other reason than for the healthy raising of their children. Parents should seek to find common ground outside of their own struggle with one another and focus on what is best for their children. They should try not to confuse what is best for the children with what is best for them. Objectively one individual parent may not be best for them at all times and in all ways. Even though the relationship between the husband and wife has failed, ex-spouses should still seek to empower one another in their parenting where possible.

Open communication is essential, especially as new marriages add stepparents into the mix. Although there will naturally be an abundance of areas for disagreement, parents and stepparents serve the needs of their children best when they are able to come together and find common ground. This is essential specifically in the area related to matters of faith. Scripture challenges the faithful to avoid being unequally yoked (2 Corinthians 6:14). This means Christians are to avoid joining as one flesh in marriage with those who do not share a similar faith in Christ. A parent whose ex-spouse left the faith or simply fell in love with a non-believer and chose not to heed this warning may find it all the more challenging to teach the faith to his or her children. However, such parents should avoid fighting over this issue. As critical as it is, open fighting over how faith is to be a part of a child's life is counterproductive.

A parent who makes it a priority to attend church and teach the faith at home should not belittle the other parent for not doing likewise. While it would be best for the child to have both parents modeling in similar fashion, there is little gain in adding this issue to other points of conflict. Parents should support one another, even if only by refraining from speaking ill of the priorities of the other parent. Where possible, parents should structure custody so that their children can faithfully attend church with them and participate in the life of the congregation. This may mean that other concessions may need to be made in order to make this a priority.

A Stepparent's Role

Another area of potential conflict involves the role of the stepparent in teaching the faith at home. Especially when children are older—preteens and teenagers—the parenting of a stepfather or stepmother is in and of itself complicated. It is far too easy for children to argue that they do not have to listen to someone whom they do not view as having any real authority. Just as it is essential for a father and mother to parent children as a unit, when there is a stepfather and stepmother involved, they all need to parent as a unit. It may be challenging to build enough trust in a former spouse, let alone his or her new spouse; however, doing so helps to provide a solid disciplinary foundation upon which to build.

From a united foundation, stepparents are able to contribute to the catechizing of their stepchildren. Stepfathers, along with fathers, are especially to take a lead role in this effort. Stepfathers should never seek to undermine the leadership of a child's father, but this does not mean that they should shy away from leading spiritually within the blended family unit. Stepfathers should seek to open lines of healthy communication with fathers so that they can affirm one another in their leadership. If a stepfather places a higher value on teaching the faith to the children than the father does, he should make an effort to reassure the father that he does not intend to undercut his leadership. They should spend what time is possible helping each other understand the goals that they have for their children.

Stepmothers should support and encourage fathers to take leadership in matters of faith. They should encourage the kind of communication described above between fathers and stepfathers. Further, stepmothers should develop a nurturing relationship with the children that supports and extends the catechizing efforts of the children's father, as well as mother and stepfather if possible. Many times, mothers and stepmothers spend a good deal of time reading the Bible to their young children. Both should be encouraged to share with one another the stories that the children have been hearing and about the teaching provided related to those stories.

Children will naturally make comparisons. That is just a part of who they are and what they do. The more often parents and stepparents can be on board with one another, the better. Where you must disagree (for example, on matters of doctrine and church practice), do so agreeably.

Where this is not possible, make sure to keep personal issues as far out of the discussion as possible and seek to keep the children themselves from having to navigate a minefield between their parents.

Blended Families

Blended families are not merely blending sets of parents, but they are often blending children from prior relationships and perhaps eventually children from the new marriage. When we talk about "yours, mine, and ours" with regard to children, all kinds of conflict may arise. Children of one parent may feel slighted by what they receive from their parents as compared to what they perceive their stepsiblings receive. The blending of a family takes time and is often a rather messy process. Hurt feelings may be a regular occurrence for both children and adults.

Participation in the life of the local church can serve as a foundational way to help blend a family into a single unit. The rituals associated with the practice of the faith not only bond one generation in faithfulness with another, but those practices are also able to bond members of the same generation as they seek to understand the nature of this new construct they are told is their family. This means that it is especially important for the family to worship, pray, and study God's Word together. The practice of their faith can become common ground from which to build unity as a newly blended family. Blended families can spend time walking through Luther's Small Catechism just as any family can. However, as a blended family, time should be spent talking about the contributions of the traditions from both prior families and how that informs and furthers the traditions and practice of the faith that all members of the family hope will be a part of their new unit.

When walking through the catechism, biological parents can affirm the leadership of stepparents by finding intentional ways to involve them in the process. Mom can start the process by asking Stepdad to lead prayer or to take the lead in asking questions from the catechism. Dad may still maintain the lead, but the family will be blessed by his encouraging Stepmom to have her own intentionally active role in the discussion. Plan this out ahead of time. Be willing to make adjustments if the kids are not quite ready for the particular role or approach selected.

In situations where there is a stronger tradition of family faith life on one side of the new family than the other, some care may be needed to avoid making children who are less familiar with family faith practices feel uncomfortable or even alienated. Talk to children who are old enough about helping their new siblings grow to know the traditions they hold dear. Talk to them about how they might develop faith traditions and practices together as a new family together.

Grandparents can be of tremendous help when seeking to blend a family in the Christian faith. Grandparents who are able to maintain a trusted status with their grandchildren, and who do not demean their own son or daughter's ex-spouse, may be in a great position to speak to the potential for a happy future in their new family. Grandparents can provide a safe place for older children to express the frustrations that they may not be prepared to share with their parents. Grandparents can offer support for both parent and child as they struggle to find a new normal. They can provide a bridge to the past. Grandparents can present a legacy of faith to their grandchildren and help to ensure that the Christian faith lives on for generations after them. Time spent with grandparents can help provide a connection to past feelings of stability. Connecting those times with intentional nurturing of the faith can buttress the faith of children struggling to understand their new lives.

The church can also be a stabilizing support for blended families. Church leaders should make sure that they work with, not unintentionally against, the catechizing efforts of blended families. Get to know the contours of the family structures in your church. Support efforts of parents and stepparents alike to teach the faith to the children in their lives. Find intentional ways to involve all parents in confirmation and other ministries. Struggle with children as they try to get used to having the addition of a stepparent(s) in their lives. Affirm God's presence in their lives despite the loss of security they may feel with the breakup of their parents' marriage. Provide a safe place for them to mourn as their parents remarry, ending their hopes that their parents might reconcile.

THE CHURCH

The church can provide critical support for parents who must raise their children alone, due to divorce or the death of their spouse, by helping such parents feel less alone. Connecting moms to other moms or dads to other dads can help provide a much-needed sounding board for the single parent. When children take part in formal confirmation instruction, consider pairing the single parent with another single parent or another family for support. Encourage grandparents to be a part of the confirmation process when possible. Churches who assign mentors or "godparents" to provide support during the confirmation years can connect those people with single parents, with all parents for that matter, so that they can help pray for the child going through confirmation.

Teaching the faith to young children as single parents can be challenging. Churches might consider expanding their existing mentoring programs to connect another adult to the lives of these children sooner. Teach both single parents and mentors to support one another in prayer, as well as basic practices of the faith. If single parents have multiple children of differing ages, the mentor may help with the younger kids at times to provide relief and to allow the single parent a chance to talk with the older children about matters of faith at a more advanced level. Mentors can also help train a parent on family devotions and other faith practices by inviting the single parent and children to participate with their family. A mentor's family and the single-parent family can also team up during worship, helping the single parent to manage the kids in church. This reinforces essential faith practices that have been noted already.

Much more can be included as there are so many varieties of families these days. The point here is not to provide an exhaustive list of family structures or every potential way to address how a family and church can support one another in catechizing their children. The purpose here has been to make note of the potential diversity of family structures found in a local church and to affirm for both family and congregation that the task of catechesis does not have to be overwhelming. There will be challenges for blended or single-parent families that other families will not as likely encounter. But God remains faithful and through His Church is able to provide the support needed to teach the faith even in this form of brokenness. In truth, all families experience some element of brokenness. Christ, who makes us whole, brings restoration to each of our families, no matter the kind or depth of the brokenness.

PART 2

Embracing Lifespan Catechesis

CHAPTER 8

LIFESPAN CATECHESIS

STRATEGIES FOR THE CHURCH

The Church has the opportunity to influence young people as they grow in their faith and explore questions related to the nature of their faith and life in Christ. Despite the well-attested fact that nothing even competes with the influence that parents in the home have in shaping the faith of youth, those of us who work either professionally or voluntarily in congregational ministry and leadership do have a ministry to offer. We are called by God to pour the wisdom of the Scriptures into the lives of youth as they mature in mind, body, and faith.

For many, if not most, of the students we see in our confirmation classes, their vision for confirmation is not what has been laid out in the preceding chapters. One might even wonder if the average pastor or other called worker laboring to provide quality instruction is granted the luxury to pause and consider the full implications of the catechesis process and the connection that this process has with what is taking place in our congregations as confirmation. For much of my own ministry, it was hard to grapple with bigger picture questions when the demands of current ministry came so fast and furious.

One of the key learnings gleaned from my research on confirmation and catechesis is the need to move beyond the programmatic toward a more holistic approach to catechesis. We need an approach to catechesis that does not see confirmation as a stand-alone program, but rather as a key element of an ongoing shaping process that begins at Baptism and extends across each person's lifespan.

Rather than catechesis being set aside as a brief program for junior high students to struggle their way through and escape, a healthier, and I would argue more biblically sound, approach would be what might be seen as lifespan catechesis. As noted elsewhere in this book, catechesis is a lifelong project and should be taught as such in our churches. Church leadership should impress upon parents that catechesis truly begins as the waters of Baptism are still drying.

Walking with parents as they teach the faith to their children is essential. One of the great joys of my ministry has been meeting with families as they prepare to have their children baptized. It is always wonderful to connect with these families, talk with them about the promises they are about to make to raise up their young ones in the Christian faith, and ensure them that the church and I are committed to sharing this journey with them. Helping young parents see not only that they are capable of teaching the faith, but also that they have support to do so through the staff and ministries of their church provides them with a good deal of strength.

The implications of this approach to catechesis can be far reaching in how it affects our overall approach to ministry. Rather than making curricular decisions for programs such as Sunday School, Vacation Bible School, and other children's ministry programs independently, lifespan catechesis becomes the filter through which to evaluate and assess these programs. This helps us to view confirmation as more than the memorization of the Six Chief Parts and Luther's explanations thereof, and see it as a step in a longer journey of faith. This does not in any way lessen the value of this instruction. I remain very passionate about the critical nature of these central teachings of the faith; however, restoring a catechetical approach provides not only a vision for the work leading up to that study, but also a launching point for further growth following traditional confirmation.

By applying a lifespan catechesis approach, the church and the families of the congregation engage together over a more sustained time to form and shape the faith in our young people. Faith conversations become a natural part of life, just as Luther had envisioned with the writing of the Small Catechism. By re-empowering parents to have these faith conversations, children grow up wrestling with matters of faith. Families are able to be proactive and are supported by their churches in introducing the young to the foundations of the faith and a life of discipleship.

Hopefully by now you recognize the need for an approach to catechesis that begins when children are young rather than playing catch-up when youth show up for confirmation instruction. But, practically speaking, how can a pastor, DCE, or other church leader go about creating a church culture for lifespan catechesis? Start with intentional classes and conversations with families prior to Baptism. Lay out for them the journey ahead and the parts they and the church play in the journey. Provide for parents resources that explain the basics of the faith in a way that they are able to understand and teach to their children.

Next, establish regular classes or group meetings in which you gather together parents with children of similar ages. Walk them through the developmental stage through which their children are traveling, drawing connections with methods to approach faith talk with their kids. In the church, we often talk about the critical role parents play in the formation of faith in their children, a role that is second only to the Holy Spirit with regard to their spiritual influence. However, the counter reality is that for many parents, this role fills them with much concern and even fear. Many feel ill equipped to respond to the spiritual needs of their children. Therefore, it is the task of church leaders to equip parents to fulfill their spiritual leadership in the home.

This can begin simply by walking parents through concepts of prayer with and for their young children. Through example and practice, we can teach parents how to pray a blessing upon their children and gain confidence in praying for the needs of their children and family as a whole. Along with prayer, it is helpful to instruct parents of young children on the benefit of reading the Bible to their children. Even when kids are too young to understand or even sit still all the way through a brief passage, establishing the habit of reading the Bible is beneficial. In addition, it would be beneficial to provide parents opportunities to examine various children's Bibles and discuss different times during the day (e.g., at meals or at bedtime) when families can employ Bible reading.

When children are two to three years old, we can teach parents about what it means to share their faith with their kids. Using concrete language, churches can help parents to capture an understanding of what faith is like to a toddler so that they can also model prayer. At three years old, my youngest son began to offer his own prayers at bedtime just as he had heard his older brother and I doing. At times the prayers seemed to ramble and appeared to be a recounting of the events of the day, but in retrospect a prayer life that examines the events of the day is a prayer life that entrusts all of life to the care and guidance of our Lord.

Four- and five-year-old children are developmentally ready to learn about worship in a basic manner. This is why the children's worship at Shepherd of the Hills (see chapter 4) was structured to include children starting at age 4. Children can learn about the faith of their parents by observing what happens in worship and through the questions they ask during Bible reading times. Resources like *My First Hymnal* (St. Louis: Concordia, 2011) can help parents guide their children through what goes on in worship. This is beneficial for parents to refresh or sharpen their understanding of what takes place in worship, while introducing children to the ability to experience and learn about their Creator through worship. Churches should provide resources and training for parents to help them feel comfortable bringing their little ones into the sanctuary for worship and talking about what takes place in the service.

As the attention span of their children grows, parents of six- and seven-year olds can move beyond Bible reading and begin adding devotions to their daily routines as a family. Again, parents will need resources and training to help them develop the confidence to lead family devotions. There are an overwhelming number of resources available. The challenge for parents is knowing where to look for quality, theologically appropriate material. Knowing how to evaluate the appropriate use of Law and Gospel and how to keep Christ central in their family's devotional life will help parents lay a foundation for the faith of their children that will stand a far better chance of surviving and, in fact, thriving until, throughout, and beyond confirmation.

Finally, churches would do well to present their young members with their own Bibles. They can do this in kindergarten to get ahead of most readers or wait until children are perhaps seven years-old and are more confident in their reading. With either approach, it is helpful to make sure parents realize this is not a ploy to get them and their children into worship one additional Sunday; it is an essential step on the road of faith formation for their sons and daughters. The gift of a Bible to a child should focus on the giving of God's Word from one generation to another. Just as parents have Bibles that they read regularly,[1] now their children are able to have their own Bibles so that the habit of Bible reading moves naturally from something done exclusively within family devotional time to an activity that the children themselves are able to initiate and practice.

As children enter into Christian education (Sunday School, VBS, etc.), programs should be structured to work with the family to lay out the basic content of the faith. Remember that young children are naturals at memorization. Their minds readily drink up phrases that they can repeat back (just watch a Disney movie with them and you will see what I mean). Focus on memorizing the elements of the Six Chief Parts of the Small Catechism. Teach the books of the Bible through song.

As children grow and mature, provide tours of the church to help them get to know the space in which they worship. Walk children in early elementary grades through the order of worship. Show them the connection between Lutheran liturgy and Scripture. Have a discussion with children about worship while standing in the church sanctuary. Talk to them about what happens when, where in the service, and why. Pastors should consider working with kids in the worship service not just in a "children's sermon" but throughout the service with asides that teach them what is taking place. This can actually be very instructive for all in attendance, as the days in which one can assume everyone knows what is happening in worship may well be over. These asides can be delivered in print in the bulletin as well as by taking a moment to provide commentary for the kids during the service itself.[2]

As children progress through Sunday School, lay out the story of Scripture with quality curriculum that not only provides all the key stories of both the Old and New Testament, but also helps students understand how these individual stories tell one larger story. God speaks to us

---

[1] This is a great opportunity to encourage parents in their own reading of Scripture. For many this may be a sore spot as they have not been as regular in their habit of Bible reading as the church is asking of them and their kids. Make sure to apply to Gospel here—this is an opportunity to make a fresh start and to lead by example. This applies in Bible reading, Bible study, and worship attendance. In each of these simple practices, parents demonstrate the value of their faith in Christ. This has a lasting impact in the lives of their children.

[2] See Concordia Publishing House's *Growing in Worship* children's worship folders for an example of this approach (www.cph.org/t-topic-wr-giw.aspx).

in the Bible to tell us the story of our relationship to Him and with Him. In that single story, we learn of His desire to create us and make a home for us. We learn how we, as humanity, marred that creation with sin. However, the largest portion of the story focuses on how God determined to bring us back to Him, to redeem us from our sin, and to restore us to a right relationship with Him in this life and for eternity. The whole of Scripture points to the promised coming of the Son of God, Jesus the Christ, whose life, death, and resurrection worked for us our salvation. When teaching the individual stories of the Bible in Sunday School, teachers should always seek to connect individual stories to this meta-story of sin and redemption through the life, death, and resurrection of Christ.

Having laid this foundation, confirmation instruction naturally moves to a more developmentally appropriate level. Rather than empha-sizing memorization as children become teens and develop abstract thinking, spend time helping them to wrestle with the questions of faith to which they are beginning to be exposed. Create that thinking climate in which they are able to work through their doubts freely but within a faith-nurturing church environment.

Following the Rite of Confirmation, continue to wrestle with the cen-tral doctrines of the Church with your high school students. Engage them apologetically with guided learning on topics that surface in their high school classrooms, such as evolution, world religions, sexual identity, and more. Confront these potentially controversial topics head-on, ground-ing your reflections in Scripture. Provide older high school and young college students with training in critical thinking. Basic logic training can go a long way toward providing students with the ability to grasp the dis-tinctions between Christian beliefs and competing systems of thought. Walk them through basic logic skills, such as the law of identity, the law of the excluded middle and the law of non-contradiction. With logic training, young people are able to develop the skills needed to identify properly a good argument from a bad argument. With so much of public discourse on religion and topics with religious implications being "ar-gued" based on emotion, it is critical that we equip our teens with the ability to not only connect emotionally but also to intellectually compre-hend presented arguments.

Throughout the rest of its members' lives, the church should provide opportunity for continued reflection upon the basics of the Christian faith. It should also provide the chance to push deeper, so that members can apply those foundational doctrines further into their lives and delve ever more intensely into God's Word.

This ongoing catechetical discipleship that is lifespan catechesis could take a number of forms. It should take place in Sunday School as well as in youth groups for elementary, junior high, and high school youth. Through this ongoing approach, a confirmation program might structurally look more like reinforcement and formal affirmation of progress rather than a stand-alone program with a firm beginning and end. Some would argue that merging youth ministry with confirmation could serve as such an approach.[3]

We need to have a two-pronged approach that (1) provides space in our ministries for one-on-one and small group discussions on catechetical topics with discipleship applications; and (2) provides ongoing large group or mass-targeted instruction to ground those discussions in the Scriptures and Lutheran Confessions. We can all too easily select one option or the other, but I would argue that this is a both/and situation. We need both the core teaching of well-trained church workers to continue calling the faithful back to God's Word and out of potential heresy or heterodoxy as well as time in smaller groups led by seasoned and well-trained laity to give this teaching further legs in the lives of those to whom we are called to serve.

This aligns with the approach used by Christ. The making of disciples is a messy process to say the least. From the outside, the apostles themselves did not appear to be the right choices, yet through the ministry of the Holy Spirit, these less than stellar leaders turned the world upside down. They took a message of grace and love to the far corners of the world through proclamation of the Word and the making of disciples.

Through lifespan catechesis, we, too, continue to make disciples, even when it gets messy, even when they ask difficult questions and have doubts that are hard to eliminate. By enlisting others in our churches to join us in that task, we extend the model of our Savior, raising up new generations of disciples and perhaps a few new church leaders.

---

[3] See Steve Christopher and Timothy Potthoff, "Youth Ministry as Confirmation," in *Confirmation Basics* (St. Louis: Concordia, 2009), 96–108.

Once, when my son was five years old, I was sitting in my office at Concordia University Irvine as I overheard him in the hallway engage in a conversation with a couple of my colleagues. He explained in great five-year-old detail just what took place when David killed Goliath. Listening to him expound upon his understanding of Scripture with a pair of theologians was something to hear. He spoke with great confidence and provided precise details, which is a part of his God-given personality. What a proud dad moment!

Moments like this remind us why it is so important to instill in our children a love of Christ and His Church at a young age. Having both the habit and natural love for the faith is essential. Developing and nurturing this as a habit is what makes failing to be involved in church feel not quite right, even in the teenage and young adult years. These habits echo in the minds of our children and call them back to the comfort that is their faith. The love of their faith in Christ is what encourages our children to pick up their Bibles and read (even as toddlers not yet truly able to comprehend the words). This love can draw teens with growing questions to seek out answers from both their own research of God's Word and the counsel of others. What a great reason to make lifespan catechesis a part of family life and the life of our congregation!

The last task to which we turn our attention is the equipping of parents to become catechists in their own homes. In the final chapters of this book, we will walk through the content of Luther's Small Catechism for that very purpose.

CHAPTER 9

LUTHER'S CATECHISM IN THE HOME

ATTENTION PARENTS: What follows is for you! While much of what you have been reading in the previous chapters was also of benefit for you to read and digest, these next few chapters were written especially for your benefit as you develop as a catechist in your own home. As has been demonstrated previously in this book, parents have a far greater influence in the formation and practice of their children's faith than anyone else, even more so than pastors, DCEs, elders, and other church leaders. Ideally, we ought to join together as a team. When the church and the home echo one another in how the faith is taught and lived, the impact grows exponentially.

Our children are well able to memorize when they are young. Their minds are designed to take in and repeat back what they encounter in the world. That means that we are able to teach our kids the Apostles' Creed and the Lord's Prayer, even in their preschool years. We are also able to talk through elements of the Ten Commandments with our kids, digging deeper as they grow and mature. Confession is natural for our children, even when they are young, as they experience their own need to be forgiven. Finally, we can also examine the Sacraments with our kids.

Therefore, we will walk through the text of Luther's Small Catechism and offer thoughts and recommendations on how you might incorporate learning from the Small Catechism into the life of your family. It may have been a while since you last opened your old copy of the Small Catechism. You may still have the old blue edition from your own confirmation instruction. Whether you make use of that, order a new edition, or download the catechism app from Concordia Publishing House[1] on a smartphone or other mobile device, get a copy or simply make use of the text as presented in the following chapters as a starting point.[2]

---

[1] See catechism.cph.org or search for "Luther's Small Catechism" in the iTunes store.

[2] I would recommend getting a copy of the current edition of *Luther's Small Catechism with Explanation* (St. Louis: Concordia, 1991, 2008). It contains additional helpful explanatory material that will not be reviewed directly in this book.

CHAPTER 10

THE TEN COMMANDMENTS

As the head of the family should teach them
in a simple way to his household

The Ten Commandments, traditionally taught first in confirmation instruction, serve as a natural starting point for our children. As Lutheran doctrine makes clear, we are all born sinful and in need of a Savior. Our kids might look cute and innocent, but we know that they are anything but truly innocent. Rather than needing to learn how to sin, our children take naturally to violations of both God's Law as well as the rules that we establish in our own homes. Thus talking to our children about the Ten Commandments can lay a foundation for their moral formation.

As parents, we should approach the moral formation of our children in such a way that we try to avoid doing so in a form that might degenerate into mere moralism. We need to be careful so that we do not confuse our own efforts as the source of our salvation or cause such confusion in our children. When I was serving in my first church, a gentleman in our congregation suggested that we really do not need to consider theology when it comes to teaching children. He proposed that we join in with the Episcopal Church down the street from our Lutheran congregation. I simply could not disagree more with his premise that theology is not essential for designing our approach to teaching the faith to children and youth. It is important that we as parents lay the proper foundation. When beginning our teaching of the Ten Commandments, we ought to make it clear that we strive to obey the commandments out of gratitude to Christ, since we have been saved by Him. We do not do so out of obligation in an effort to justify ourselves.

Practically speaking, this means that we need to be a bit redundant. We need to invest in the joy of purposeful repetition. We need to remind our children regularly that they should seek to keep the commandments not because failure to do so will upset us as parents or make God mad (an approach too often used), but because God has created us to keep them and do good works in His name through them. This is not conceptually a simple thing to achieve with young children. Developmentally, they may only be ready to respond out of a desire to please us as their parents. Even so, our teaching should not reinforce this stage of their development but gently push them to move beyond it. Teach and remind them that obeying the Ten Commandments is our response to the love of God in Christ's saving work, but recognize that this often will not be what they do in practice. In this way, you lay a motivational foundation for keeping the commandments that properly aligns with a Lutheran understanding of the Christian faith.

THE FIRST COMMANDMENT

You shall have no other gods.

What does this mean? We should fear, love, and trust in God above all things.

There is much going on in the First Commandment. Where should you begin in walking through this with your children? First, you should make sure you remember that the very idea of God, as well as many doctrines related to how the Christian faith explains who God is, are abstract, making it difficult for children to truly or fully understand. However, it is important to begin, even when they are young, to talk in trinitarian terms about who God is. Personally, I like to avoid using the phrase "God and Jesus." It is a rather popular phrase in Christian circles, but I believe that this does not help our kids truly come to understand God as the Trinity. Talk instead about God the Father, God the Son, and God the Holy Spirit. Reinforce with such language that the Father, Son, and Holy Spirit are each truly God. In parallel with this, emphasize that we believe in one God, not three.[1]

---

[1] What is of most importance here is consistency. Figure out how you will approach the topics of the Trinity and naming God, and stick with that approach. This will prevent confusion in children who are not able to handle frequent changes in

I know what you are thinking here—sounds too simple, right? Well, if we keep our language clear and simple and do not introduce our own struggles in understanding the Trinity, children as young as three years of age will be able to comprehend the basics of this doctrine. They are able to deal with the concepts, accepting what we see as a logical paradox, without nearly the same struggles as we have. Simply focusing on the basic facts that there are three persons (you do not really have to use this term, simply noting each individually as God will do), and then noting that we worship only one God, will often suffice. Beginning with this simple approach lays a foundation upon which they can develop a more complex understanding of God later in life.[2]

At this point, it is important to return to the wording of Luther's explanation, "*What does this mean? We should fear, love, and trust in God above all things.*" Here Luther helps us to understand what it means for us to treat God as God, and conversely what it would mean to treat anyone or anything else as a god. For older children, talk about what else might be a "god" to us. Talk about how those things that we most desire can become "gods" to us, whether we value celebrities or our social status. If we put more trust and love into these other things than we put into our relationship with God, then they have become our gods.

In unpacking the phrase "fear, love, and trust," we can carefully make use of an analogy to ourselves as parents. Our relationship with our children is ideally marked with elements of each, depending on our interactions. Certainly, when my two boys disobey, they have reason to fear not only punishment but also my disappointment, the latter of which is a far bigger threat to our firstborn than to his younger brother. Additionally, they might fear me when they run quickly around a blind corner only to be shocked and surprised as they run headlong into me. Simply being so much larger than they are is a legitimate reason for the kind of fear that we might also call respect. God is similarly so much larger and more powerful than we are that this fear ought to be a natural reaction. However, this is not the full aspect of fear that Luther speaks about. With that fear, he combines love and trust.

---

terminology. Concordia Publishing House has a great resource to help teach this concept: *3 in 1: A Picture of God*, by Joanne Marxhausen (2004).

[2] "Brain Architecture," developingchild.harvard.edu/key_concepts/brain_architecture (accessed July 13, 2015).

Love is a fundamental part of the bonding between parent and child. We can teach our children about the love of God, despite the imperfections of our own love. Pointing to ways in which we love our children, they can see a reflection of the love of God. We can then teach our children to love God in return, as He has loved us, just as they grow to love us as we show our love to them. As our kids grow older and begin to understand more about the effect of sin on the world, they may struggle to comprehend God's love when He allows evil things to happen to those for whom they care. When encountering this challenge, it is important not to claim to know more about the mind of God than we actually do or than is even possible to know.

We can talk to our children about God's love as well as His justice. Unpacking God's justice, we remind our children that the world is full of sin, and God requires that this sin be accounted for. Out of love for us, God does not make us atone for our sin, but sent Jesus to pay for sin on our behalf. However, this does not mean that there is no consequence for sin. A painful example of this happened in my home one morning. Our younger son was upset that he was not allowed to watch television when he wanted. He expressed his anger in a sinful way, by throwing a toy. Unfortunately, that toy connected with his brother's forehead just above his right eye. When he realized how he had hurt his brother, he was quick to say that he was sorry. However, even with my wife's and my love working to heal the relationship between all members of the family, the physical damage done to the forehead of our oldest remained. The consequences of our sin remain. Even in the lives of the sinless in that situation, the impact of sin can never be fully removed. We are forgiven by His grace, and yet we remain burdened in this life by the consequences of our own sins and the sins of others, even those we will never meet or with whom we will never have direct interaction.

Building on the love that we receive from God and in turn have for God, we grow to trust God. Loving us as parents involves our children trusting us. They know we love them and desire to do the best for them, despite our imperfections. God, whose love is perfect, is thus worthy of our complete trust, as He will always act in accord with His love for us.

Parents should ask older children who are more abstract in their thinking to begin considering how they might generalize the concepts of "fear," "love," and "trust." They can ask their children to move from specific examples of what each means toward more universal principles.

For example, parents can talk to their children about who and what they trust. Children may talk about trusting their own parents or other adults they know well, like teachers or relatives. From there, parents can talk about how their children develop trust, asking them what it is about those people that makes them trustworthy. Finally, parents can then talk to their kids about how we develop trust in others and ultimately in God.

As children move toward their preteen and teenage years, parents should ask them to apply each of these concepts together as they grapple with what it means to fear God but also love and trust Him at the same time. In this way, they draw together and build upon prior learning. Then they will be able to see these concepts not merely as three individual ideas, but as reflections of the same truth about our relationship with God.

THE SECOND COMMANDMENT

You shall not misuse the name of the LORD your God.

What does this mean? We should fear and love God so that we do not curse, swear, use satanic arts, lie, or deceive by His name, but call upon it in every trouble, pray, praise, and give thanks.

If we love someone, we are likely to want to treat that person well. This applies to our friends, our family, and most importantly, our God. Therefore, building on what we already know from the First Commandment, God commands us in the Second Commandment to use God's name appropriately. When teaching this commandment to our children, there is both a positive and a negative aspect of the commandment to keep in mind. When I talk about a negative approach to God's Law, I am talking about what actions we are to refrain from doing according to the Law. On the other hand, a positive approach to God's commandments means that there are those things that we are to actively engage in in order to attempt to fulfill the Law.

From the positive side of the equation, we can teach our children that we use God's name, as Luther suggests, as we "call upon it in every trouble, pray, praise, and give thanks." We can teach them this in our modeling of prayer and in our modeling of worship. By giving them the opportunity to express their faith and grow in relationship with God as they pray and worship their Creator, we teach our children how to make sure God's name is used properly.

From the negative side, we naturally begin by instructing our kids to avoid casual use of God's name or any use that is meant to demean God or others. It is almost cliché to site the misuse of the Lord's name in childhood sports, but cliché or not, the unfortunate practice is still all too prevalent. It would be foolish to think that our kids are not going to encounter this kind of crass usage of the Lord's name. Therefore, we need to work with them to know how to respond. Children, especially when they are young, are natural imitators. It continues to amaze me how words and phrases coming out of our boys' mouths have their origins in my wife's or my speech patterns. They have and will continue to pick up other phrases. I find that it does not help to overreact. When said in an unthinking, reflexive manner, we can simply bring what our children said to their attention. I tend to find that they will understand and feel guilty enough, once they are reminded about whose name they are using.

Moving from discipline to a more proactive catechizing of our children, we can talk with kids about how improper use of the Lord's name insults whom He is. Perhaps you could illustrate this with your son or daughter by using his or her own name as an example. At first, this might seem silly, but if you can illustrate how using their own name(s) as an insult ends up insulting them, it can help them to see how this happens in their use of God's name.

As our children grow older, they may begin to do what many people do when caught in a lie or challenged with regard to their honesty: they default to using God's name to demonstrate their truthfulness. This may seem logical, but in Matthew 5:33–37, Jesus instructs us to avoid oaths in His name. We are instead to be so honest in our dealings with others that there is no need to call upon God's name to encourage people to believe us. We can illustrate this by asking our children if they would rather be trusted by what they say or if they would prefer we check with someone else to verify what they are saying is true. If we always have to verify with someone else, this results in our children feeling as though they will never be believed at any point on their own merits or that they are not trustworthy of their own accord. As Christians, we are to reflect the life of Christ. Swearing in God's name draws attention to the continuing effects of sin rather than having us deal with them by being so honest that no such swearing is necessary. That should be the kind of honesty to which our children aspire.

Teens and preteens can begin to discuss how the use of God's name reflects the way in which people view and value God. Having established a more personal concrete example, older children are able to start discussing how what tears us down emotionally also tears down God. Talk with teens and preteens about how the language people use to describe God shapes their understanding of who God is. Have youth pretend to be non-Christian and then ask them to create a list of God's attributes as they would see them from outside the faith. Talk with them about what kind of a God they have fashioned in their minds through this exercise. Compare that with the attributes of God found in Scripture (creative, holy, loving, just, omniscient, omnipotent, etc.). Discuss how these two lists give a very different image of God and thus how our use of language has a direct impact on how we, and those around us, view God.

THE THIRD COMMANDMENT

Remember the Sabbath day by keeping it holy.

What does this mean? We should fear and love God so that we do not despise preaching and His Word, but hold it sacred and gladly hear and learn it.

The Third Commandment is one that may not seem like much of a challenge. It is just the "go to church" commandment. How hard could that be? It means that we as parents need to be consistent in our enthusiasm for worship, which is not always easy. We best teach the Third Commandment by living it out. By actively participating in the worship life of our local church, we teach our children its importance. By finding a church in which to worship or worshipping in some form as a family while on vacation, we teach our children that worship and the keeping of the Sabbath really is a priority.

In our busy lives, it is easy to excuse the occasional "Sunday off." However, what we ought to demonstrate is a desire to worship God, and to nurture a love for God's Word and the preaching of it in ourselves as well as in our children. By implication, this means that the habit of many American church-going parents of dropping their kids off at Sunday School while they attend a worship service will not do. Not only does this practice cut off our kids from learning to love worship, but it also confuses them on our priorities.

Only by making both worship as a family and attendance of Sunday School (Bible class for adults) a priority will our children fully understand how to keep this commandment and develop the habits needed to do so. Anything less and our kids will eventually see through it. When we do not value being in Bible class, they will learn that there is a time when they are done with that sort of thing. In addition, if they do not learn while they are young to appreciate worship, then you will find it more than a little challenging to transition them into worship as teenagers.

However, if church participation has not yet been established by the time they are teenagers, there is still hope. The struggle will be to help teens see their time in worship and other church related activities as something more about God than about themselves. Draw a connection between the time they spend with their friends and the time they spend with God. Teenagers are generally social creatures. They invest this time with their friends out of a desire to belong. In Christ, we belong to the Church and to God the Father. Therefore, we should desire to spend time with God.

Teens do not always see worship as spending time with God. Help them to see how their time in prayer with the rest of the congregation is like time with a group of friends getting to know one another. Talk with them about the Scripture readings, the sermon, and even the songs and hymns sung in worship. If parents are engaged, they can help their kids learn how to engage and grow in the knowledge of Christ.

This is not the time for guilt. Parents may be able to get short-term positive responses through guilt trips, but in the end, that motivation has more to do with mom and dad than their son or daughter. Creating an encouraging and engaging environment where the family as a whole takes part in worship and engages in learning and application following the worship service lays a foundation for teens to more readily carry with them a lifelong connection to Christ and His Church.

THE FOURTH COMMANDMENT

Honor your father and your mother.

What does this mean? We should fear and love God so that we do not despise or anger our parents and other authorities, but honor them, serve and obey them, love and cherish them.

Now for the parent's favorite! Oh, how I long to be honored by my boys. One of the truly maddening things about being a parent is the sheer number of times I have to make the same request for good behavior from my children. At times, I really wonder to what or to whom my boys are listening, because it certainly is not me.

Before we get ahead of ourselves, we as parents need to pause and notice that Luther's explanation both expands and enlightens this commandment. You might wonder why Luther makes a point to move from a commandment merely about parents to a commandment that covers all aspects of authorities. Understanding this will shed great light on this commandment and point us in the right direction in teaching our children how to keep it.

Although our kids do not always see us as such, we parents are gifts to them from God. Our role in providing for and protecting them, and raising them in accordance with God's commands is, properly understood, His gift to them. Therefore, our children should understand that we, as their parents, and all other authorities in their lives have been properly placed into their lives as gifts of God for their protection. Our parental authority is God-given and intended for the benefit of our children.

Ephesians 6:2–3 points out that obedience of this commandment comes with a promise to our children of long life. How is this so? God gives authorities their roles in order to guide and protect those over whom they exercise authority. Thus, parents are to put the needs of their children first, ahead of their own. We are to share our wisdom to help keep them safe as they grow in knowledge and wisdom of how this life and this world work. The same is true for all other authorities. This is why we teach our children to respect and obey the police, their teachers, and others in authority. God gives each of them these roles in order to look out for those in their care. By doing so, the promise that Paul notes in Ephesians is fulfilled as we are protected from many evils in this world that might otherwise shorten our time this side of eternity.

The Fourth Commandment calls us to do more than just obey. Luther points out that we are not to "despise or anger our parents and other authorities." Children are likely to see correction as a wrong done against them, when in reality, what motivates us as parents is often a desire to protect them from their own immaturity or from other people who might harm them. Furthermore, Luther says to "honor," "serve and obey," and "love and cherish" one's parents. I do not often cherish those who restrict my freedom. American culture thrives on the nature of unrestricted freedom. However, I need restraints for myself, and I am called by God to offer similar restraints to my children. I am called to love those who exercise authority over me, even when I would rather not be under anyone's authority. In like manner, our children are called to love us as well as others in authority as they fulfill the vocations to which God has called them. Honestly, this is easier for children to accomplish than for adults.

With the approach of the teenage years, this can become a rather challenging commandment. In their preteen years, children may begin to question their parents' knowledge. Often a youth's experience with new technology will far outstrip that of their parents. This may cause youth to push back against what they may see as the flawed authority of their parents. If this begins to take place, parents should engage in discussions with their children on what it means to be respectful of them, even when they realize that they possess information that their parents do not.

The key here is to emphasize the use of wisdom on the part of parents, and their role in helping their teenage children cultivate wisdom of their own. It may be helpful for parents to draw upon their experience learning wisdom over the years from their own parents as a way to bridge generations and relate to their children. The goal here is not to question the new knowledge that teens are learning, but to walk along with them, and even learn from them, while helping them to evaluate the source of the new knowledge they are gaining. In this way, teens may better maintain a level of respect for the place God has for their parents in their lives.

THE FIFTH COMMANDMENT

You shall not murder.

What does this mean? We should fear and love God so that we do not hurt or harm our neighbor in his body, but help and support him in every physical need.

Many current issues intersect with the Fifth Commandment, which can make talking to your children about it a challenge as they grow up. On the surface, the commandment is straightforward. However, it will help to clarify for our children that the wording of the commandment refers to the prohibition of murder, not killing. For older kids this becomes a critical distinction. The reason I make this distinction is to avoid the implication that being a member of the military is inherently at odds with the Christian faith.

Children who look up to soldiers and police should not feel conflicted when they learn that in both vocations there are times when it might become necessary to take another's life. For older children grappling with questions related to the use of deadly force by the police and military, it might be helpful to note that governmental authority, in light of the Fourth Commandment, has the moral ground from which to use deadly force in the preservation of others' lives. Put another way, when seeking to secure the protection and lives of individuals under their care, the police and military are morally justified in taking the life of anyone whom they deem poses a serious danger to others.

Try to avoid getting too deep into the weeds on this issue unless you have done a good deal of study on your own and deeply understand all the moral mechanics going on here. While there are generalizable moral principles that we can and should use, each situation presents its own complicated set of realities. Unless your children are mature enough to dig into these various variables, try not to go deeper than the level of maturity for which they are prepared.

As with other commandments, there is both a positive and a negative side to the Fifth Commandment. While it might be simpler to see this commandment from the negative side, I believe it to be more fruitful to teach children from a positive standpoint. Luther stresses the double-sided nature of the Fifth Commandment in his explanation, noting how we are not to "hurt or harm our neighbor in his body" but are to "help and support him in every physical need." This latter positive approach may prove more beneficial when teaching our children.

By focusing on the positive side of the matter, we instruct our children to understand the reason behind the prohibition of murder at a deeper level. We also turn our attention to the value that God has for each person in His creation. The Bible is full of passages that pronounce the value God places on His creation. Beginning in Genesis 1, where

God's addition of humanity to creation caused Him to declare His work very good, the pages of Scripture consistently point to the love and value God places on us as His children.[3]

From a viewpoint that values life, we look at issues such as abortion, euthanasia, and suicide and affirm the sanctity of life rather than merely object to the taking of life in its most vulnerable state. We affirm our children of their value and, through that, the value of others. We affirm the value of the unborn, the elderly, and those struggling with life's deepest challenges. In each case, parents should use good judgment with respect to the maturity of their children. For younger children who are more easily disturbed by the thought of death, the focus on the positive preservation of life can help avoid conversations for which neither child nor parent are ready. For older children who are starting to ask questions about why people kill other people, be sure to focus on answering the questions actually presented by your son or daughter. Try to avoid bringing in areas of consideration or struggles that you have had. However, be willing to explore this difficult topic as openly and honestly as you can.

As children enter their teenage years, the struggle for their identity can often bubble over into frustration and anger. Teens may begin to push back on parental, school, and societal restrictions, not seeing how they benefit them. In these years, it may be beneficial to reflect as parents with teens on how Christ expanded this commandment to include hating our neighbor just as it includes taking their life (Matthew 5:21–26). Teenagers may desire to vent their anger and frustrations, which can be healthy. Parents, however, should help them to avoid allowing that anger to metastasize into hate for others.

If a teen is learning to drive, talk to him or her about the frustration that often happens when someone driving around us does something foolish or reckless. In the privacy of the car, we may be tempted to say things that we would not be comfortable saying directly to the person. Out of frustration, teens may engage in their own reckless behavior. Parents can use this as an example of how our anger can lead to hate and how hate can lead to the harming of others around us. They may not initially desire to hurt anyone, but in anger, all people are capable of much destruction.

---

[3] See 1 John 3:1; John 3:16; 1 John 4:10; Ephesians 2:4–5; Romans 5:8.

THE SIXTH COMMANDMENT

You shall not commit adultery.

What does this mean? We should fear and love God so that we lead a sexually pure and decent life in what we say and do, and husband and wife love and honor each other.

Can we just skip this one? Do you really want to go there with your kids? Much as we might like to avoid the topic, the realities of our society suggest that spending time discussing this with our children, as well as modeling a healthy marriage, is critical. However, for many, perhaps even you, there is no model of a healthy marriage from which to draw from.

I believe when teaching children about the Sixth Commandment that the focus should stay on how to keep the commandment rather than what it means to break it. This is especially true with younger children. I am sure I do not have to mention that discussing sex, as Luther does ("lead a sexually pure and decent life"), is territory that, despite trends in public education, is not age appropriate for young children. It is, however, necessary to offer a vision of the love of a husband and wife that our children can see and emulate. If you are a parent for whom this is not a reality, seek the assistance of those in the congregation who are married to provide a model from which children may learn.

There is a need for our children to have mature role models of both genders, who have a solid concept of what it means biblically to be a man and a woman. Our children need to see Ephesians 5:21–33 lived out in their lives so that they are able to grow up in accord with this vision of married life. I know that this sounds like a lot of pressure. No one's marriage fully lives up to this standard, even at its best. However, this model is of benefit not only for our own married life, but also for the future for our children. The mutual submission of this passage teaches married couples how to place their spouse's needs ahead of their own and vice versa. In turn, by witnessing healthy mutual submission and having role models who exhibit what it means to be a Christian man and a Christian woman our children are presented with a vision of a fulfilled life that will help to demonstrate the shallow nature of extra-marital sexuality.

As children become teenagers, discussing the Sixth Commandment doesn't get any easier. Rather than dealing with a lack of knowledge, parents may begin to find that their teenagers have an excess of knowledge, though perhaps little understanding of that knowledge. This knowledge may also be grossly inaccurate. Thus, the discussion with teens should move to what our behavior and dress say about us as well as how we appropriately treat one another, especially those of the opposite sex.

It is no secret that many youth take part in youth group because there they may find members of the opposite sex. This means that temptation may still present itself to youth who take part in the wholesome activities that their parents desire of them. As uncomfortable as it may be, parents need to have conversations about God's design for sex. Resources such as Concordia Publishing House's Learning About Sex series can be great tools to prepare parents for these conversations.[4]

Youth need to understand that God designed sex for marriage and through sex bonds the two who have become one flesh (Mark 10:8). When people engage in sex outside of marriage, that bonding still takes place, just without the commitment of marriage. Eventually, when people engage in sex with multiple partners, they will begin to lose their ability to bond. Through God's grace, this can be restored to some degree, but lasting emotional and relational damage is likely.

God's design for marriage avoids this damage. Rather than youth viewing the Sixth Commandment as God restricting them from enjoying sex, parents can help them to see how true enjoyment and lasting relational happiness are preserved by listening to and respecting the workmanship of God.

THE SEVENTH COMMANDMENT

You shall not steal.

What does this mean? We should fear and love God so that we do not take our neighbor's money or possessions, or get them in any dishonest way, but help him to improve and protect his possessions and income.

Once, when I was teaching about the Seventh Commandment in a confirmation class, one of my students turned in a PowerPoint presenta-

---

[4] See cph.org/las for more information, including free videos for parents.

tion on the Ten Commandments. One of the slides had a watermarked graphic, indicating that the image was available for sale. This student did not purchase the graphic but simply copied it following a Google image search. The prevalence of accessibility to digital media has complicated our children's understanding of what it means to steal. There is a widespread belief that if you are able to access it on the Internet, it should be free. Nice as that might sound, the creators of the images, music, and other files, who put time and effort into their creation, may not necessarily agree with this.

To illustrate the universality of the Seventh Commandment, I once asked a youth in confirmation class who had been challenging whether this always applies if I could see his wallet. Once I had it, I thanked him, put the wallet in my pocket and returned to my teaching. As his discomfort grew, I eventually asked him what might be troubling him. He then asked if he was going to get his wallet back. I let him know that since he had given me access to it, I thought it fair that I get to decide if I wanted to give it back or not. At this point, he became rather upset. "But that's stealing," he said. "Exactly my point," I told him. It is not up to me to determine if I am able to claim something that was not previously mine as my own. The owner of the property must agree. This applies to his wallet as well as to digital media we find online.

God calls us not only to not take what belongs to others, but also to protect and in fact improve the possessions of others. We can best teach this to our children by keeping things personally connected to them. If our children are to learn not only to avoid taking things that do not belong to them (a true challenge for a toddler) but also to care especially for the possessions of others, then they need to see from their own perspective the value of taking such care of their own possessions.

My youngest is truly all boy. He is physical by nature and as such often destructive. We have to spend a good deal of time working with him to help him realize that not everything he breaks will be replaced. We are attempting to teach both his older brother and him that if they do not take care of each other's toys, then they will find a dwindling number of them available for their enjoyment. Asking them how they feel when the other damages a favorite toy is a great teachable moment to reinforce for both of them the value of caring for and protecting the property of others. By doing this with both boys present, both the offender and the harmed learn the consequences of their action. Although they need help making the connection, their natural outrage at having their own toys damaged or lost helps them to learn the impact violations of the Seventh Commandment can cause.

THE EIGHTH COMMANDMENT

You shall not give false testimony against your neighbor.

What does this mean? We should fear and love God so that we do not tell lies about our neighbor, betray him, slander him, or hurt his reputation, but defend him, speak well of him, and explain everything in the kindest way.

The Eight Commandment is a natural follow-up to the Seventh. Social media is teaching us far more about the nature of one's reputation than any of us likely anticipated. Today, the idea of managing one's image like a personal brand is pervasive. When Yelp reviews make or break a restaurant, you know that the influence of image has become powerful indeed.

Well before these social media perils, God laid out the standard that we are not to testify falsely against others. Luther unpacks this to include betrayal, slander, and damaging one's reputation. He further turns to the positive, instructing us to defend and speak well of others. Luther points out that God is calling us to "explain everything in the kindest way."

Kids are naturals at tearing one another down. It amazes me how my oldest is able to turn just about any phrase into something that sounds like an insult. Often the insulter does this in order to feel better than the insulted and thus feel better generally. However, our experience as adults tells us that this never lasts. The result is a negative cycle that simply brings both parties further down as the insults continue to fly back and forth.

Once again, helping our children to empathize with others often requires us to help them see and truly feel the damage as it is done to them. Teaching our children to stop before they react is essential. Teaching them to pause before tearing someone else down for a perceived slight can often help avoid unnecessary escalation or even misunderstanding. As our children grow and mature, their desire for relationships grows with them. Their desire to be seen in a certain way can be used to build upon prior lessons of how their own harsh words or those of others can damage reputations and friendships. Helping our children learn to think before they speak (or post something online) is essential.

Many teens love gossip. Hearing the latest dirt on their classmates helps distract from their own issues. Talk to your teens about how they feel when they learn that they are the subject of gossip. Do not let them get away with bluffing their way through this conversation. If the response is that they do not care, push harder. Teens are naturally concerned about what others think of them—obsessively so at times. How might they want to have their friends think and talk about them? Gossip has the tendency to feed upon itself. One story about one person soon becomes many more about many others. There is perhaps an element of addiction to the hearing and sharing of gossip. Like a temporary high, teens seek more gossip to feel good about themselves repeatedly.

Rather than feed this cycle, challenge teens to focus on building one another up just as they would like to be build up in the eyes of their peers. Talk specifically about what they can do to uplift rather than tear down. There are youth groups that have a "No J/K rule." That means youth are not allowed to make fun or tease someone and get away with it by saying "Just kidding." Help teens realize that the good feeling is truly short lived, especially when compared with the deep bonds of friendship available to those who focus on building one another up in the eyes of their peers.

THE NINTH COMMANDMENT

You shall not covet your neighbor's house.

What does this mean? We should fear and love God so that we do not scheme to get our neighbor's inheritance or house, or get it in a way that only appears right, but help and be of service to him in keeping it.

THE TENTH COMMANDMENT

You shall not covet your neighbor's wife, or his manservant or maidservant, his ox or donkey, or anything that belongs to your neighbor.

What does this mean? We should fear and love God so that we do not entice or force away our neighbor's wife, workers, or animals, or turn them against him, but urge them to stay and do their duty.

We do not often use the word *covet*. However, we do covet all the time. Just watch kids with their siblings and cousins at Christmas. You are likely to see coveting on display. Kids love to get new toys but may struggle with others receiving a toy that they might perceive as better. All too often, after having unwrapped a huge pile of gifts, we hear our children ask what else they are going to get or complain that they did not receive a gift that someone else did.

The key to avoiding coveting is contentment. I believe that one way to teach our children contentment is to teach them how to give. By giving to others, we are able to take on an element of God's character, who is ultimately the giver of all good things. As our children experience giving to others, they gain an appreciation of the effort and sacrifice behind the act of giving.

These final two commandments that explore various aspects of coveting are connected to our understanding of the Seventh Commandment's concern over the property of others. Coveting is in many ways the fertile ground in which the desire to take from others grows. Instead of harboring a desire for the possessions of others, our children are better served when they are able to nurture an attitude of satisfaction in the blessings God has given them. Otherwise, these desires may develop into more unhealthy desires resulting in theft or damage of others' property.

As the toys get bigger and more expensive, the temptation to covet grows as well. The toys of the teen years may include phones, cars, tablets, TVs, and much more. Often friendships in these years are reshaped by who has what toys. This makes coveting all the harder to avoid. Who doesn't want a great new car or the latest iPhone? The challenge is that satisfaction becomes harder to achieve when chasing after the possessions of others. Teens who take part in both local and global service have a better chance of understanding the true value of what God has blessed them with. With a larger perspective on our material blessings, teens are able to come closer to being satisfied and may find themselves desiring more for others and less for themselves.

THE CLOSE OF THE COMMANDMENTS

What does God say about all these commandments?

He says, "I, the LORD your God, am a jealous God, punishing the children for the sin of the fathers to the third and fourth generation of those who hate Me, but showing love to a thousand generations of those who love Me and keep My commandments." (Ex. 20:5–6)

What does this mean? God threatens to punish all who break these commandments. Therefore, we should fear His wrath and not do anything against them. However, He promises grace and every blessing to all who keep these commandments. Therefore, we should also love and trust in Him and gladly do what He commands.

It is important that we as parents reinforce the overall purpose of the commandments with our children. As has been explored above, there is both a positive and a negative side to God's commands. In the passage from Exodus above, God makes it clear that He is a jealous God, one who desires that we keep Him first in our hearts, minds, and lives (see commandments 1–3). The Lord continues by stressing how His love also extends across generations for those who do just that and keep Him in His rightful place in their lives.

This begins with the fear aspect of our relationship with God, as noted throughout Luther's comments in the catechism. However, we do not merely remain in fear of God and His power to punish. We should teach our children to grow to "love and trust" God and to "gladly do what He commands." Our ultimate goal is to teach our children to love the commands of God. In order to do this, we need to help them to see how the Ten Commandments reflect the order that God has placed into creation. We should talk to our children about how God has designed the Ten Commandments to provide a structure for our lives that is ultimately to our benefit both now and in eternity. They are a set of instructions for how we are best to interact with the world God created and the sinful corruption that we as humanity have introduced into it.

CHAPTER 11

THE APOSTLES' CREED

As the head of the family should teach it
in a simple way to his household

THE FIRST ARTICLE: CREATION

I believe in God, the Father Almighty, Maker of heaven and earth.

What does this mean? I believe that God has made me and all creatures; that He has given me my body and soul, eyes, ears, and all my members, my reason and all my senses, and still takes care of them.

He also gives me clothing and shoes, food and drink, house and home, wife and children, land, animals, and all I have. He richly and daily provides me with all that I need to support this body and life.

He defends me against all danger and guards and protects me from all evil.

All this He does only out of fatherly, divine goodness and mercy, without any merit or worthiness in me. For all this it is my duty to thank and praise, serve and obey Him.

This is most certainly true.

In a brief twelve words, the Early Church packed much of the essential teachings of the faith. To begin, we make a radical claim that God is our Father. So many centuries later, we hardly seem to flinch at the mention of God as Father, but to the disciples and others who first heard

Christ speak this way about God, this was more than a mere new novelty of teaching. The personal nature of our ability to claim God as our Father speaks of a relationship that the Lord desires with us that is not to be found in other religions. A level of intimacy is implied that is unprecedented in religious life. Further, this relationship is only available from a God who claims His fatherhood over us and bids us actually call Him Father. What this means for the relationship of our children to their God is that they enter into a relationship with a God who desires intimacy and love. They enter into a relationship initiated by God, who as a loving Father comes to us to free us from sin and death.

In addition, this means that we are entering into a relationship with a Father who provides richly for His children. I know as a father myself how much I desire to provide for my own sons. But in Luke 11:11–13, Christ contrasts the gifts we earthly fathers give with the gifts that God as our Father gives. He uses a rhetorical question (who gives their kids a scorpion?) to help us understand how far better God's gifts for us will be. If our earthly sinful fathers give good gifts, imagine how much better the gifts are that God has in store for us!

This does not mean, as many of our children might hope, that God will give us everything we desire. Rather, as Luther points out, our Father, the Creator of all things, will give to us richly to support our daily needs. Therefore, we can teach our children how the many things in our lives that keep us fed, clothed, warm, and safe are provided by God. Notice that Luther writes here about daily needs. Unlike the rich fool in the parable of Jesus from Luke 12, who desired to store up increased riches for himself, we are instead reminded of the people of God who were left to rely upon His promised manna on a daily basis. In Exodus 16, they received instructions to collect only enough for a single day, other than the day before the Sabbath when they were to collect twice as much. Those who did not trust in the daily provision of God found that what they stored up for themselves was full of rot and decay.

Therefore, we teach our children to trust God our heavenly Father, thanking and praising Him for all His many blessings. One great way to do this is to work with your kids to develop a list of all the various things that they have. Then take the list and work out how those things are created and made available to us. Your children will find that a great many people are involved in getting something as simple as a loaf of bread onto their kitchen table. Walk with them to examine how God the Father has created each of these individuals, giving them the necessary gifts that allow them to be a part of what brings us our food, clothing, and other daily needs plus all those fun things that we really do not "need" for daily life.

As teenagers approach adulthood, the call to trust in the provision of God grows ever greater. Preparing to step into adulthood can be a frightening reality as each step on the road tests their ability to trust more fully in God. Remind your teens that their heavenly Father still abides with and provides for them even as they begin the shift from their daily needs being fulfilled by the efforts of their parents to being fulfilled through their own resources. Getting a job should not just be about adding to their disposable income. Teach your teens how God provides for their needs by walking them through a plan for the money that they earn. Budget with them, stressing firstfruits giving to God and saving for more immediate and future needs, and allow them to gradually take on responsibility for their own expenses. The car is a perfect starting point—regardless of whether they own or borrow. Entering into the process by which God provides for us helps teens acquire a more intimate understanding of the tangible ways that God's creation is used to sustain His children.

THE SECOND ARTICLE: REDEMPTION

And in Jesus Christ, His only Son, our Lord, who was conceived by the Holy Spirit, born of the Virgin Mary, suffered under Pontius Pilate, was crucified, died and was buried. He descended into hell. The third day He rose again from the dead. He ascended into heaven and sits at the right hand of God, the Father Almighty. From thence He will come to judge the living and the dead.

What does this mean? I believe that Jesus Christ, true God, begotten of the Father from eternity, and also true man, born of the Virgin Mary, is my Lord, who has redeemed me, a lost and condemned person, purchased and won me from all sins, from death, and from the power of the devil; not with gold or silver, but with His holy, precious blood and with His innocent suffering and death, that I may be His own and live under Him in His kingdom and serve Him in everlasting righteousness, innocence, and blessedness, just as He is risen from the dead, lives and reigns to all eternity.

This is most certainly true.

In the Second Article of the Apostles' Creed, we find the central doctrines of the Christian faith. It begins by defining who Jesus Christ is. Much in this first portion of the Second Article may be over the heads of younger children, but it is still worth the work to familiarize them with it, even if only in a basic sense. You can walk through this portion of the Creed step by step with your kids, unpacking the many rich elements included about the life, death, and resurrection of our Savior.

Begin with who Jesus is and how He became incarnate. For that matter, take a step back and walk through what it even means that Jesus became incarnate. To do that you might make use of the Marvel movie *Antman*. What would it be like if we were able to enter into the world of the ants? What would it be like to be one of them? Jesus became one of us. More than just putting on a suit that looked like one of us, Jesus actually became a man.

In one relatively quick phrase, the Creed notes that Jesus Christ is the Son of God, but unlike our claim to being children of the Father, Jesus is uniquely the Son. Jesus is the Father's only Son from eternity. This is an overwhelmingly big concept for adults, let alone children, so you might unpack a word like *eternity* by using a simpler term like *forever*. The Son has always been the Son of the Father. Unlike the time before our children were our kids, there was never a time when Jesus was not the Son. However, there was a time when the Son was not a part of humanity. It was only when Mary conceived Jesus that He became man as well as God.

How was this possible? Well, the Creed reflects the teaching of Scripture that our Lord "was conceived by the Holy Spirit." We do not know how Jesus was physically conceived, but, by faith, we believe that it happened. Resist the temptation to speculate; it is not likely to help. Instead, focus on the miracle that Mary conceived while remaining a virgin. In children's books, the question of defining virginity is often sidestepped by talking about Mary being unable to have a child due to her not having a husband. This move reinforces God's design for the family and conveys the spirit of teaching without having to unpack in detail concepts of a more mature nature for which younger children are not ready.

Especially for children with an enthusiasm for history, the phrase "suffered under Pontius Pilate" may be quite intriguing. Until 1961, we had no evidence outside of the biblical record of who Pontius Pilate was. Then, what is now known as the Pilate Stone was found in the ruins of Caesarea Maritima, proving not only that there was such a man but also verifying his role as Prefect of Judea. This seemingly inconsequential phrase grounds the Christian faith in history in a way that no other faith can claim. Arming your children with this knowledge can help them to feel more secure when their faith is mocked as mere mythology.

Connected with Pilate in the Creed are the suffering, crucifixion, death, and burial of Christ. It is important to impress upon our children the reality of not only the historical existence of Jesus Christ but also the historical reliability of His suffering, death, and resurrection. Paul teaches in 1 Corinthians 15:12–19 that if the crucifixion and resurrection had not been historic events, then we would have no hope and should be pitied. When the Creed says "on the third day He rose again from the dead," it is talking about an essential tenant of our faith that must be historically true in order for our faith to have validity. Arming our children with the knowledge of the historicity of the Christian faith on these points especially prepares them for the dismissiveness they are likely to encounter from those who believe all religion to be merely personally relevant and not universally true. Naturally, this element of teaching requires some maturity on the part of our kids in order to be beneficial for them.

It is important to note that Jesus' resurrection was of such central importance to the early Christians that they were willing to alter their understanding of the custom of worship to accommodate it. They originally met on the Jewish Sabbath, maintaining their connection to the faith fulfilled in Christ. However, early Jewish Christians eventually began to make Sunday, not Saturday, the central day for worship as a celebration of the resurrection of Christ.

Following His resurrection, Jesus spent forty days with various disciples and groups of disciples. Following that time, Christ "ascended into heaven and sits at the right hand of God, the Father Almighty." We believe that Jesus did not cease to be fully God and fully human at any time and that He remains eternally both God and human while now present with the Father in heaven.

Finally, we believe that Jesus will have a role in our judgment. This is great news! For those of us with faith in Christ as our Savior, there is reason for confidence when we finally stand before the Father. Scripture teaches us that the Son will speak on our behalf. Jesus will claim us as those for whom He died, and thus, when the Father looks at us, rather than seeing our sin, He will see the innocent blood of the Son.

We can illustrate this for our kids by describing a situation in which they get caught breaking the window of a neighbor, but we as parents take the responsibility and pay what cannot be paid by our children to repair the damage. From a parenting standpoint, we do want our children to take responsibility for their actions eventually, but the key teaching element here is their inability to make the payment. Christ does that for us. There is no greater reason for joy than to know your eternity is secure. No wonder we teach our children to love and obey God with a joyful heart. Considering what He has done for us, how could we not desire to respond with joyful obedience, flawed as that obedience might be?

The Third Article: Sanctification

I believe in the Holy Spirit, the holy Christian church, the communion of saints, the forgiveness of sins, the resurrection of the body, and the life everlasting. Amen.

What does this mean? I believe that I cannot by my own reason or strength believe in Jesus Christ, my Lord, or come to Him; but the Holy Spirit has called me by the Gospel, enlightened me with His gifts, sanctified and kept me in the true faith.

In the same way He calls, gathers, enlightens, and sanctifies the whole Christian church on earth, and keeps it with Jesus Christ in the one true faith.

In this Christian church He daily and richly forgives all my sins and the sins of all believers.

On the Last Day He will raise me and all the dead, and give eternal life to me and all believers in Christ.

This is most certainly true.

At first, the Third Article of the Apostles' Creed may appear like somewhat of a hodgepodge of leftover doctrines. However, taking a closer look shows us more of a connection than might first seem evident.

While the First Article focuses on God the Father, and the Second on God the Son, the Third centers on the work of God the Holy Spirit.

Conceptually, teaching our children about the Father and Son is far simpler, and yet, the work of the Holy Spirit touches us all the more intimately now between the first and second coming of Christ. While we are familiar with the work of the Holy Spirit, we generally are not so familiar with the nuances of who the Holy Spirit is.

Our focus as we teach our children should begin with the Holy Spirit as the third member of the Trinity, as fully God, just as the Father and Son are fully God. Jesus sent the Holy Spirit to be with us following His ascension. The Holy Spirit is responsible for inspiring the disciples to proclaim boldly the risen Christ, risking their lives in order to convince others of the truth that Jesus is the Messiah, our Savior.

We will touch on this later, but it is helpful to mention to children that in Baptism, it is the Holy Spirit who gives all Christians faith in Christ as their Savior, even to those who are not intellectually capable of fully comprehending what that entirely entails. This is why Luther begins his explanation stating, "I believe that I cannot by my own reason or strength believe in Jesus Christ, my Lord, or come to Him." The Holy Spirit gives us faith, strengthens that faith, helps us to grow in and understand our faith more fully, and sustains us in the faith even as we are tempted to doubt or abandon our faith.

When talking to your kids about the work of the Holy Spirit, it is helpful to focus on how the Holy Spirit is there for us and helps us to trust and follow Jesus. This gives our children someone specific to turn to when they struggle with sins or doubts. Just as it is helpful for us as adults to know that we have the Holy Spirit not only to give us faith but also to rely upon as we live out that faith, our children need the Holy Spirit as well.

We can see the further work of the Holy Spirit in "the holy Christian church, the communion of saints, the forgiveness of sins, the resurrection of the body, and the life everlasting." Connected together as the Church, we have communion with one another. This is not simply a reference to the Sacrament of Holy Communion, but it is a connectedness found in the Christian community. We have a spiritual unity and togetherness with our fellow believers through the Holy Spirit. It is in that context that we experience forgiveness. As will be explored later, this forgiveness, as given to us by Christ through the Holy Spirit in the context of the

Church, should mark our lives in the forgiveness we offer to others. As parents, we can teach and reinforce this practice of forgiveness in our families and in our children's lives more broadly.

We can teach our children about forgiveness when we say "I forgive you" after they confess their sins against us. The practice that my wife and I use in our home to reinforce a culture of forgiveness in Christ centers around our use of timeouts. When placed in a timeout, we require our boys to explain to us, as best they are able, the reason why they were put in timeout at the conclusion of that time. Once they identify what they did, they hear a pronouncement of forgiveness and receive a hug, often with a reinforcement of the love that we as parents have for them. It is critical for them to hear verbally that they are forgiven. Too often we are used to simply telling each other, "It's okay," when someone tells us they are sorry. However, is that really true, or is there something more needed? You can reinforce this with your children by insisting that they go to those whom they have wronged to confess their sin and ask for forgiveness. The person wronged should then say, "I forgive you."

Finally, we profess and confess a belief that death is not our end. Through the faith given us by the Holy Spirit, we know that we will live for eternity in heaven with the Father, Son, and Holy Spirit. While we recognize that the resurrected body is yet to come, eternal life is ours now, not something for which we look in the future. This should give us great confidence. Knowing that eternity is secure and that death is not the end can help us work with our children as they come to grips with the loss of a loved one. Whether it is the death of a beloved grandparent or perhaps a school classmate taken far too young, we have comfort in knowing that God—who created the universe—has promised to those who trust in Him that death no longer has the ultimate power over us.

CHAPTER 12

THE LORD'S PRAYER

*As the head of the family should teach it
in a simple way to his household*

Our Father, who art in heaven, hallowed be Thy name, Thy
kingdom come, Thy will be done on earth as it is in heaven.
Give us this day our daily bread; and forgive us our trespasses
as we forgive those who trespass against us; and lead us not
into temptation, but deliver us from evil. For Thine is the
kingdom and the power and the glory forever and ever. Amen.

We may at times need to be reminded of this, but prayer is a wonderful gift. To be encouraged and to be able to come with our needs and requests before our Maker is remarkable. As a father heading my household, nothing gives me more joy than to see my boys making this precious gift their own. Listening to them explore what it means to pray is a true joy. Thus, the Lord's Prayer is a fantastic gift to the family, as it exemplifies what prayer is all about.

When the disciples asked Jesus how they should pray, Christ taught them to pray by teaching them the Lord's Prayer. Luke notes for us that Jesus Himself had been praying when the disciples asked for His input on their own prayer life. Seeing something in how Jesus prayed that was beyond their experience, they were wise to seek His teaching. The faithful have benefited from their inquiry ever since.

Just as the Church makes use of the Lord's Prayer in worship, we, too, should use Jesus' model prayer as a guide and foundation for our own prayer life. We should also use it to teach our children how to pray. By making use of the Lord's Prayer, we are able to instruct our children not only to pray for their needs, but also to offer thanks and praise to our Lord.

THE INTRODUCTION

Our Father who art in heaven.

What does this mean? With these words God tenderly invites us to believe that He is our true Father and that we are His true children, so that with all boldness and confidence we may ask Him as dear children ask their dear father.

As discussed previously, the belief that we can approach God as Father is unique to the Christian faith. In prayer, knowing we are praying to our Father helps us approach this action of faith with appropriate boldness. Prayer to the Almighty is one thing, but if we view the Almighty also as our loving heavenly Father, then there is far less reason to fear bringing our wants and needs to His attention.

We should teach our children that God our heavenly Father desires to hear from us. He listens to our prayers with a loving desire to care for us. Luther calls us "dear children" who pray to "their dear father." This is truly intimate language. In order for prayer to be that intimate, it should not be something restricted to Sunday morning corporate prayers in worship. Rather, if our children are to learn from us to see God as their dear Father, they need to be shown through our prayer lives a frequent return to the Father for all our daily thanks, praise, needs, and desires.

Fathers in particular are able to have an impact in teaching their children about God as Father in the Lord's Prayer. We can talk to our children about all the things that we encourage them to bring to us. This, of course, might mean that we need to work on our openness to listening to our children. However, if we are able to model for our children the type of open listening God our heavenly Father exemplifies, how much more trust will our kids be able to develop in their prayers?

As children grow older and enter their teenage years, the role of a father in many ways becomes even more critical. Teens, who are working to understand more fully for themselves what it means to be a Christian, will at some point grapple with the concept of God as Father. Fathers are able to help shape their teens' understanding of God the Father by engaging in intentional conversation about how they as fathers relate to both their earthly father and heavenly Father. Fathers should talk to their teens about ways in which their own father modeled the love of their heavenly Father. They can talk about the love shown to them as children as well as the necessary discipline that helped to shape them into men capable of being good fathers themselves.

This is a good time to talk about the changing roles between father and child that take shape in the teenage years and on into young adulthood. Dads can talk about how they have been there supporting their children and will continue to do so, but will now allow more space for both success and failure—just as God is there for us, yet allows space for us to grow through both our failures and successes. Because God is still our Father into adulthood, dads are able to comment on how the way in which they relate to their children changes, but their love does not. Fathers are still there for their children when they need them just as God remains available to us through prayer, even as our needs get far more complicated.

THE FIRST PETITION

Hallowed be Thy name.

What does this mean? God's name is certainly holy in itself, but we pray in this petition that it may be kept holy among us also.

How is God's name kept holy? God's name is kept holy when the Word of God is taught in its truth and purity, and we, as the children of God, also lead holy lives according to it. Help us to do this, dear Father in heaven! But anyone who teaches or lives contrary to God's Word profanes the name of God among us. Protect us from this, heavenly Father!

The holiness of God's name seems to be so self-evident that it might not require much discussion. Even so, as we discussed above when walking through the Second Commandment, the name of God is not universally understood as something that is to be treated as sacred. As the old nursery rhyme goes, "Sticks and stones may break my bones, but words will never hurt me." Used as a childhood taunt, kids may attempt to show indifference by repeating it when someone else uses language to tear them down. However, the thinking that words do not hurt is severely flawed. We all know words can hurt and destroy, as we discussed in connection with the Eighth Commandment. This applies to the use of the name of God and the preservation of His name in the hearts and minds of humanity.

The phrase "that it may be kept holy among us also" indicates our role in working to uplift the name of the Father in our lives. We do this by making sure to teach the faith correctly from generation to generation. Just as the pastor is charged with the necessity to teach members of the church the Word of God properly, parents are called similarly to be careful in how we teach our children. This means that at times, when our kids ask questions for which we do not have solid answers, we should avoid offering our own speculation as though it were the Word of God. Rather, we should take the risk and admit to our kids that we do not actually know how to answer their question, but we will join them in exploring the Bible to seek the wiser counsel of others for answers. I know that this can be hard to admit. We like to be able to provide answers. I know I do. Nonetheless, the name of the Father is uplifted not when we carelessly speak on His behalf but rather when we take the time to know what it is we are really teaching our children. Have I made my case for you to join a Bible study at your church yet?

We additionally teach our children that we uplift God's name and keep it holy among us as we live lives consistent with His will. This is a challenge. As sinners still needing forgiveness, we are not capable of perfect obedience. We cannot fully live our lives consistently with the will of God. However, as we seek to rely upon the guidance and strength of the Holy Spirit, we are empowered to respond to the grace that has freed us from our bondage to sin by attempting to live in accordance with the will of God. This uplifts the holiness of God's name as those around us see His image in our lives. They may see it imperfectly, but the *Imago Dei* (image of God) is still there to be noticed.

As noted previously, God's name is not always treated with appropriate reverence. My wife has taken to attempting a bit of humor when someone says "Good God" in her presence. Her response is, "Yes, He is." The attempt is to avoid scolding, as those who make the statement may not be followers of Christ. With our own children, we make sure to point out when they carelessly make use of any of the names of God. Simply asking our boys, "Is that the way we talk?" can help draw attention to the issue and offer a loving correction. The goal is to keep our minds focused on the way in which we use God's name. When we, and our children, unthinkingly use the name of God, we get into trouble.

In high school and college, students are at times mocked for their faith. The very idea of there being a God may become a subject of scorn and mockery. God's name is not made holy when belief in Him is mocked. One possible way for parents to prepare their teens to keep the name of God holy is to dig into apologetics. Those who mock Christ and His faithful may do so armed with the arguments of secular intellectuals. Exposing teens to basic training on how to respond to these arguments not only with well-thought-out responses but also with the love of Christ helps to witness to the love of a God who cares even for those who reject Him. Parents should keep track of the topics being discussed in class by their teens and, where possible, find resources that they can read with their son or daughter to help equip them to give a God-honoring answer (cf. 1 Peter 3:15).

THE SECOND PETITION

Thy kingdom come.

What does this mean? The kingdom of God certainly comes by itself without our prayer, but we pray in this petition that it may come to us also.

How does God's kingdom come? God's kingdom comes when our heavenly Father gives us His Holy Spirit, so that by His grace we believe His holy Word and lead godly lives here in time and there in eternity.

In order to help our children understand what the Second Petition of the Lord's Prayer means, we should begin by trying to understand what is meant by God's kingdom. There are three aspects to the kingdom of God to keep in mind as we talk to and teach our children. First, there is the kingdom of power. By this, we mean that God rules in His power over all that He has created, which is everything. When we pray for God's kingdom to come in this sense, we are asking for those in authority (recall the Fourth Commandment discussion) to exercise that authority as God desires for them to do so. Thus, we are asking for parents, police, mayors, etc., to fulfill their vocations seeking to serve and protect those over whom they have authority and not to serve and enlarge their own "kingdoms."

The second aspect of God's kingdom is His kingdom of grace. This is the special role of the Church. Through the ministry of the Church, the grace of Christ is shared with a world that is in desperate need of it. It is the Church that offers the Means of Grace (God's Word and Sacraments), which the Holy Spirit uses to create and sustain faith in us. We, as a part of the Church, experience and share in God's grace. We share that grace in how we deal with our children, forgiving them when they disobey. We share that grace when we share our faith in Christ with those who need to know the grace of the Savior themselves. As parents, we can encourage God's kingdom to come by making God's grace a central part of what family in our home is all about.

The third aspect of God's kingdom is His kingdom of glory. In this life, we only receive a foretaste of this aspect of God's kingdom. This kingdom is heaven. God's kingdom comes when people believe in Christ as their Savior and thus receive the promise of eternal life in God's kingdom of glory. This is the ultimate and final coming of the kingdom. As Paul points out in 2 Timothy 4:18, the Lord rescues us from evil. What a hope we have in God's kingdom! We can teach our children about the joy we have knowing God's kingdom will be ours as Jesus promised (John 14:2).

Luther notes that a part of God's kingdom comes to us as we live godly lives. For younger children this is learning the Ten Commandments, as through them we understand the basics of right and wrong (recall the good boy and good girl stage of development from Kohlberg in chapter 4). As their children mature, parents can add complexity by moving beyond mere morality to the true center of godly living—our identity in Christ. In Christ, believers are able to receive the kingdom of God through the Means of Grace (the Sacraments and hearing of God's Word). This is why we gather together as the Church to receive this grace from God and receive His kingdom.

THE THIRD PETITION

Thy will be done on earth as it is in heaven.

What does this mean? The good and gracious will of God is done even without our prayer, but we pray in this petition that it may be done among us also.

How is God's will done? God's will is done when He breaks and hinders every evil plan and purpose of the devil, the world, and our sinful nature, which do not want us to hallow

God's name or let His kingdom come; and when He strengthens and keeps us firm in His Word and faith until we die.

This is His good and gracious will.

"But, Dad, if God is all powerful, why do we need to pray for His will
to be done? Won't that happen anyway? Who's going to stop Him?" This
might be a way in which our children voice a natural question that arises
when considering the Third Petition. We pray for God's will to be done,
but as Luther points out, "The good and gracious will of God is done
even without our prayer." Luther goes on to stress that the emphasis
should therefore be on God's will being "done among us also," or put
another way, that we would follow the guidance of the Holy Spirit and
live according to God's will.

In heaven, God's will is done perfectly. On earth, God's will is often
simply disregarded. When talking with our children, it should not take
much to help them understand that even though they might desire to
make their parents happy, they do not always make the good choices necessary in order to make that happen. In the same way, God's standards
are so high that there is really no way we or our children could ever reach
them. This is why in 2 Corinthians 12:9, Paul points out that Christ
taught him that His grace is sufficient for Paul and for all of us as His
children. The perfect power of God is, in fact, seen in our weakness. It is
only the power of God that enables us to follow God's will at all.

As parents, we pray with our children that we all as a family might
follow God's lead and do His will. We can talk about the implications of
what doing God's will has on life together as a family, on what it means to
be a student in school, a friend in the neighborhood, and all the other
situations in which our children find themselves. This is where the call to
pray unceasingly (1 Thessalonians 5:17) comes into play. We keep the
will of God in our minds as we keep God in our hearts and on our lips.
Teaching our children to establish habitual prayers that ask God for His
guidance in doing His will helps them focus their lives on God as the center of who they are in Christ.

As they grow older, children can be taught to make the will of God
their own more deeply. Teens will naturally find themselves in conflict
between their own selfish desires and the will of God as they have come
to know it in their youth. Parents can help teens dig deeper by suspend-
ing the impulse to offer their own thoughts and conclusions on tempta-

tions faced by their children; instead, seek more openly to talk through issues with them allowing them to think things through and reach their own conclusions. This does not mean leaving them to reach just any conclusion. Parents would be wise to ask questions that push their teens away from unsound conclusions toward an understanding of the will of God. However, there must remain enough freedom for youth to struggle and reach agreement with God's will based on the conviction and guidance of the Holy Spirit and not parental pressure, which is far shorter lived.

THE FOURTH PETITION

Give us this day our daily bread.

What does this mean? God certainly gives daily bread to everyone without our prayers, even to all evil people, but we pray in this petition that God would lead us to realize this and to receive our daily bread with thanksgiving.

What is meant by daily bread? Daily bread includes everything that has to do with the support and needs of the body, such as food, drink, clothing, shoes, house, home, land, animals, money, goods, a devout husband or wife, devout children, devout workers, devout and faithful rulers, good government, good weather, peace, health, self-control, good reputation, good friends, faithful neighbors, and the like.

As we explored in the First Article of the Apostles' Creed, God our Creator is the giver of all good things. In the simple concept of our daily bread, Luther unpacks a plethora of needs for daily life. Notice that after listing twenty-three items, Luther concludes his comments on the Fourth Petition of the Lord's Prayer with the phrase "and the like." This is his way of saying etc., etc., and so on, and so forth. In other words, this is not even a complete list. It may well not even be a remotely complete list. So why take the time to enumerate twenty-three items at all? Why not just say, "everything you need?"

Luther teaches us through this enumeration how to assess the enormity of just what we are praying for in this simple phrase, "Give us this day our daily bread." I sometimes change the words of our dinner prayer from "daily bread" to perhaps "daily waffle" or "daily taco." While it is funny, slightly, the point is not humor as much as it is to illustrate what is meant by "daily bread." I want our kids to know and understand that what we mean by this is more than just requesting some toast with breakfast. Rather, we are asking a blessing at our meal for all that we eat.

However, we are not to stop there. "Daily bread" is not just about food. As you can see from Luther's list, everything from our home, to our pets, to our health, and even our neighbors is included as gifts for our daily sustenance. Take time to talk about the various things listed. Perhaps take time to make your own list. Then talk about how each of those items ends up in your home or neighborhood. Talk about all the various people and situations needed to make that happen. God's hand is in all of that.

As noted in the discussion on the First Article of the Apostles' Creed, God does this daily. Not all of us are blessed with an abundance of God's blessings all at once. For many, unfortunately, their need is so great that it seems as though they are not being blessed with their daily needs. This is one impact of sin. This is an area of potential discussion with your child as they grow older and possibly begin asking questions related to poverty and wealth. If your son or daughter is struggling with issues related to poverty and the idea that we pray for our daily needs, you can make use of passages like Hebrews 13:16, which instruct us to share from the blessings that we receive from God in order to provide for people who appear to have less. In this way, God provides for the daily needs of those who are not able to work or make enough money for themselves. If this topic comes up, it might be a good time to meet with your pastor to talk about what your church does to provide for those in need and to find out how you as a family can take part.

It is more than wise to help teenagers start the process of providing for their daily needs. Parents will still provide the bulk of what they need to sustain their lives, but as teenagers mature, a part-time job along with a contribution to the work around the house can reinforce how God provides daily bread through the means of our labor.

THE FIFTH PETITION

And forgive us our trespasses as we forgive those who trespass against us.

What does this mean? We pray in this petition that our Father in heaven would not look at our sins, or deny our prayer because of them. We are neither worthy of the things for which we pray, nor have we deserved them, but we ask that He would give them all to us by grace, for we daily sin much and surely deserve nothing but punishment. So we too will sincerely forgive and gladly do good to those who sin against us.

Kids are all about things being fair. I have to take great care in how I slice pieces of pie in my house lest one son think that his brother got a bigger piece. "That's not fair!" It is a regular occurrence to hear complaints followed by tattling, as our boys want to make sure that if one is not getting away with something, then for sure the other brother should not either. We desire justice, sort of. We desire justice as long as we end up coming out on top.

Forgiveness is great, but we get a bit uncomfortable with the implication in the wording of the Fifth Petition of the Lord's Prayer that we are to forgive as God forgives. Yet, that is an implication that is hard to miss. Even as young children, we like to hang on to the anger and the hurt that others cause in us. We want to make sure that they get what is fair, what they deserve. We want justice. However, as the parable of the unforgiving servant teaches us in Matthew 18:21–35, we ought to forgive others out of gratitude for the far greater forgiveness given freely to us in Christ.

As Luther points out, because of the sacrifice of Christ, when the Father looks at us in judgment, He does not see our sins. It is interesting to note that what we are asking for is not something that we at all deserve; yet, Jesus tells us not only that we should pray for forgiveness, but He also promises that we will receive that undeserved forgiveness.

This is again one of those lessons best learned by making it personal. Talk with your kids about how they experience forgiveness and how good it makes them feel when they truly know that the wrong they did is forgiven. You can also talk with them about what it is like when someone is not willing to forgive them and continues to remind them of what they did wrong. None of us enjoys hearing repeatedly about something that we know we did, especially if there is nothing we can do to erase or change it.

We should teach our children about the joy of forgiving. I have at times illustrated in confirmation class the burden of being unforgiven by having kids try to hold ever-increasing amounts of luggage. Once weighed down, they start to have a hard time moving around. They cannot interact with others well. They bang into people and things in the house. This illustrates what it is like to carry our hurts (i.e., the sins of others against us that we have chosen not to forgive) with us. When we refuse to forgive, we carry each hurt like a piece of luggage weighing us down. Forgiveness removes those hurts from us and gives them to Jesus, who nails them with Him to the cross. Freed from these burdens, we are free to care for others. In the freedom we have received from Christ, we are able to help others let go of their own burdens and experience the forgiveness of Christ as we have. What a joy to share with our children!

THE SIXTH PETITION

And lead us not into temptation.

What does this mean? God tempts no one. We pray in this petition that God would guard and keep us so that the devil, the world, and our sinful nature may not deceive us or mislead us into false belief, despair, and other great shame and vice. Although we are attacked by these things, we pray that we may finally overcome them and win the victory.

Would God really lead anyone into temptation? If not, what is this Sixth Petition getting at? It is not so much that we are asking God not to tempt us as much as we are asking the Holy Spirit to strengthen us when we do face temptation. We pray that the Holy Spirit would empower us to resist. Some parents once told me of a technique they used to empower their daughter in this way when they found out that she was struggling to say "No" to a friend who wanted her to do something she knew was wrong. The parents told their child that she could let her friend know that her parents specifically told her she was not allowed to do the particular thing. For teenagers, this technique might take shape as a parent steps in to play the bad guy for a youth who would rather not go to a party but does not want his friends to think less of him. At times, our kids need that type of backup.

God provides us with His backup. In this petition of the Lord's Prayer, we get a fantastic reason why we should be familiar with the Ten Commandments. They provide the moral framework that helps us keep out of bad situations. Encourage open conversation with your kids to explore things that are particularly tempting for them. Do this in a way that ensures them they will not get in trouble merely for the temptation.

Work to create an open environment in which your children are able to comment on their temptations. In this way, you will be more aware and better able to offer ideas to help them make wise and morally honorable choices. When they succumb to temptation, work through the issue with them, seeking to restore them through grace and forgiveness. If you start doing this when they are younger, it will build trust that will be of great benefit in their teenage years.

We quite instinctively teach our children how to keep themselves out of situations in which they are more likely to make poor choices. We talk to them about the choices they make regarding their friends and the places they go with their friends. I recall my mother always asking to see pictures of the friends whom I mentioned to her while I was in high school. It took me years to appreciate the logic of doing so. At the time, I wondered what use it was for her to see a picture. It was not as if she was meeting them. In some cases she never did. What I later realized was that she wanted to know as much as possible about the people with whom I spent my time. For her, seeing a picture made them real. It connected them legitimately to my life through school. Although I attended a private Christian high school, I was in a school unfamiliar to her. All throughout my elementary and junior high years, I attended the Lutheran school of which my father was principal. My parents knew who was there and could thus know more about what I was doing. That knowledge helped them know if I was getting myself into situations that had potential for temptation.

When our children pray not to be led into temptation, they are in a way authorizing our looking out for them, which in reality we know is a God-given authority parents receive along with their other responsibilities. Through the Lord's Prayer, our children are acknowledging their need for guidance. Consequently, we are able to provide them that guidance, helping them learn how to make wise choices and grow into mature followers of Christ who are capable of avoiding temptation and handling it when it cannot be avoided.

As children grow older, the temptations that they face may become more complicated. The pressure of their friends may become harder to resist. Building on a solid foundation laid when they were young, parents of teens should talk with their children about the reality of the temptations that they face. Hard as this might be, parents need to be willing to hear the painful struggles that their teenagers are going through without passing judgment for their struggle. The parental impulse to step in and guide should at times be set aside to create space for teens to share how they struggle and at times fail. This is done in order for them to grow in their trust of their parents so that they might remain open to hearing from the wisdom gained over their parents' years of life.

THE SEVENTH PETITION

But deliver us from evil.

What does this mean? We pray in this petition, in summary, that our Father in heaven would rescue us from every evil of body and soul, possessions and reputation, and finally, when our last hour comes, give us a blessed end, and graciously take us from this valley of sorrow to Himself in heaven.

The Seventh and Final Petition of the Lord's Prayer follows thematically from the Sixth Petition. Having just asked God to keep us out of tempting situations and to give us strength to withstand those to which we succumb, we now ask for deliverance from the evil we encounter in the world. The purpose in this petition is to ask God to see us through to the end. Temptation will come. Evil is a reality in this world, as is the corruption of sin. These things can be limited but not entirely eliminated. Therefore, we pray that God would do what can be done either to remove evil from our lives or sustain us when it comes.

Job's story exemplifies one way in which God delivers us. Satan asked to have free access to Job so that he could tempt him to forsake God. The Lord granted this, but with limits. Initially God limited Satan's actions against Job to his property and family, but not to his person. Later God allowed Satan to harm Job, but not to kill him. Although we may experience evil in our lives, God may be restraining greater evil from harming us.

Luther points out that God delivers us not just physically or spiritually, but that He also works to protect our reputation as well as our possessions. He protects our reputation by giving us the Eighth Commandment, which instructs Christians to avoid speaking falsely about others. He protects our possessions by giving us the Seventh Commandment, instructing Christians not only to refrain from theft but also to help preserve our neighbors' property. My own neighbor does this when he comes by to let us know that we accidentally left our garage door open.

Simple acts like that help preserve valuable items, such as our son's new bike.

We cannot always understand why God allows evil in some situations and not others. We struggle, as will our children as they grow, to understand perhaps why a tornado hits a neighborhood and leaves only a home or two standing. Why did it happen to them and not others? Why are they protected and not us? Our heavenly Father, with wisdom we cannot hope to comprehend, knows far more about each of us than we even know about ourselves. Why is evil restrained sometimes and not at other times? When your child asks something like this, avoid speculating when you really have no answer. Church leaders too often get in trouble for claiming that a particular natural disaster is connected to a particular sin. This takes place in the home, too, when parents make connections with weak evidence. It is wiser to simply point to what we *do* know about God and His character and the confidence that we can have in that. We can pray with our children that God will let us in on His motivation. We can continue to pray that God deliver us from evil, even evil we are feeling or others we know are still experiencing. Finally, we can pray for the patience and wisdom to trust God, even as we continue struggling to understand. Perhaps these will make great questions to ask Jesus when we meet Him in eternity.

The Conclusion

For Thine is the kingdom and the power and the glory forever and ever.* Amen.

What does this mean? This means that I should be certain that these petitions are pleasing to our Father in heaven, and are heard by Him; for He Himself has commanded us to pray in this way and has promised to hear us. Amen, amen means "yes, yes, it shall be so."

*These words were not in Luther's Small Catechism.

The Conclusion or doxology of the Lord's Prayer is not text that we find in Matthew and Luke.[1] It was a common practice of the Early Church to conclude prayers this way. Over time, this doxology was

---

[1] The Orthodox churches have this phrase in their manuscripts.

adopted by some, but not all, Christian traditions. For example, not all Catholics include this doxology when they pray the Lord's Prayer. So why do others include it?

By praying this doxology, we lend our voice affirming the petitions as Jesus gave them to His disciples. We acknowledge God as the ruler of His kingdom with all power and glory due to Him. Finally, we pray that all that was just prayed would be done in accordance with the will of the Father who has the power to do so and that what is done would be done to His glory.

"Amen" simply means, "so shall it be." We do not use *amen* to end prayers as a way to hang up the phone or a way to say goodbye to God. Rather, we conclude prayers this way in order to affirm once again our desire that our prayer be heard and that God's will be done with regard to our prayer. It is tempting to skip over this element of the Lord's Prayer as we teach it to our children. However, we should take a moment to affirm what we say in the doxology.

In the doxology, we reinforce the idea that the words of our prayer are not mere passing recitation of an ancient, no longer relevant, liturgy. Some branches of the church are less attached to the repetition of ancient customs. Even biblical prayers such as the Lord's Prayer do not receive as central a position in their worship design. Nonetheless, the doxology is a reminder to us all that this prayer is not merely a reply to the disciples' questions, relevant only to their time, but rather a timeless structure that guides us as we address our heavenly Father.

There is perhaps less here that we might draw upon to teach our children, but more for our inspiration as we seek to teach them. Let it be so. Let us always return to this timeless prayer and inspire in our children a love and deep abiding within its profound structure and contours. May we seek to help our children grow in the faith expressed within the Lord's Prayer that it may be so within our homes.

CHAPTER 13

THE SACRAMENT OF HOLY BAPTISM

As the head of the family should teach it
in a simple way to his household

As we are now moving into a discussion of the sacraments, it might be good to pause before explaining each of them individually, and explain the concept of a sacrament generally. *Sacrament* is a word derived from the Greek word for mystery, μυστήριον (*mysterion*). No matter what we can know about the two sacraments of the church, they remain a mystery of God's design.

We define a sacrament using the following criteria:

1. Instituted by God

2. Includes a visible element

3. Involves God's gracious forgiveness of sins

The churches of the Reformation determined that of the seven sacraments practiced by the Roman Catholic Church, only two sacraments meet these criteria. Those are Holy Baptism and Holy Communion. Some consider Absolution (to be discussed under the Confession section below) to be a possible third sacrament. It is generally not included due to a lack of a visible element. We can use this helpful formula to teach our children what a sacrament is and what a sacrament does.

FIRST

What is Baptism?

Baptism is not just plain water, but it is the water included in God's command and combined with God's word.

The physical element of Baptism is water, yet it is clearly not mere water. The power in Baptism is the promise of God spoken during one's Baptism. The Word of God is what makes the water able to deliver on the promise of grace and forgiveness. We are commanded to baptize in Matthew 28:19–20, in what is known as the Great Commission. The disciples were charged with making disciples of all nations. They were instructed to do so through Baptism and teaching. Their calling is our calling. We are to continue the work, seeking to make all of humanity disciples of Christ through water and the Word. While all disciples are able to baptize, the congregation delegates this authority to its pastor, since he has the calling to care spiritually for the church.

Although pastors usually baptize, this is not due to any power of their own. Their own spirituality does not aid them in performing a Baptism. It is God who acts in Baptism. Neither the pastor nor those being baptized are truly active participants. God calls us into faith. Likewise, it is God who gives faith and forgiveness in the waters of Baptism.

Since it is the Holy Spirit who is active in Baptism and is the giver of faith, there is no need to be concerned with what we bring to the table. When Jesus called His disciples to baptize all nations, He did not make distinctions in age or gender. All are able to be baptized, and God wants all to be baptized. This is why we as Lutherans practice infant Baptism. Even babies like my oldest who fell asleep during his Baptism are able to be brought to faith in Christ through the waters of Baptism, because the efficacy of Baptism is not something we bring, but rather something entirely up to the work of our triune God.

This is an important teaching about which parents should talk with their children. There is comfort in knowing that the reason they have faith is not because they have done anything, but rather because of what God has done for them. We find comfort in this fact because God's actions are far more reliable than our own. We find comfort in knowing that our salvation is based on the promises and action of God and not on our own merits and accomplishments.

A great time to talk about this with your kids is when there is a Baptism at church. Make Baptism something special for your family every time someone is baptized. You can celebrate and pray for the newly baptized while reminding your children about the meaning of their own Baptism. If your children have not yet been baptized, set down this book, pick up the phone, and call your pastor to arrange for them to be baptized.

Which is that word of God?

Christ our Lord says in the last chapter of Matthew: "Therefore go and make disciples of all nations, baptizing them in the name of the Father and of the Son and of the Holy Spirit." (Matt. 28:19)

There are a couple of key things taking place in this passage. Jesus commands His disciples to make other disciples. In order to do that, they are to do two interrelated things. They are to baptize and they are to teach. As parents, we bring our children to be baptized, perhaps when they are only a few days or weeks old. A part of the baptismal liturgy is our promise as parents along with that of the sponsors to ensure that we will provide the proper teaching of the faith throughout our child's life. This is one reason why this section of this book is so very critical. As parents, we promise to raise our children in the faith. This begins with parents teaching the faith in the home through reading the Bible together, family devotions, as well as talking about matters of faith throughout the week. Additionally parents can make sure that their kids participate in church-led Christian education that is designed to support the home, be that Sunday School, VBS, or by sending them to a Christian school for their general education.

A second key element of the Great Commission has to do with the content of the teaching that is to take place. We are not simply to teach morality. It is good to have well behaved children, especially as we take them out in public, but the Christian faith is fundamentally about so much more. You may have noted a particular formula in the passage used in all Christian Baptisms: "Baptizing them in the name of the Father and of the Son and of the Holy Spirit." We baptize in the name of and into the faith of the Trinity. Thus, we can share with our children that their Baptism united them with a personal God who is our Father, who is Jesus the Son and our brother, and who is the Holy Spirit who gives us faith through Baptism.

Second

What benefits does Baptism give?

It works forgiveness of sins, rescues from death and the devil, and gives eternal salvation to all who believe this, as the words and promises of God declare.

As cute and adorable as children are, they are born in sin. This is a hard thing to see at times in the lives of our children, but the Bible is clear. Paul teaches on this matter in Romans 5:12–21 when he discusses the impact that Adam's sin had on all of humanity. Death came through sin and has affected all who live. Thus, we are all under the judgment of sin.

Baptism washes our sins away (Acts 22:16). Through this washing, we are born into the new life promised through Jesus' sinless life, death, and resurrection. We no longer need to fear death as we might have otherwise. We still feel the loss of loved ones, while at the same time we look forward to eternal life together with Christ in heaven.

As parents, we are able to help our children live out the reality of their new life through Baptism with a daily (at times minute-by-minute) reminder of forgiveness. We will touch on this again when discussing confession, but we have the opportunity to demonstrate the power of forgiveness in our children's lives. Our kids generally desire to please us. It is true that at times they might stubbornly give the impression that they really couldn't care less. However, deep inside, even the most stubborn, rebellious child still desires the affirmation of his parents.

Especially when our children are young, we are able to teach forgiveness by using very clear language. Our culture is often uncomfortable actually stating, "I forgive you." We tend to say things like "That's okay" or "Forget about it," rather than directly offering forgiveness. This sends a mixed message to our children. They need to know that if they do something wrong, the Bible calls that sin. We need to be comfortable calling sin *sin*. By doing so, we teach our children not only the seriousness of sin, but also the joy of forgiveness. In chapter 11, I explained how my wife and I reinforce the concept of forgiveness with our boys. We always make a point of saying "I forgive you" when they have done something wrong, and we also make sure they say the same when they have been wronged. By doing this, they know that what they did was not "Okay," but it is also not something that they need to carry with them. They are forgiven, and we can now move on in right relationship with one another, just as God's forgiveness restores us to a right relationship with Him.

As they grow older, children continue to need to hear forgiveness. They may not respond the same way as they did when they were younger, but even teenagers need to hear words of forgiveness. The consequences for specific sins still need to be felt, but just as in Baptism, when they seek the forgiveness of their parents, they need to hear that they are forgiven and know that they are washed clean of all their sin.

Which are these words and promises of God?

Christ our Lord says in the last chapter of Mark: "Whoever believes and is baptized will be saved, but whoever does not believe will be condemned." (Mark 16:16)

If we are going to make the claim that Baptism saves, then we need to back it up when we teach. When talking with our children, we can talk about passages like Mark 16:16. At first, a passage like this might not seem very promising. It clearly offers salvation to those who believe, which is good news. The passage offers condemnation to those who do not believe in Christ for their salvation, which is not good news for unbelievers. So how can we know if our children have faith?

The good news is that Baptism gives faith to our children, even when they are not able to respond themselves. Faith is a gift freely given and not something that we as fallen sinners are capable of gaining on our own. In addition, the Holy Spirit sustains our faith. This, then, truly is a comfort to teach our children. God gives them faith and sustains that faith through the Holy Spirit. Even when God does not feel close, He is with us. Even when we run from God, He is faithful and calls us home. Like the father in the parable of the prodigal son (Luke 15:11–32), God does not simply leave us to return to sin but eagerly seeks to restore us when we fail. If faith were up to us, there would be little hope. However, since faith is up to God, we can have ultimate confidence.

This faith has lasting effects. Even through the teenage years, the faith given to our children when they were young endures and links them with their heavenly Father. Unlike the many things teens are asked to achieve on their own, faith is a gift, not something they have to be concerned about as to whether they got it right or not. God got it right for us all.

How can water do such great things?

Certainly not just water, but the word of God in and with the water does these things, along with the faith which trusts this word of God in the water. For without God's word the water is plain water and no Baptism. But with the word of God it is a Baptism, that is, a life-giving water, rich in grace, and a washing of the new birth in the Holy Spirit, as St. Paul says in Titus, chapter three: "He saved us through the washing of rebirth and renewal by the Holy Spirit, whom He poured out on us generously through Jesus Christ our Savior, so that, having been justified by His grace, we might become heirs having the hope of eternal life. This is a trustworthy saying." (Titus 3:5–8)

Having a three-year-old in your lap during a Baptism is fun. They are so curious about what is going on. As they get older, this curiosity has potential to produce great questions like the one above from the Small Catechism. "How can water do such great things?" The short answer is that it cannot. Really, there is no power in the water itself. However, water and the Word, now that is a different story.

When our kids start asking about what is taking place in Baptism, they will inevitably get around to this issue. We can share with them that the water is the means through which God has chosen to work to give faith and forgiveness. We are washed with water, but not the same washing that we do each day in our bathtubs or showers. Water is used in both, but by including the Word of God in Baptism, far more takes place. Water on its own can cleanse our outside. Water and God's Word cleanses us from the inside. We are cleansed of our sin and all of its filth. Water is used because it is a washing, but God's Word is used so that this washing is able to cleanse us spiritually from the inside out.

As children get older, the mystery of Baptism may fade. The wide-eyed joy of seeing someone baptized may no longer be readily present. One way to help teens appreciate Baptism, and how mere water can have such an impact, is to have them talk with adults or other teens who have recently been baptized. For example, there is a teen girl in the youth group at my church. She is new to the faith and it shows through her enthusiasm. This affects the faith of those whose Baptism is years in the past, because as she talks about her interest in growing in her faith, it becomes infectious to those around her.

FOURTH

What does such baptizing with water indicate?

It indicates that the Old Adam in us should by daily contrition and repentance be drowned and die with all sins and evil desires, and that a new man should daily emerge and arise to live before God in righteousness and purity forever.

Our kids sin daily. We forgive them daily. Thus, there is opportunity to remind them about their baptismal identity on a daily basis. Maybe it is at bath time at the end of the day. Maybe it is first thing in the morning when they are washing their face to get ready for school. Maybe it is a shower after soccer practice. Whenever this works in your family's schedule, it is worth the effort to help our children recall their Baptism by the reapplication of water. When we pour the water on our child or when they stand in the shower, we can encourage them to recall the cleansing power of Baptism. Each day we are able to live in the light of the forgiveness that is ours in Christ. Perhaps you can say something to your younger child like, "Just as this water cleans your body, the water and the Word of God in Baptism continually cleanses you of your sin." Use language that makes sense for you and for your kids. By choosing to use the same language each day, you further ground them in the practice of baptismal remembrance, making the daily living in their Baptism even more a present and conscious reality for them.

When old enough to help wash the car, we can connect the washing of a really dirty car with Baptism. The difference being that each new car wash is not like a new Baptism—there is no need for a new Baptism. Rather, we need a reminder to bring us back to the cleansing that took place in our Baptism. Each new car wash returns the car to a state of cleanliness that was already achieved. When we remember our Baptism and receive again God's forgiveness, we remember and return to the sinless state of Christ given to us on the cross in order to restore us before the Father. We drown the old Adam just like we wash the dirty car, in order to continually seek to return to our trust in Christ and the forgiveness that is ours in Him.

Where is this written?

St. Paul writes in Romans chapter six: "We were therefore buried with Him through baptism into death in order that, just as Christ was raised from the dead through the glory of the Father, we too may live a new life." (Rom. 6:4)

The Old Adam in us, that part of us lost in sin and bound to death, was buried with Christ in His death. This was the entire purpose for the crucifixion. We can teach our children that Jesus took all our sins upon Himself, and in so doing, He put to death that part of ourselves that keeps us from loving Him. We are then raised to new life, which means that we now are filled with the love that God has always had for us. Our children are now able to pray to God to thank Him for His love and for everything in their days. Spend less time on the topic of death with younger children, focusing more on putting sin behind us and living a new life in Christ free from sin and free to love God and one another.

As children mature and are able to grapple with the concept of spiritual death and new life, talk to them about the imagery of drowning the Old Adam that connects with Baptism. Focus then on the new life we have. In Christ, we make a break from the past and enter into something new. We are no longer bound to the bondage of sin. Remind your children at all ages that in Baptism their sins are no longer their concern. Christ has washed them clean, and each day we can be reminded of our Baptism as we seek forgiveness for those ways we failed to remain the holy new creation Christ has made us.

CHAPTER 14

CONFESSION

How Christians should be taught to confess

What is Confession?

Confession has two parts. First, that we confess our sins, and second, that we receive absolution, that is, forgiveness, from the pastor as from God Himself, not doubting, but firmly believing that by it our sins are forgiven before God in heaven.

The Christian home should be a place for confession and forgiveness. The Christian family should regularly participate in confession and receive absolution when the Body of Christ gathers each Sunday for corporate worship. We each have a need to hear the words of forgiveness from our pastor, who speaks on God's behalf, offering us forgiveness for every offense we might have incurred and restoring us to a right relationship with God.

Within the family, each of us individually may offer forgiveness of sins for those things that are done to us. This forgiveness restores us to a right relationship with our fellow family members. It is for this reason that we have children apologize for specific things they do to wrong family members, friends at school and in the neighborhood, and others. However, when our children sin against God, we are not in the same position to offer forgiveness. I cannot absolve the sins of my children when they take the Lord's name in vain. Rather, I, as a parent, am merely to call my children to repentance and assure them of God's forgiveness. Christ, on the other hand, offers forgiveness for all of our sins. Each time we sin against our brother or sister, we are in fact sinning against God and are thus in need of His forgiveness.

We should teach our children to value the liturgical practice of confession and absolution that we experience each Sunday. The pastor speaks on God's behalf and announces complete forgiveness to young and old alike. Those things we have done to break the commands of God are wiped clean. We are now able to begin anew, stepping into a new day and new week, unburdened by past sins.

A colleague, who was once my professor, told the story of his father buying him a new car following an incident in which he drove recklessly and totaled his first car. In that moment, he learned forgiveness at an astounding depth. Having confessed his wrongdoing, he was restored even more fully than seemed remotely likely. When we confess our sins, God restores us to a right relationship with Him. This applies to the relationship between teenagers and their parents. Teens will push boundaries. They will seek to find out just how much they can get away with. When caught, and when they are able to understand the seriousness of what they have done, the sweet taste of forgiveness will be all the sweeter. However, this is not possible without confession. No matter what their children's age, parents should insist that their children confess before moving toward forgiveness.

What sins should we confess?

Before God, we should plead guilty of all sins, even those we are not aware of, as we do in the Lord's Prayer; but before the pastor, we should confess only those sins that we know and feel in our hearts.

During the week, we do innumerable things that transgress the will of God. This was Luther's burden. Having studied law before he turned to the study of theology, his legal mind was acutely aware that he was in need of some atonement for his sins. Thus, he spent hours confessing his sins in exacting details to the priests on confessional duty. He may have gone so far as to turn right around and return to the confessional if he discovered that he missed anything immediately after finishing his latest round of confession.

If our children learn to take their sin seriously, we, too, might feel a similar burning to specifically confess each of our sins. Thankfully, each week we are able to receive absolution for all of our sins in corporate worship. We ought not to doubt that we have received forgiveness. Moved to confess our sins, God is faithful and promises to forgive our sins (1 John 1:8–9). We need not list each sin or even recall them all specifically, though when confessing, it is of benefit to recall those sins most burdensome to us.

Notice that Luther even notes that we are still able to bring specific sins that we know and feel in our hearts to the pastor, so that we might hear specific forgiveness for these individually. There is no requirement for this practice in Lutheran teaching as there is in Catholicism. However, this is a much-neglected gift of the Church. Being able to bring specific sins that particularly burden us to our pastor so that we can hear the words of forgiveness spoken by him on behalf of God are a true blessing. Our children should learn of this practice and be encouraged to make use of it, especially as teens, so that as they struggle through life, the church is seen as a source of healing rather than a place of judgment.

In their teen years, sins may become less comfortable to hear about. Parents still need to be able and willing to hear the confession of their children. Even when challenging, parents need to be willing to hear them in order to offer forgiveness and unburden them of their sins. Sometimes teens may find it too difficult to confess certain sins to their parents. In these instances, it may be better to encourage enough of an open relationship with their pastor that they feel comfortable confessing those sins to him, so that they can receive forgiveness. If possible, however, once forgiven, teens should still be encouraged to be open with their parents. Parents then, in consultation with their pastor, DCE, etc., should work to balance consequences with forgiveness.

Which are these?

Consider your place in life according to the Ten Commandments: Are you a father, mother, son, daughter, husband, wife, or worker? Have you been disobedient, unfaithful, or lazy? Have you been hot-tempered, rude, or quarrelsome? Have you hurt someone by your words or deeds? Have you stolen, been negligent, wasted anything, or done any harm?

What sins are we to confess? A simple answer might be all of them. However, especially when teaching our children about confession, it helps to provide a prompt that gets them (and us) thinking about just what sins we might need to confess and be forgiven. The questions that Luther includes here ought not to be taken as an exhaustive list. As parents, we might talk through the past week with our kids to help them reflect back on the vicissitudes of their lives. We might ask them how they interacted with their siblings, teachers, friends, parents, etc. In this way, we prepare them for confession.

A SHORT FORM OF CONFESSION

[Luther intended the following form to serve only as an example of private confession for Christians of his time. For a contemporary form of individual confession, see *Lutheran Worship*, pp. 310–11 or *Lutheran Service Book*, pp. 292–93.]

Here Luther provides a structure for private confession that pastors can use with those who come to them for private confession. However, we as parents may also make use of this form, or that which is found in *Lutheran Service Book*, to help our children know more about what it means to confess our sins and perhaps to encourage them to see the benefit of private confession.

The penitent says:

Dear confessor, I ask you please to hear my confession and to pronounce forgiveness in order to fulfill God's will.

I, a poor sinner, plead guilty before God of all sins. In particular, I confess before you that as a servant, maid, etc., I, sad to say, serve my master unfaithfully, for in this and that I have not done what I was told to do. I have made him angry and caused him to curse. I have been negligent and allowed damage to be done. I have also been offensive in words and deeds. I have quarreled with my peers. I have grumbled about the lady of the house and cursed her. I am sorry for all of this and I ask for grace. I want to do better.

Right from the start, you can tell that Luther is not messing around. We are not used to using language like "poor sinner," but that is what we are. We ought to teach our children to seek forgiveness with sincere contrition (feeling remorseful) and not arrogant entitlement. The list prompts us to consider all the ways in which we have sinned before God.

This is helpful to teach our children. It is easier to see how we have hurt someone standing in front of us. My sons know they have done wrong when the other brother is crying (at least when I point it out, they see the connection). It is harder to reflect on the ways in which we sin against God since we do not see the distress that it causes Him directly. Luther's list helps focus our attention on the ways in which we can and do sin against God.

A master or lady of the house may say:

In particular, I confess before you that I have not faithfully guided my children, servants, and wife to the glory of God. I have cursed. I have set a bad example by indecent words and deeds. I have hurt my neighbor and spoken evil of him. I have overcharged, sold inferior merchandise, and given less than was paid for.

Parents, note that we have a part in this order of confession and absolution. As a parent, I model the behavior that my sons learn. For good or for bad, they mirror much of what they see in my wife and me. When parents take the lead in confessing their sins to one another and before God, we teach our children to do likewise.

[Let the penitent confess whatever else he has done against God's commandments and his own position.]

Moving from corporate to private confession, things get more personal. Now is the time when we seek to examine ourselves individually and confess the specific sins that burden us. Take the time to talk with your child before meeting with your pastor so that the specific sins that call for the private confession are clearly understood and can be articulated.

If, however, someone does not find himself burdened with these or greater sins, he should not trouble himself or search for or invent other sins, and thereby make confession a torture. Instead, he should mention one or two that he knows: In particular I confess that I have cursed; I have used improper words; I have neglected this or that, etc. Let that be enough.

> But if you know of none at all (which hardly seems possible), then mention none in particular, but receive the forgiveness upon the general confession which you make to God before the confessor.

Luther presents a right and proper caution not to seek private confession legalistically. If we, as parents, choose to instruct our children in the benefits of private confession, we should let this serve as a warning. We should not use private confession in a way that adds to the burden of sin carried by our children. Instead, we should focus on its use as a way to help the young find forgiveness and release from such burdens. Thus, as we prepare children for confession, we should only do so by focusing on sins that burden them, not in any way add to their list of sins.

Then the confessor shall say:

God be merciful to you and strengthen your faith. Amen.

Why is it now important for the confessor to offer a prayer for the strengthening of the faith of the penitent? The reason is simply so that the one confessing his or her sins would have the increased strength of faith to receive forgiveness. It is not unusual for children to question if they are really forgiven. Are we as adults any different? We all seek some assurance. The pastor here offers a prayer for the strengthening of faith so that when absolution is pronounced, those receiving forgiveness will trust all the more that their sins are truly forgiven.

Furthermore:

Do you believe that my forgiveness is God's forgiveness?

Yes, dear confessor.

There is a certain power in speaking that which we are trying to believe. It may be helpful as we teach our children about forgiveness to take a lesson here and ask if our kids believe they have been forgiven. Only when we no longer hold onto the burden of sin are we able to trust in God's forgiveness. Verbalizing that belief helps reinforce its reality in our children's hearts and minds.

Then let him say:

Let it be done for you as you believe. And I, by the command of our Lord Jesus Christ, forgive you your sins in the name of the Father and of the Son and of the Holy Spirit. Amen. Go in peace.

Having had their faith strengthened by the promises of God, the pastor now speaks forgiveness to the penitent. He does this in the same trinitarian name of God we heard at our Baptism. This is another important connection we can make for our children. The same God who gave us the gift of faith in our Baptism restores us repeatedly, forgiving our sins as we seek to live out our imperfect lives in His name and by His will. We can teach this great comfort to our children.

A confessor will know additional passages with which to comfort and to strengthen the faith of those who have great burdens of conscience or are sorrowful and distressed.

This is intended only as a general form of confession.

Just as your pastor is able to offer additional comfort from the Bible, we, too, as parents, are able to offer the same as we talk about forgiveness with our children. Some particularly helpful passages include Matthew 9:2; 18:18; John 20:23; Psalm 103:12; 32:2; 1 John 1:9; Acts 3:19; and Ephesians 1:7 among many others.

What is the Office of the Keys?*

The Office of the Keys is that special authority which Christ has given to His church on earth to forgive the sins of repentant sinners, but to withhold forgiveness from the unrepentant as long as they do not repent.

The Office of the Keys is given to the Church. The Church delegates the administration of the Office of the Keys to its pastors. This is not likely a topic to discuss with younger children. At a young age, it is more helpful to keep the conversation focused on corporate and individual forgiveness rather than on withholding forgiveness.

As they get older, we might begin to discuss with our preteens what might happen if we refuse to repent and seek forgiveness. True repentance is a turning away from the sins of our past. It is more than a glib,

"I'm sorry"; it is a heartfelt personal examination and desire to sin no more. We can indirectly teach this when they are younger as we insist on apologies to end a timeout, but it is not helpful to connect this to God until children are more mature. Walk through Matthew 18:15–20 with your children. Help them to see how at each turn, the Church should seek to restore sinners by seeking to help them realize the seriousness of their sin. Further, help them to see the necessity of not offering cheap grace by offering forgiveness without repentance. A heart hardened to the reality of sin within it offers no fertile ground for the growth of God's grace.

Where is this written?*

This is what St. John the Evangelist writes in chapter twenty: The Lord Jesus breathed on His disciples and said, "Receive the Holy Spirit. If you forgive anyone his sins, they are forgiven; if you do not forgive them, they are not forgiven." (John 20:22–23)

Why does the Church have this authority? It is not authority the Church takes upon itself but authority given to the Church by Christ. Jesus was known as one who taught and forgave with authority. This authority was given to Him by the Father. The Church is now given that authority to exercise in the name of Christ and on His behalf.

What do you believe according to these words?*

I believe that when the called ministers of Christ deal with us by His divine command, in particular when they exclude openly unrepentant sinners from the Christian congregation and absolve those who repent of their sins and want to do better, this is just as valid and certain, even in heaven, as if Christ our dear Lord dealt with us Himself.

*This question may not have been composed by Luther himself but reflects his teaching and was included in editions of the catechism during his lifetime.

Many of us may never have had experience dealing with a church exercising its discipline to the point of excommunication, but this is a good and right practice of the Church. When talking with our children about this, we can provide context for them to understand by making a comparison to friendships. We always desire that our friends remain true and our friends. However, there are times when the behavior of our friends makes it necessary to no longer keep them close for our own protection. Likewise, the Church must at times remove from its midst unrepentant sinners who are not willing to hear the reality of their sin and their need for repentance. For the sake of the whole, out of love, the Church may need to remove individuals from fellowship. This is done using a process similar to that noted in Matthew 18, with the goal always being the restoration of full trust and fellowship.

CHAPTER 15

THE SACRAMENT OF THE ALTAR

As the head of the family should teach it
in a simple way to his household

What is the Sacrament of the Altar?

It is the true body and blood of our Lord Jesus Christ under the bread and wine, instituted by Christ Himself for us Christians to eat and to drink.

We know the Sacrament of the Altar by many names: Holy Communion, the Eucharist, the Lord's Supper, and others. As Lutherans, we approach this special meal with a particular reverence. As a sacrament, the Lord's Supper is to be given proper respect as we prepare individuals to partake in it. An essential element of that preparation is an understanding of what we believe takes place in this very special consumption of the bread and wine.

When we talk with our children about Holy Communion, we should take care, as there is a good deal of mystery related to the elements involved. When Jesus instituted this sacrament during His last supper with His disciples, he took bread and wine and presented them as His body and blood. Some theological traditions have held that we receive only the body and blood of Christ, which are no longer bread and wine (Roman Catholic). Many Protestants hold some variation of a symbolic view in which either the bread and wine are representations of Christ's body and blood or that we merely partake spiritually in the body and blood of Christ. In either case, they do not believe that there is any physical eating of the body and blood of Christ.

Teaching our children as Lutherans means speaking to the simple language that Luther insisted had to be respected. Luther argued with Zwingli that the word *is* must be taken at face value. "This is My body" thus means that what we receive is indeed the body of Christ. Luther further taught, as we should, that what we see, feel, and taste (bread and wine) is truly present as well. We say that the body and blood of Christ are in, with, and under that bread and wine. As Lutherans, we talk about the real presence of Christ in the Lord's Supper. By this, we mean that Christ is truly present in the bread and wine that we consume. Not in merely a spiritual manner, in which the bread and wine represent the body and blood of Christ, nor, as the Roman Catholic Church teaches, in the bread and wine becoming the body and blood and no longer being bread and wine. As Lutherans, we believe that we truly receive both the bread and Christ's body along with the wine and Christ's blood.

It may be helpful to explain the nature of our view of the Sacrament of the Altar to our children when they are young. As early teenage reasoning skills take shape, it becomes more challenging to introduce counterintuitive mysteries like the real presence of Christ in the Lord's Supper. Therefore, I believe it to be beneficial to begin to explain Holy Communion to children when they are young. Teaching our children about the nature of Holy Communion when they have the faith of a child gives them a foundation of faith upon which to build as they more rationally wrestle with this doctrine later in life.

Where is this written?

The holy Evangelists Matthew, Mark, Luke, and St. Paul write:

Our Lord Jesus Christ, on the night when He was betrayed, took bread, and when He had given thanks, He broke it and gave it to the disciples and said: "Take, eat; this is My body, which is given for you. This do in remembrance of Me."

In the same way also He took the cup after supper, and when He had given thanks, He gave it to them, saying, "Drink of it, all of you; this cup is the new testament in My blood, which is shed for you for the forgiveness of sins. This do, as often as you drink it, in remembrance of Me."

Use a copy of *Lutheran Service Book* (if you don't have one, ask your pastor if you can borrow one from your church) to take your children on a tour of the liturgy of Holy Communion, pointing out the passages from the Bible like Matthew 26:26–30 that are used. Your pastor can expand this by helping you walk through larger portions of the liturgy noting the use of Scripture all over; however, here specifically it is profitable to help our children see how our celebration of the Lord's Supper is directly shaped by the Word of God.

What is the benefit of this eating and drinking?

These words, "Given and shed for you for the forgiveness of sins," show us that in the Sacrament forgiveness of sins, life, and salvation are given us through these words. For where there is forgiveness of sins, there is also life and salvation.

Why is participation in Holy Communion central to the practice of the Christian faith? Through partaking in the Lord's Supper and faith in Jesus' words "given and shed for you for the forgiveness of your sins," we receive forgiveness. As Luther points out, through forgiveness we receive life and salvation. We should teach our children that just as we parents find all kinds of special ways to show our love and care for them, so, too, God our heavenly Father finds special ways to love and care for us. Holy Communion is what we call a "Means of Grace." It is a way the God has promised to pour out His grace on us in a special and specific way.

When beginning to participate in Holy Communion, it might be helpful to talk with teenagers about the benefit that receiving forgiveness brings through this sacrament. The tangible nature of the Lord's Supper reminds us how truly real and tangible the forgiveness of Christ is for us. Just as the cross was real, the forgiveness we receive is real. God makes use of His creation through something as simple as bread and wine to convey to us His love and forgiveness.

How can bodily eating and drinking do such great things?

Certainly not just eating and drinking do these things, but the words written here: "Given and shed for you for the forgiveness of sins." These words, along with the bodily eating and drinking, are the main thing in the Sacrament. Whoever believes these words has exactly what they say: "forgiveness of sins."

Have you ever taken your kids to Communion with you, only to have them try to help themselves? If what was taking place was mere eating and drinking, why not allow them to take part? Because that is not what is taking place. Not only are we receiving the true body and blood of our Lord and Savior Jesus Christ, but we also receive His gracious forgiveness through the Sacrament of the Altar. (See the next question from Luther's catechism for an answer as to why not just anybody should take part in this.)

We can therefore talk to our children about how we are fed not merely physically, but spiritually in this meal. We are fed and strengthened by the outpouring of forgiveness, life, and salvation. Just as God gives us food that we eat every day to stay physically healthy and strong, we receive sustaining spiritual strength from Holy Communion through the forgiveness of sins.

Teenagers can often become enamored with the scientific method. Applying that method in this instance will only cause confusion. While we truly believe as Lutherans in the real presence of Christ in the Lord's Supper, we will not find genetic evidence of that presence. This does not mean, however, that this meal is merely representative or a spiritual form of Christ given for us. Scripture does not allow for that. Not knowing the exact manner in which God accomplishes this does not negate its reality. Instead, a mystery is preserved, through which we receive God's grace poured out for us.

Who receives this sacrament worthily?

Fasting and bodily preparation are certainly fine outward training. But that person is truly worthy and well prepared who has faith in these words: "Given and shed for you for the forgiveness of sins."

But anyone who does not believe these words or doubts them is unworthy and unprepared, for the words "for you" require all hearts to believe.

Not just anybody should be welcomed to take part in the Lord's Supper. If we take seriously the gifts given, out of respect we must reserve this meal for only those who faithfully seek forgiveness through this eating and drinking. We should teach our children about what it means to prepare to receive Holy Communion and thus to receive Christ's forgiveness as well. We do not do so casually. We should teach our children how we prepare to receive the Sacrament through self-examination, seeking once more to make sure that we are placing our sins before Christ for Him to take our burdens.

If our children do not believe that we will truly forgive them when we say to them that they are forgiven, what value do our words have? They would naturally grow to distrust our words. Likewise, if there is doubt in the promises of God, we ought to pause and consider seriously that God is both faithful and just (1 John 1:9) and thus accept the veracity of His promises. Trusting that we will receive the promised forgiveness through the Lord's Supper further strengthens our faith and trust in Christ as our Savior.

Preparation for participation in the sacrament of Holy Communion is vital but often forgotten. Talk with teens as they prepare. Instruct them that they are to examine their hearts for the following: (1) Do you trust in Christ for your salvation? (2) Do you believe that Christ is truly present in, with, and under the bread and wine? (3) Do you believe that you receive forgiveness of sins through the Lord's Supper? Using these questions, teens and their parents focus on what is taking place so that we can prepare our hearts and minds to receive this Means of Grace.

CHAPTER 16

DAILY PRAYERS

How the head of the family should teach his household
to pray morning and evening

Morning Prayer

*In the morning when you get up, make the sign of the holy
cross and say:*

In the name of the Father and of the ✠ Son and of the Holy
Spirit. Amen.

*Then, kneeling or standing, repeat the Creed and the Lord's
Prayer. If you choose, you may also say this little prayer:*

I thank You, my heavenly Father, through Jesus Christ, Your
dear Son, that You have kept me this night from all harm and
danger; and I pray that You would keep me this day also from
sin and every evil, that all my doings and life may please You.
For into Your hands I commend myself, my body and soul,
and all things. Let Your holy angel be with me, that the evil
foe may have no power over me. Amen.

*Then go joyfully to your work, singing a hymn, like that of the
Ten Commandments, or whatever your devotion may suggest.*

Just as it is essential to ensure that your children get a good breakfast,
so, too, is it important that your family begin the day spiritually fed as
well. Luther's Morning Prayer serves as a guide for us on how we may
teach our children to start their day in the Lord.

Rather than rushing forward unreflective into the busyness of the day, Luther's Morning Prayer first calls us to offer thanks that God has seen us through another night. In Luther's day, infant mortality rates were far higher than anything we know today. A family might have a dozen children in the hope that a couple would make it through to adulthood. Although we do not put our children to bed with nearly this kind of concern for their safety overnight, this is still a helpful reminder that each day is a gift from God. Starting our day in joyful thanks for the chance of a new day sets our hearts and minds on the things of God. Gratefully and with joy, we then are able to approach the tasks of the day.

It is in that joy and thanksgiving that we further pray that we might be kept from sin and enabled to serve God in our individual vocations in a manner pleasing to Him. We pray that we might be able to submit to God and do His will. This is our thank offering for the life God has granted us.

The prayer concludes by returning to a request for further protection. The modern mind is less comfortable with thoughts of Satan as a real power in the world, yet, indeed, he is. We ought to teach our children to take the existence of Satan seriously, not in the sense that they need to fear him as though every dark corner may be filled with his minions. Rather, we should instill in them a real belief that although Satan is real and a true threat for those who leave themselves open to his influence, we are able to call upon the Lord, who is easily able to protect us from the wiles of Satan. This is why we conclude Luther's Morning Prayer with this request for protection. We need it, and God desires to provide it.

Evening Prayer

In the evening when you go to bed, make the sign of the holy cross and say:

In the name of the Father and of the ✝ Son and of the Holy Spirit. Amen.

Then kneeling or standing, repeat the Creed and the Lord's Prayer. If you choose, you may also say this little prayer:

I thank You, my heavenly Father, through Jesus Christ, Your dear Son, that You have graciously kept me this day; and I pray that You would forgive me all my sins where I have done wrong, and graciously keep me this night. For into Your hands

I commend myself, my body and soul, and all things. Let Your holy angel be with me, that the evil foe may have no power over me. Amen.

Then go to sleep at once and in good cheer.

Luther's Evening Prayer takes a form similar to his Morning Prayer. We rightly begin in gratitude. Again, we should consistently teach our children to find regular ways and times to offer God thanks for seeing us through life. Luther's Evening Prayer is such an opportunity.

Our children are served well to commit the structure of this prayer to memory. Beginning in thanks, Luther then moves to seek forgiveness for his sins. Taking a moment at the end of our day to confess our sins and seek forgiveness is a great way to remind ourselves daily of our need to begin again. Our children know that they sin. They know the wrong that they do. Using this practice of daily confession, we instill in them a respect for the will of God and an understanding that the grace of God is there and available to us to remove those sins from our lives.

Finally, having received forgiveness, we pray for God once again to protect us from Satan, that evil foe, who would seek to do us harm. What a tremendous gift of comfort this provides our children to know that they are forgiven and protected. True rest can be found in Christ's grace.

How the head of the family should teach his household
to ask a blessing and return thanks

Asking a Blessing

The children and members of the household shall go to the table reverently, fold their hands, and say:

The eyes of all look to You, [O Lord,] and You give them their food at the proper time. You open Your hand and satisfy the desires of every living thing. (Ps. 145:15–16)

Then shall be said the Lord's Prayer and the following:

Lord God, heavenly Father, bless us and these Your gifts which we receive from Your bountiful goodness, through Jesus Christ, our Lord. Amen.

From my many years in youth ministry, I recall far too many times in which my holding on to a stack of pizza too long ran the risk of endangering my life. Hungry teens, especially boys, are hard to slow down when food is before them. However, if we rush past offering a blessing at meals, we risk forgetting the Source of the blessing of food that sustains us.

Prayer at mealtime is likely one of the best-kept practices of the Small Catechism. Our children may learn in preschool many cute prayers with hand motions and catchy rhythms. This helps to lay a foundation of thankful reflection before our meal.

In addition to the prayers, perhaps we might also talk on occasion to our children about where our food comes from. This would be a great time to connect our discussion from the Lord's Prayer on our "daily bread" with mealtime. As our children grow older, we can talk to them about how they can contribute to providing food by getting part-time jobs or working around the house to help us as their parents.

It is important that this practice be maintained long term. Tempting though it might be in the teenage years to forego meals and prayer together, it remains important. If we give in to the temptation that we just do not have the time, we will end up teaching our children either that these prayers are for little kids or that they are secondary to our busy lives. Neither option is great. So maintain, as best as you are able the practice of meals together begun in prayer, thanking God for the blessings before us.

Returning Thanks

Also, after eating, they shall, in like manner, reverently and with folded hands say:

Give thanks to the LORD, for He is good. His love endures forever. [He] gives food to every creature. He provides food for the cattle and for the young ravens when they call. His pleasure is not in the strength of the horse, nor His delight in the legs of a man; the LORD delights in those who fear Him, who put their hope in His unfailing love. (Ps. 136:1, 25; 147:9–11)

Then shall be said the Lord's Prayer and the following:

We thank You, Lord God, heavenly Father, for all Your benefits, through Jesus Christ, our Lord, who lives and reigns with You and the Holy Spirit forever and ever. Amen.

While Christian families tend to be good at prayer before meals, we often neglect returning thanks following a meal. Just as a prayer of thanks before a meal focuses our children on God who provides, offering a prayer of similar thanks following the meal reinforces that belief. However, notice that Luther's wording moves beyond merely thanking God for the food of the meal. We now teach our children to connect the blessings God gives in our meal with the blessings He provides in all aspects of our lives. God our Creator has furnished this world with all that humanity needs and more. By returning thanks in this way, we teach our children this truth while connecting the experience of blessing food with the blessings of home, family, friends, clothing, health, and so much more.

CHAPTER 17

TABLE OF DUTIES

Certain passages of Scripture for various holy orders and
positions, admonishing them about their duties and
responsibilities

To Bishops, Pastors, and Preachers

The overseer must be above reproach, the husband of but
one wife, temperate, self-controlled, respectable, hospitable,
able to teach, not given to drunkenness, not violent but gen-
tle, not quarrelsome, not a lover of money. He must manage
his own family well and see that his children obey him with
proper respect. 1 Tim. 3:2–4

He must not be a recent convert, or he may become conceit-
ed and fall under the same judgment as the devil. 1 Tim. 3:6

He must hold firmly to the trustworthy message as it has
been taught, so that he can encourage others by sound doctrine and refute those who oppose it. Titus 1:9

With the Table of Duties, Luther instructs the faithful on how their
Christian faith ought to inform the various vocations to which God has
called them. Our children benefit from learning the Table of Duties because in it they are able to see how God blesses particular callings and
how each of us bless others in Christ's name through those callings.

Luther begins with the duties and responsibilities of those who serve
the Church as pastors. In his Pastoral Epistles, Paul presents the Church
with standards toward which those who aspire to the pastoral office
should aim. In our families, we should teach our children these stand-

ards, not as a way to judge our pastor and his family, but as a way to prayerfully uplift and support his ministry.

What the Hearers Owe Their Pastors

The Lord has commanded that those who preach the gospel should receive their living from the gospel. 1 Cor. 9:14

Anyone who receives instruction in the word must share all good things with his instructor. Do not be deceived: God cannot be mocked. A man reaps what he sows. Gal. 6:6–7

The elders who direct the affairs of the church well are worthy of double honor, especially those whose work is preaching and teaching. For the Scripture says, "Do not muzzle the ox while it is treading out the grain," and "The worker deserves his wages." 1 Tim. 5:17–18

We ask you, brothers, to respect those who work hard among you, who are over you in the Lord and who admonish you. Hold them in the highest regard in love because of their work. Live in peace with each other. 1 Thess. 5:12–13

Obey your leaders and submit to their authority. They keep watch over you as men who must give an account. Obey them so that their work will be a joy, not a burden, for that would be of no advantage to you. Heb. 13:17

As the pastor is called to a high standard in his ministry in the Church and within his own family, our families are called to offer support in accord with the ministry offered by the pastor. This is an opportunity to teach our children about the importance of offering the Lord a firstfruits gift of our monetary blessings. As each of us works for our wages, we share those blessings through our offerings in worship to provide for the local congregation to be able likewise to provide wages for the work of ministry that our pastor and other called workers provide.

Tithing generally is easier taught at a young age. As children, we don't really have much money. Giving ten percent of five dollars is much easier to learn to do than if we need to begin this practice with our large salary. If our children understand that a primary purpose for this giving is the support of the ministry of the pastor and church staff, they will grow up understanding the biblical principles of the stewardship of God's blessings.

The tribe of Levi was set aside to serve all twelve tribes of ancient Israel as priests. Unlike the other eleven tribes, the Levites did not receive an allotment of land from which to derive their living. Instead, the rest of the nation supported them with a tithe of the produce from the lands that God did give to them. We continue this system when we weekly give a first portion of the produce of our labor to the Church.

If your children get an allowance, provide envelops for them to give a first portion back to the Lord's work. If they do not receive an allowance, let them place your offering in the plate. Create a positive association with the practice. The more this giving is treated as normal, the more it will be accepted as a normal part of their lives, even when the giving begins to feel truly sacrificial.

As they grow older, a great way to encourage youth to respect the work of pastors and other church workers is to have them shadow their church leaders for a day or portion of a day. Growing up, I was one of the few kids who understood that our pastor did not just work on Sunday. My mother was the church secretary for a time, while my father was the school principal. I had ringside seats to view how church workers went about their service. Arrange for young teens to get their own view of what it means to be in church work. Who knows? Perhaps they will find that they are called to serve in some form of ministry themselves.

Of Civil Government

Everyone must submit himself to the governing authorities, for there is no authority except that which God has established. The authorities that exist have been established by God. Consequently, he who rebels against the authority is rebelling against what God has instituted, and those who do so will bring judgment on themselves. For rulers hold no terror for those who do right, but for those who do wrong. Do you want to be free from fear of the one in authority? Then do what is right and he will commend you. For he is God's servant to do you good. But if you do wrong, be afraid, for he does not bear the sword for nothing. He is God's servant, an agent of wrath to bring punishment on the wrongdoer. Rom. 13:1–4

Children generally have a respect for police and firefighters. Many children desire to be a police officer or firefighter themselves. These identifiable aspects of the work of the government affect our lives in ways our children can easily grasp. As we discussed with the Fourth Commandment, God places government into roles of authority in a similar way as He does with parents. The authority of government is not found in the people but in God. We as the people of a nation may choose our government, and in a sense, we place them into authority, but in an ultimate sense, no government exercises any authority other than that which God has granted it.

A similar approach can be taken with teenagers here as noted above. Shadowing a police officer or firefighter may not always be possible, but having teens meet Christians who serve in government may offer a view of faithful individuals who serve God through the state.

Of Citizens

Give to Caesar what is Caesar's, and to God what is God's. Matt. 22:21

It is necessary to submit to the authorities, not only because of possible punishment but also because of conscience. This is also why you pay taxes, for the authorities are God's servants, who give their full time to governing. Give everyone what you owe him: If you owe taxes, pay taxes; if revenue, then revenue; if respect, then respect; if honor, then honor. Rom. 13:5–7

I urge, then, first of all, that requests, prayers, intercession and thanksgiving be made for everyone—for kings and all those in authority, that we may live peaceful and quiet lives in all godliness and holiness. This is good, and pleases God our Savior. 1 Tim. 2:1–3

Remind the people to be subject to rulers and authorities, to be obedient, to be ready to do whatever is good. Titus 3:1

Submit yourselves for the Lord's sake to every authority instituted among men: whether to the king, as the supreme authority, or to governors, who are sent by him to punish those who do wrong and to commend those who do right. 1 Peter 2:13–14

As they grow, our children may find themselves less enamored with the legal authority of government. They may find themselves wishing away what they might see as restrictions to their freedom. However, as Christians we know the necessity of government to restrain evil. We can talk to our children about the reality that sin makes governmental restrictions necessary. Just as teachers in their class keep students from getting out of control, the role of government is to encourage the larger society to restrain itself. Our children can understand how this works, because they know what can happen when the teacher is out of the room. This restraint helps us to deal better with one another. A stable society with laws that are consistently upheld allows for safety and prosperity just like a well-ordered classroom allows for a similar environment of educational success.

To Husbands

Husbands, in the same way be considerate as you live with your wives, and treat them with respect as the weaker partner and as heirs with you of the gracious gift of life, so that nothing will hinder your prayers. 1 Peter 3:7

Husbands, love your wives and do not be harsh with them. Col. 3:19

Fathers, there are few gifts you can give to your sons better than a model worthy of emulation of what it means to love your wife. Talk to your sons about what it means to love your wife self-sacrificially. Help them to see how you live out this ideal. When you fail, admit your failure and help your sons to see how you and they might improve.

Daughters need this modeling just as much. They need to see what it means to have a husband who lovingly cares for his wife more than for his own needs and wants. They need to see what it means to be loved self-sacrificially so that when they are deciding on a husband, they might be able to do so with wisdom.

To Wives

Wives, submit to your husbands as to the Lord. Eph. 5:22

They were submissive to their own husbands, like Sarah, who obeyed Abraham and called him her master. You are her

daughters if you do what is right and do not give way to fear.
1 Peter 3:5–6

Our modern ears do not accept words like *submit* well. Submission seems to convey a mental picture of subjugation. Biblically, however, submission is a model of love. Submission to one's husband uplifts his leadership in the home and helps to fulfill the male need to feel appreciated. This is how God made us. Husbands and wives have needs that are well matched with our roles within marriage.

When a wife is able to submit out of trust in and love for her husband, she models for her daughter the love that we all ought to have for Christ. The Church is the Bride of Christ. Just as we ought to trust in our Lord, wives ought to trust in their husbands.

Sin hinders our ability as the Bride of Christ to trust God as we ought. Sin affects marriage, causing failures of trust to enter into the relationship. However, God offers this self-giving model to us in order that we might learn to love and trust one another and, through that love and trust, grow further to understand how we can properly trust in God.

To Parents

Fathers, do not exasperate your children; instead, bring them up in the training and instruction of the Lord. Eph. 6:4

Wait, isn't it our children who exasperate us as parents? Yes, it might feel that way at times, but consider the lifetime of exasperation that we might cause our children if we fail to train them to know how to live according to the will of the Lord. Parents need to help children learn how to live the love of Christ in their lives. We need to teach them to forgive, to care for the sick, and to love others more than themselves. That really is what this book is all about.

To Children

Children, obey your parents in the Lord, for this is right. "Honor your father and your mother"—which is the first commandment with a promise—"that it may go well with you and that you may enjoy long life on the earth." Eph. 6:1–3

Here Luther returns to the Fourth Commandment. It is the duty of children to honor and obey their parents. By so doing, they are able to learn from the wisdom collected by their parents. As a parent, I might not always feel terribly wise, but my time in this world and the way in which God has shaped me does provide for the necessary wisdom to shepherd my children.

To Workers of All Kinds

Slaves, obey your earthly masters with respect and fear, and with sincerity of heart, just as you would obey Christ. Obey them not only to win their favor when their eye is on you, but like slaves of Christ, doing the will of God from your heart. Serve wholeheartedly, as if you were serving the Lord, not men, because you know that the Lord will reward everyone for whatever good he does, whether he is slave or free. Eph. 6:5–8

Slavery is an evil institution of our past, right? Why, then, is this topic retained in our catechism? Is this not hopelessly out of date? We apply the teaching here to "workers of all kinds," as the heading notes. Our children need to learn a good work ethic in order that they might become better and more ethical employees. It is very tempting to cut corners in today's work world. Ethically going about our work may not always seem to net the gain that we may desire. As they grow up, our children might see others gain more on the short term through unethical practices. However, we know that we serve not only our earthly bosses, but we also serve our heavenly Boss in all that we do in our vocation as employee.

It is worth our time to talk to our children about the work that they do around the house. When we start to give them an allowance for chores in the home, we need to attach seriousness to the quality of what they do, not in a way that over-burdens them with notions of unattainable perfection, but in a way that calls them to do their best. The goal is not merely to have the trash taken out, though that would be nice, especially without having to nag, but rather to form a work ethic that will carry over into their adult lives, which ought to distinguish them in their employment and serve them well in their chosen careers.

To Employers and Supervisors

Masters, treat your slaves in the same way. Do not threaten them, since you know that He who is both their Master and

yours is in heaven, and there is no favoritism with Him. Eph.
6:9

We all want to have a boss who will be good to us, one who is fair
and decent, and one who understands us well. These kinds of bosses do
not come from just anywhere. Parents may be able to form a few in how
they teach their children to lead their peers. There is a good deal of emphasis on leadership in school. When we talk with our children about the
leadership principles they might be learning, we can talk to them about
the concept of servant leadership. A servant leader seeks to serve and care
for those they lead. Therefore, we are to have what is best for them in
mind as we guide them in what we ask them to do.

Children learn to be bossy at an early age. My sons do not need to be
taught how to boss each other around. Rather, I need to reinforce with
them appropriate ways by which they ask someone to do something. This
is just as important as what to tell them. A kind word can go a long way
in making someone desire to be the model employee discussed previously. We should teach our children how to use their tone of voice and word
choice in a way that wins people over to them rather than pushes them
away. It is fairly clear which is taking place when listening to children.
Learning to hear this tone enables parents to guide their children gently
to learn how to present themselves better.

To Youth

Young men, in the same way be submissive to those who are
older. All of you, clothe yourselves with humility toward one
another, because, "God opposes the proud but gives grace to
the humble." Humble yourselves, therefore, under God's
mighty hand, that He may lift you up in due time. 1 Peter 5:5–
6

I warn my DCE students that they might be in for a rude awakening
when they return to youth group as a leader. The respect that they once
had as a peer can rapidly vanish. Although we may at times look at the
past with a distorted sense of idealism, it is true that society once respected age more than youth. In our culture today, this has been reversed. Rather than seek the wisdom of their elders, youth today approach adults
with the attitude that adults will have to earn their respect. As adults, we
ought to focus on earning their respect rather than bemoaning that we do

not automatically receive it. Over time, we can teach youth that respecting their elders is beneficial.

Parents can aid this process by intentionally involving other adults in their children's lives. From a young age, parents should insist that their children treat all adults with respect. If this becomes difficult as their kids approach their teenage years, parents should find adults who are able to connect and care with youth in a way that breaks down their walls before they solidify too much. The church's pastor or DCE could be ideal choices, as might other youth ministry volunteers who have a heart for youth and the skills to listen to their struggles and hurt. This earns their respect and teaches them how to offer respect to other adults more readily.

To Widows

The widow who is really in need and left all alone puts her hope in God and continues night and day to pray and to ask God for help. But the widow who lives for pleasure is dead even while she lives. 1 Tim. 5:5–6

We should not neglect those who are most vulnerable, especially in our churches. I love when my boys interact with the older women of our church. This teaches them respect for and how to interact with elderly members. What a joy it is for us as parents to see the enjoyment that these interactions bring to both our boys and these older women.

There is rich potential in providing opportunities for intergenerational ministry within the church. Intentionally providing space for children and teens to interact with older adults may help them grow in appreciation of the wisdom that their elders can share. Older adults who personally know more of the children and youth in a congregation become great supporters of youth and children's ministry. The church should be a place where the generations interact and learn from one another. The care of widows is a great opportunity for that to take place.

To Everyone

The commandments ... are summed up in this one rule: "Love your neighbor as yourself." Rom. 13:9

I urge ... that requests, prayers, intercession and thanksgiving be made for everyone. 1 Tim. 2:1

Let each his lesson learn with care, and all the household well shall fare.

What a world it would be if we could each manage to care for one another with the same love that we generally have for ourselves. Rather than having to seek to defend our positions and possessions, we would have many more people defending us, and we would do the same for those around us.

Watching preschool children interact with one another is a great way to see original sin in action. A good deal of time and effort is needed to teach children how to share. Not nearly as much effort is needed to teach them how to say "Mine!" or "I was playing with that!" Developmentally, preschoolers have a hard time understanding that when they put down a toy, someone else could pick it up and use it. They have an even harder time understanding that they cannot keep a claim on all toys they have played with in the past half hour, though they make great efforts to defend those claims.

This is why parents should spend time teaching their children to share. Sharing is a first step toward a deeper understanding of the needs of others. Parents should seek to train their children to develop a sensitivity to others so that they might "Love [their] neighbor[s] as [themselves]." This interest in the lives of others will serve them well as they grow and mature. In fact, a concern for others is itself a sign of maturity. The ability to look beyond oneself and see the needs of others is an indication of maturation.

Moving toward adulthood and preparing for relationships means maturing to seek the desires of others over one's own. Parents help their teens see this as they grow into the dating years. Talk with your teenage son or daughter about what makes them feel loved and cared for, since this is easier to assess. Help them apply the things they share to others in their groups of friends as well as potential romantic interests. There may be a need to redirect or reshape responses that lack understanding of the needs of others, but having an ongoing discussion creates fertile ground for growing mature young adults with stable friendships.

Final Thoughts

Reading through these last several pages might cause those of us who are parents to feel overwhelmed. There is a lot of material. We might be tempted to panic, thinking that we have no hope to teach every element of the Small Catechism accurately. If that is what you are feeling right now, let me offer you comfort. As parents, we are not able to teach our children everything. If we think of the catechesis of our children as a life-long journey together, we will come to realize that we will be working on these foundational teachings throughout our entire lives this side of eternity.

Fathers, you are called upon to take the lead, but do not go this alone. Together as parents, spend intentional time discussing how you will talk with your kids about the Christian faith. For those of you who do not have a spouse to rely upon, seek support in your church from your pastor and other staff, as well as from other parents. Allow them to come alongside you and your children to support your efforts to teach the faith in your home.

When you notice that you missed an opportunity, make a note of it, ask for forgiveness, and move ahead. In Philippians 1:6, Paul reminds us that God will bring our faith to completion. Our work teaching our children is something we will never complete, and that is just as God has planned. It is not our job to bring their training to completion. We will be the primary shapers of their faith from a human standpoint. However, God began and will complete the good work of faith in our lives and in the lives of our children. Therefore, each time we prepare to teach a faith lesson to our children, we should pray that our words might be God's Word, and that we might faithfully assist in the formation of faith that God is accomplishing in our children's lives. What a privilege it is to join with God, speaking His truth into my sons' lives. I pray that you have many years of blessedness as you do the same. May you consider it a joy that God has chosen you and given you the privilege and responsibility to speak the Word into the lives of your own children.

APPENDIX

CHRISTIAN QUESTIONS WITH THEIR ANSWERS[1]

Prepared by Dr. Martin Luther for those who intend to go to the Sacrament

The questions listed in this fourth section of the Small Catechism offer a diagnostic tool that parents can use to examine the developing beliefs of their children. Perhaps as parents we can make use of these questions at the dinner table following the evening meal, or maybe they can be asked as a part of evening or morning devotions. Either way, the purpose is not to test but to assess the faith of our children in order that we might provide instruction where it is most needed.

After confession and instruction in the Ten Commandments, the Creed, the Lord's Prayer, and the Sacraments of Baptism and the Lord's Supper, the pastor may ask, or Christians may ask themselves these questions:

1. Do you believe that you are a sinner?

Yes, I believe it. I am a sinner.

Why is it important that our children know that they are sinners? This is foundational knowledge. If they know they are sinners, they can then come to know of their need for a Savior. Knowing the need for a Savior sets the stage for us to introduce our children to Christ as Savior.

2. How do you know this?

From the Ten Commandments, which I have not kept.

Our children need to know that they are sinners, and there is a need to ground that reality in specific ways. We can use the Ten Command-

---

[1] The "Christian Questions with their Answers," designating Luther as the author, first appeared in an edition of the Small Catechism in 1551.

ments to assist our children in identifying their sin. We can teach our children to confess their sins through their knowledge of how they sin.

3. Are you sorry for your sins?

Yes, I am sorry that I have sinned against God.

Once we help our children come to an accurate understanding of their sin, we need to guide them to the point that they have remorse for their sin. As parents, we know the difference between a child who is sorry for what he has done and a child who defiantly continues to disobey. Our role as parents is to instill in our children a respect for the commandments of God in such a way that they have true remorse and desire forgiveness.

Children can learn through interaction with us when we as parents demonstrate our own sorrow for sin and seek God's grace and forgiveness. We can model for our children a joyful desire to keep God's commandments, perhaps by returning extra change given to us at the supermarket; and at the same time we can model our trust in God's grace as we allow our children to see us seek forgiveness from God and when appropriate from them. Young children especially have a developmental desire to please their parents. This lays a foundation of behavior that is in accord with our will. Through the guidance of the Holy Spirit, we seek to keep our will in line with the Lord's. By extension, our children learn about seeking the will of God as they seek to conform to our will and see how we seek to conform to God's will.

4. What have you deserved from God because of your sins?

His wrath and displeasure, temporal death, and eternal damnation. See Rom. 6:21, 23.

God's grace is cheapened when we fail to realize that God would be entirely justified in punishing us. We might not want to talk with our young children about the eternal consequences of their sin, but as they grow and come to understand the nature of death in this sinful world, we should teach them the connection between sin and death. God created the world in a state of perfection. In that perfection, there was no death. We were designed to live with Him for eternity. However, when sin entered the world through the fall of Adam and Eve (see Genesis 3), death

came with sin. Sin separated humanity from God, which resulted immediately in spiritual death and ultimately in physical death. Just as our
children know that our relationship is damaged (not lastingly) when they
disobey us, they can learn that our relationship with God is also damaged
when we disobey Him (again not lastingly, as Christ restores this frac-
tured relationship).

5. Do you hope to be saved?

Yes, that is my hope.

Our children should know the hope that is found in Christ. Through
the sinless life, death, and resurrection of Christ, that break in the bond
between God and humanity was restored. On the merits of Christ alone
our sins are forgiven. When we and our children sin, we are no longer in
a right relationship with the Father, and this is why we seek to receive
God's grace and forgiveness through Christ as often as possible. Through
Christ, that relationship with the Father is restored and we are again welcomed into His kingdom both in this life and in eternity. Just as our children experience the joy of hearing us speak words of forgiveness to them
and embrace them with our arms and our love, so, too, can they learn to
experience the joy of forgiveness in Christ.

6. In whom then do you trust?

In my dear Lord Jesus Christ.

Our hope for salvation rests not on just anyone or anything, but on
Christ alone. In Christ alone are we able to have the hope and confidence
of salvation. We should teach our children to know Christ as Savior.
They should know that their only hope of salvation rests on His life,
death, and resurrection and not on our own merit. In Romans 3:23–24,
Paul talks about the reality that all have sinned. We all fail to live up to
the expectations that God has for us. In a similar way, our children learn
that they will not always live up to our expectations. We can model grace
for them by speaking words of forgiveness when they fall short. In such
times, we can talk to them about how Christ our Savior has won for us
forgiveness that we could not otherwise gain for ourselves. We can use as
an example furniture that is broken by kids when they roughhouse. It
cannot restore itself but requires someone else to save it and fix what has

been damaged. In the same way, Christ removed from us our sins by His shed blood, sins that we cannot remove ourselves.

7. Who is Christ?

The Son of God, true God and man.

Young children will naturally have a simple faith regarding who Jesus is. More complex notions of the paradox of the God who became man can wait until they are older and ready to understand them. Their child's faith is enough. As they grow older, we should talk to our children about that paradox. The ministry of the Holy Spirit in our children develops in them a desire to know more about who Christ is. This can be presented with simplicity in their early years and with increased sophistication as they grow older. Take the time to listen to their questions. Try not to add on to what they are asking until you are sure that what you have to offer them is really what they are asking and ready to comprehend.

There will always remain an element of mystery in this teaching. We will never fully understand what it means for Christ to be both God and man. We can, however, take care to teach our children that in Christ the fullness of God was present even when He took on the flesh of our humanity. What this means is that Christ was 100 percent God and at the same time 100 percent man. By becoming incarnate (becoming a man), Jesus did not lose any element of His divinity. Christ was no less God as a man on the earth than before His birth. How is this possible? That is where the mystery must remain. We know it is so because of what God has taught us in the Bible. What we do not know is how God accomplishes this. We can, however, point to the all-powerful nature of God, which gives Him the capacity to make what seems to be an impossibility become reality.

The Church has come to understand this important doctrine as being necessary for our salvation. Only a member of the human race would have been able to die on behalf of another's sins. Only true God would have been able to do this on behalf of all humanity. As man, Christ had the ability to sin, but He did not. As God, Christ was born without the taint of original sin. It is because Christ is both God and man that only His sacrifice could save us from the wrath of God. Only the shedding of His innocent blood could pay the price for our sins, once and for all.

8. How many Gods are there?

Only one, but there are three persons: Father, Son, and Holy Spirit.

The doctrine of the Trinity is another complicated mystery that we as parents ought to teach with an element of simplicity to our children. We can talk with even preschool-aged children about the Trinity if we keep our language simple. While the Early Church Fathers had to spend time working out the difference between substance and essence within the Godhead, as a father, my only goal is for my sons to know that the Father is God, the Son is God, the Holy Spirit is God, and that there is but one God. I want them to know that the Father, Son, and Holy Spirit are three individual persons, but each is a part of a single God. Teaching the Trinity to our children may appear complicated. If we spend too much time working out nuances beyond their understanding or answering questions they have not even asked, then this teaching will end up rather complicated. However, keeping things simple and to the point, we are able to provide the foundation needed to distinguish a Christian understanding of God from other monotheists and even polytheists.

What, then, do we know about the Trinity? If you really want to dig in, look up the Athanasian Creed. In it, you will find a wonderful exposition of the nature of the persons of the Trinity and how they relate to one another. The essential elements to talk to children about regarding the Trinity are the following:

1. The Father, Son, and Holy Spirit have been God together as the Trinity from the beginning.

2. The Father, Son, and Holy Spirit will always be God.

3. The Father did not create the Son or the Holy Spirit.

4. We worship one God, not three gods.

5. The Father, Son, and Holy Spirit are each individual persons but one God.

It is tempting to use analogies to try to explain the Trinity. I would counsel against this. Most analogies fall apart fast and end up pointing you in the direction of many of the classic trinitarian heresies. Stick to the basics and when you get in over your head, bring your pastor in to help out.

9. What has Christ done for you that you trust in Him?

He died for me and shed His blood for me on the cross for the forgiveness of sins.

Our faith and trust in Christ is based on historical fact. Christ lived on this earth in history and suffered and died on a Roman cross to pay the price for our sins. Our children should know that our salvation in Christ is based on the life, death, and resurrection of Christ, a historical set of events that took place roughly two thousand years ago in and around Jerusalem. Here we want to make sure that we distinguish between Christ who entered into our world and walked among us and other stories that we tell our children. Now I am not going to argue that you should not talk to your kids about Santa Claus or the Easter Bunny, or even the Tooth Fairy. I will note that we should do so with caution. The Jesus whose birth we celebrate at Christmas was and is a real person. Growing up to discover that Santa is not real and that he does not bring you presents should be carefully distinguished from our Savior's birth.

As kids grow older, you can talk to them about the archeological and historical evidence for the life of Christ.[2] Through a review of the evidence for the life of Jesus, we distinguish Him from other gods and religions that lack such a contact point with our world. In this our children can grow up to know their faith in Christ as founded on historically verifiable facts, which can go a long way in supporting the further claims of the Christian faith found in the pages of the Bible.

10. Did the Father also die for you?

He did not. The Father is God only, as is the Holy Spirit; but the Son is both true God and true man. He died for me and shed His blood for me.

Why is this at all a critical question? If we make sure to teach our children that Christ died for our sins, why would we need to ask them a question about the Father dying for our sins? The purpose of this question is to ensure that we do not cause confusion in our teaching of the Trinity with our children. Both the Father and the Son are God, but both

---

[2] A classic book that can help you research this is John Warwick Montgomery's *History and Christianity* (Downer's Grove, IL: InterVarsity Press, 1971).

did not die for our sins. If our children confuse this, they are perhaps confusing what the unity of the Trinity truly means. In all likelihood, parents will most likely never face this question. However, just in case, an attempt at offering an answer is included.

In the Trinity, there is both unity and diversity. There is unity in that there is only one God. There is diversity in that this one God is three persons: Father, Son, and Spirit. The full Godhead may together act, or individual members of the Trinity may act on their own. The Father was present for the death of Christ, but the Father did not die. The Father was at the crucifixion, turning His back on the Son. It would be illogical for the Father to turn His back on Himself. One person of the Trinity may turn His back on another, but the same member cannot do so to Himself.

In short, it is important to assign correctly the roles of the Trinity in our salvation. It was to the Father that we owed the debt of our sin. It was the Son whose sinless life, suffering, death, and resurrection paid that debt. It is the Holy Spirit who gives us faith to trust that this is true.

11. How do you know this?

From the holy Gospel, from the words instituting the Sacrament, and by His body and blood given me as a pledge in the Sacrament.

We are saved through Christ alone. We know this through Scripture alone. It is only through the words of the Bible that anyone is able to reliably know anything about the Christian faith and the details of the Gospel. God's Word is reliable. Through the years of repeated copying and translation, God has preserved His Word in truth and accuracy. We can trust that what we have in the Bibles in our homes and on our phones is the message God intended.[3]

We need to teach our children to form their ideas about who God is and what God is like according to how the Bible answers these questions. Our individual opinions about these questions, while perhaps interesting and personally appealing, fail to shape reality. I cannot get to know my wife in the absence of gathering information directly from her. At best, I am limited in my ability to learn about my wife from the input from oth-

---

[3] However, there are issues with certain translations. For information on Bible translations, go to www.cph.org/pdf/esv/011946study.pdf.

ers who have themselves directly learned about my wife from her. I cannot ponder who my wife is by merely gazing at her picture and never conversing with her.

God speaks to us in the Bible. God teaches us about who He is in those pages. This is a precious gift. We insult God and spurn His gift when we fail to seek our relationship with God in the pages of His communication to us. Our children cannot know Christ outside the Word of God. Therefore, our homes should be places where the Bible is faithfully, or better yet daily, read together as a family.

12. What are the words of institution?

Our Lord Jesus Christ, on the night when He was betrayed, took bread, and when He had given thanks, He broke it and gave it to the disciples and said: "Take eat; this is My body, which is given for you. This do in remembrance of Me."

In the same way also He took the cup after supper, and when He had given thanks, He gave it to them, saying: "Drink of it, all of you; this cup is the new testament in My blood, which is shed for you for the forgiveness of sins. This do, as often as you drink it, in remembrance of Me."

What is it that makes mere bread and wine not only bread and wine, but bread and wine along with (in, with, and under) the very body and blood of Christ? It is the very Word of God. Teaching our children the Words of Institution provides for them a reminder of the reality offered in the Lord's Supper. When they hear these words, they are reminded of the teachings related to the Lord's Supper and are therefore comforted in knowing that Christ is truly present in this meal and truly provides forgiveness through its consumption.

13. Do you believe, then, that the true body and blood of Christ are in the Sacrament?

Yes, I believe it.

Why is it important for us to believe that the body and blood of Christ are really present in the Lord's Supper? By trusting that the real presence of Christ is in the Sacrament of the Altar, we take seriously the words of Christ concerning what it is that we consume. Christ is clear when He tells His disciples to take and eat His body. This is important to teach our children so that they learn to take the words of Christ seriously, as they are presented and in their context. In a similar way to the questions related to the Trinity and the nature of Christ, the Lord's Supper will retain an element of mystery. Luther resisted attempts by other reformers to resolve the tension between the words of the Bible that called the bread the body of Christ, and the bread they saw before them. He insisted that though we do not know with certainty how God accomplishes this, we can know that the body and blood of Christ are truly present and consumed. The bread is still bread, but it is now also Christ's body. In similar fashion, the wine is still wine, but is now also the blood of Christ. Although the "how" questions cannot be answered, we can remain faithful, as Luther did, to the text of Scripture, which clearly states that what Jesus presented to His disciples on Maundy Thursday was not merely bread and wine, but was in fact His very body and blood, in, with, and under the bread and wine.

14. What convinces you to believe this?

The word of Christ: Take, eat, this is My body; drink of it, all of you, this is My blood.

The very words of Christ Himself, if taken seriously and in the context in which they were presented, lead us to the conclusion that what we are consuming is not just bread and wine, but the body and blood of Christ in, with, and under the bread and wine. We should teach our children that "is" here clearly means just that: "is." Although we do not know precisely how it is that Christ is truly present in the Lord's Supper, we believe that as God, His words are absolutely true and thus to be trusted.

As noted above, there will always remain a mystery on this point of teaching. However, we can point to the reliability of God to provide the foundation for trusting that which we cannot fully verify or comprehend. We can talk about how our children may trust us and take us at our word on things that they do not understand on the basis of those things that they know and understand well. In like manner, we take God at His Word, based on what we learn about His trustworthiness in those areas of Scripture that we understand more clearly.

15. What should we do when we eat His body and drink His blood, and in this way receive His pledge?

We should remember and proclaim His death and the shedding of His blood, as He taught us: This do, as often as you drink it, in remembrance of Me.

Eating and drinking the body and blood of Christ should not be something that we do without a good element of reflection. Christ calls on us to remember Him and to participate in remembrance of Him. Remembering Christ in this way calls to mind His suffering and death, and therefore the very real cost that Jesus paid for our salvation. By remembering Christ in this way, we recall with joy the love of Christ and are reminded that we ought to love one another with a self-sacrificial love.

Many people spend a brief time in private prayer following the Lord's Supper. Parents can take that time to talk with their children about what it is they are praying about, since often those prayers are a prayer of thanks to God for the gift of forgiveness through participation in the Lord's Supper. We reflect upon and remember the sacrifice of Christ when we pray following Communion. Perhaps the next time you take Communion, you can reflect in prayer together with your child.

16. Why should we remember and proclaim His death?

First, so that we may learn to believe that no creature could make satisfaction for our sins. Only Christ, true God and man, could do that. Second, so we may learn to be horrified by our sins, and to regard them as very serious. Third, so we may find joy and comfort in Christ alone, and through faith in Him be saved.

Each week in our churches, we should hear Christ crucified. Some might be wrongly concerned that if we cover the same thing each week, we might tire of hearing about Christ crucified. Yet, this is the very message that we need to hear because it is the message of life for those dead in sin. Our children should be taught to appreciate the regular hearing of the preaching of Christ crucified in our churches and not to find the repetition boring. Our children, just like us, need to hear this message as often as we can to avoid any thought of our own merit creeping in. We need to hear this message regularly in order that we do not find our sins less of a stain and so that we instead find comfort in Christ and in Christ alone.

Children cannot learn to appreciate the preaching of God's Word if they do not regularly hear it preached. Although it can be frustrating and distracting to have children with you in worship, it is critically important that they are present and see their parents attentive to the sermon. From this modeling, children learn that the sermon has value as does worship generally. I sometimes take my young family to sit toward the front of the church so that my boys are better able to see and hear what is going on. There have been times when they have verbally responded to the pastor preaching, laughing, or offering an answer to a question loud enough for the folks around to hear. I find that if people are taught appropriately, most can learn to accept and welcome children in worship.

When they are regularly present in worship, they will be present for a regular diet of Christ crucified (or they should be). When they notice that they are hearing this same message week after week, parents are able to talk to them about how centrally important that message is to our faith. Just as we need to work on memorizing the alphabet and numbers when we are young, we also need to be reminded of the cross of Christ, lest we risk forgetting.

17. What motivated Christ to die and make full payment for your sins?

His great love for His Father and for me and other sinners, as it is written in John 14; Romans 5; Galatians 2; and Ephesians 5.

Love is an amazing thing. My wife likes to remind me that love is a verb, meaning that love is seen in our actions. When we claim to love and yet do not act out that love, it is not truly love. Christ's love is beyond all other love. Christ loved us to the point that, while we were still sinners, He died for us (Romans 5:8). This is a love that we should talk about with our children. We should stress that this love demonstrates the true value that God places on each of us. No matter what we think of ourselves, or what others might say about us, Christ loved us so much that He died for us. That is truly valuing us as God's special creation.

Our kids can see in our love for them a model of God's love for us. They are not loved because they are good kids, though it might be easier to love them on those days. Rather, we love them because they are our kids. God loves us in a similar manner. He does not love us based on our obedience. If that were the case, we would be in serious trouble. Rather, God loves us because He created us in His likeness to be His children. Parents can talk to their kids about the love God has for us by comparing our imperfect love for them with His perfect love for us all.

18. Finally, why do you wish to go to the Sacrament?

That I may learn to believe that Christ, out of great love, died for my sin, and also learn from Him to love God and my neighbor.

The Sacrament of the Altar reminds us of the love of Christ demonstrated in His death. Through this reminder, we should be inspired to love God in return and to love our neighbors as equally loved children of God. We should teach our children that the remembrance of Christ in the Lord's Supper is a reminder of Christ's love for us.

19. What should admonish and encourage a Christian to receive the Sacrament frequently?

First, both the command and the promise of Christ the Lord. Second, his own pressing need, because of which the command, encouragement, and promise are given.

If I am able to receive God's grace through partaking in the Lord's Supper, why would I not desire to partake as often as I am able? This section started with a reminder of our sinful nature. As a sinner, I have a need for God's grace. Therefore, we should teach our children that we should desire to take part in the Lord's Supper because it is another way in which Christ is present in His grace among us, giving us forgiveness and strength. As noted above, we need to receive expressions of one another's love on a regular basis. With that in mind, we can talk to our children about why we regularly attend worship and participate in the Lord's Supper.

20. But what should you do if you are not aware of this need and have no hunger and thirst for the Sacrament?

To such a person no better advice can be given than this: first, he should touch his body to see if he still has flesh and blood. Then he should believe what the Scriptures say of it in Galatians 5 and Romans 7.

Second, he should look around to see whether he is still in the world, and remember that there will be no lack of sin and trouble, as the Scriptures say in John 15–16 and in 1 John 2 and 5.

Third, he will certainly have the devil also around him, who with his lying and murdering day and night will let him have no peace, within or without, as the Scriptures picture him in John 8 and 16; 1 Peter 5; Ephesians 6; and 2 Timothy 2.

There will be unfortunate times in which our children will lack the motivation to seek after the gifts of God. These are not easy times for a parent. We struggle to know what to say or to do. Luther calls upon individuals in such a state to take stock of their reality. If we are truly open and honest, we will see our own sin. We will see the influence of Satan around us in the evil of our world. Seeing these realities, we hope that God will motivate our children to return to a state in which they seek after and desire the blessings of God, if not out of a loving response, then for a time out of a fear for what the devil might desire to have in store for us.

This is not likely to be something that a parent can proactively teach to a child. Rather, as our children grow older and test out their independence, these words of Luther serve to offer us a way of talking to our children about how they can reconnect to the need for God and His grace that they may have discarded or forgotten.

Note: These questions and answers are no child's play, but are drawn up with great earnestness of purpose by the venerable and devout Dr. Luther for both young and old. Let each one pay attention and consider it a serious matter; for St. Paul writes to the Galatians in chapter six: "Do not be deceived: God cannot be mocked."

There are a good number of other questions that Luther could have provided in this section. In the twenty that he chose to include, we see what Luther believed to be essential elements of our faith. There is plenty of additional material that we have covered in the Small Catechism, but here Luther seeks to provide us with a tool that we can use to examine the core of our faith.